THE NATURAL
SHADE GARDEN

THE NATURAL
SHADE GARDEN

KEN DRUSE

PHOTOGRAPHS BY KEN DRUSE
ASSISTED BY VICTOR NELSON

DESIGN BY BARBARA PECK

Clarkson Potter/Publishers
New York

DEDICATION:

To the Wildflowers.

Conserve them.
Protect their habitats.
Enjoy them where they grow.
Rescue them when their homes are threatened.
Propagate and plant them in new places
all over the world.
These are the plants that make our
natural gardens in the shade.

Published by Clarkson N. Potter, Inc., 201 East 50th Street, New York, New York 10022. Member of the Crown Publishing Group.

CLARKSON N. POTTER, POTTER and colophon are trademarks of Clarkson N. Potter, Inc.

Manufactured in Japan

Garden plans by Natalie Siegel

Library of Congress Cataloging-in-Publication Data
Druse, Kenneth.
The natural shade garden/by Ken Druse; photographs by Ken Druse; assisted by Victor Nelson; designed by Barbara Peck.
p.   cm.
1. Gardening in the shade.   2. Woodland gardening.   3. Natural gardens, American.   I. Title.
SB434.7D78   1991
635.9'54—dc20   *90-20276*
CIP

ISBN 0-517-58017-9

10   9   8   7   6   5   4   3   2   1

First Edition

ACKNOWLEDGMENTS

When I finished The Natural Garden, *I thought that I would never write another book. That lasted about two weeks. Soon I had several ideas for new projects, but I didn't do any of them. Books like this one come from a passion, a need to share. I left a sunny garden in New York City and was plunged into a small garden that had a lot of one thing: shade. I've always loved the woodland wildflowers, so I saw this not as a problem but as an opportunity. The painter Robert Goldstrom, who gardens in similar circumstances, said, "Write about shade." And I did.*

So many people have helped me along the way. At Clarkson N. Potter there's Carol Southern, Lauren Shakely, Howard Klein, Tina Zabriskie, Karen Nagel, Teresa Nicholas, Laurie Stark, Michelle Sidrane, Bruce Harris, Gail Shanks, Barbara Marks, Joan DeMayo, Phyllis Fleiss, Jo Fagan, Robin Strashun, Chip Gibson, Barbara B. Kantor, and Jim Walsh. I want to thank Gretchen Salisbury, who started this project, and Amy Schuler, who carried it along. Also, Alexandra Enders, my indefatigable coach, and Barbara Peck, who designed this book, turning pictures and prose into this beautiful work. Their efforts show in what you see before you.

I'd like to thank so many gardeners who inspired me and shared their wisdom and garden art. Among them: Suzanne Bales and Martha Kraska, Louis Bauer, Felice Frankel, John Trexler, Bobby Zeleniak, Mary Anne Conroy and Steve Griffin, Pamela Lord, Barbara Pryor, Jim and Conni Cross, Marco Polo Stufano, and Charles Cresson. Thanks too to supportive friends and colleagues, Linda Yang, Betsy Kissam, Keith Crotz, Tom Koster and CP Campagna-Pint, and Margaret Roach, and my parents, Helen and Harold Druse. And thanks to my agent, Helen Pratt, for her unfailing support.

I especially want to thank Victor Nelson, my cheering section, critic, and friend; and Jim Doyle for putting up with the years of work that went into this book. I can't thank Isolde Motley enough for her undaunted contribution to this project. She simply doesn't accept the phrase "It can't be done." It was she more than anyone who brought The Natural Shade Garden *to light.*

CONT

E N T S

INSPIRATION

FROM THE WILD

MANY OF OUR SHADE GARDEN PLANTS COME FROM THE FOREST FLOOR AND
blossom in spring. The deep-pink-flowered native Dicentra eximia, *however, blooms through fall.*
OPPOSITE: *The hardwood forest shows its colors in autumn.*

A WALK IN THE WOODS

Imagine a walk in the woods. You might begin in the sunny meadow, where a stream cuts a line through the waist-high flowers. Follow its path and you'll come to the edge of the woodland. This half-shade is the habitat of the evergreen and deciduous shrubs: mountain laurel, blueberry bushes, and deciduous rhododendrons, for example. The small trees that line the forest—dogwood, redbud, and shad-blow—mingle with the spreading shrubs. Pass into the darkness and you'll find more woody plants of the understory blooming in turn: witch hazel, *Fothergilla,* and oakleaf hydrangeas. Farther along, the middle layer fades, except by the streambed, where waterside plants capture every bit of sunlight that

filters through the slash in the treetop canopy.

Sun still pierces through where the stream pools and forms the woodland pond. Along the edges of this quiet lagoon, pitcher plants, irises, and marsh marigolds bloom. Beyond, you'll come to another clearing—filled with a sea of jade green ferns that have colonized a drier spot in dappled shade. Spring in the deciduous forest explodes with masses of flowers that bloom and fade before the emerging leaves veil the light from above. And it's the darkest place—this floor —that in spring supports the most precious botanical jewels: wildflowers such as trilliums,

MAGNOLIA VIRGINIANA *grows among the shrubs and the small trees that live on the edge of the forest.* OPPOSITE: *The woodland pool is an open place within the shaded habitat where moisture-loving plants welcome a few hours of midday sun.*

dogtooth violets (*Erythronium* spp.), celandine poppies (*Stylophorum diphyllum*), bellwort (*Uvularia perfoliata*), and lady-slipper orchids (*Cypripedium* spp.). But there's always a summer straggler (*Lobelia cardinalis,* for example) to add brilliant color in a moist spot or among the warm brown of fallen leaves that form the mulch of the forest floor. This place, this woodland, will inspire your shade garden.

THE NATURAL GARDEN

In a sense, the shade garden is the most "natural" garden. It's true that nature tends to indulge

her plantings in the sun. The vigorous meadow is an example. Yet a meadow could not compete indefinitely with a forest's spreading blanket. Tree and shrub seedlings take hold—the first step toward reclaiming open land. Even the meadow, in order to stay meadow, must be cut down once a year by fire, drought, or man. The forest does quite well on its own, for nature favors the woodland most of all.

The trees dominate because they create an environment that favors the land. They cast shade to keep the forest floor cool and moist. Their leaves break the force of the rain to gently drip moisture to the soil below, and

A WALK TO THE WOODS passes through the sunny meadow and by the small trees and shrubs that line the forest's edge.
OPPOSITE: *Beneath the forest canopy, the American bulb,* Camassia scilloides, *or wild hyacinth, flowers in spring.*

roots fight erosion from running water. Fallen leaves contribute to the humus-rich soil, and decompose to return nutrients to the earth. The wood itself stores the energy made by the trees, while the sheltered woodland is home to all manner of flora and fauna. The goal is to learn from this self-sufficient model and bring some of this comfortable world to our gardens in the shade.

THE GLOBAL GARDEN

We've all heard of global warming. That's primarily the result of burning fossil fuel, which increases the levels of carbon diox-

VERY LITTLE CAN GROW IN THE DENSE SHADE OF THIS BAMBOO GLADE AT
Blithewold in Rhode Island. OPPOSITE: *Trees, like this one at the Brooklyn Botanic Garden, will be among the*
saviors of our planet. Their leaves provide cooling shade in summer and consume carbon dioxide.

ide in the atmosphere. (Another cause is the destruction of tropical rain forests, still slashed and burned at a rate of thirty million acres a year.) If current consumption continues, the level of carbon dioxide could double in the next few years; scientists theorize that the earth's temperature could rise between six and twelve degrees Fahrenheit. You don't have to imagine the polar ice cap melting or picture Ohio beachfront to make that a startling reality: think of your 1997 air-conditioning bill.

There isn't one clear solution. But shade is at the root of an appealing idea. Trees, especially young trees, gobble up carbon dioxide. And of course as the trees take in contaminants, they spew out their waste product—

oxygen. The American Forestry Association, a citizens' group, suggests we plant enough trees over the next several years to slow global warming—reversing the current practice. Today, we plant only one tree for every four that are harvested, destroyed, or die of old age.

A tree-planting campaign helps the globe in less direct ways, too. Trees help cut down the consumption of energy. A shade tree is one of the best ways to cool a house, reducing the need for air-conditioning. (A deciduous tree, losing its leaves in winter, will allow the warming sun into the house. Evergreen trees, used as windscreens, can reduce heating costs in the colder months.) The five hottest summers of this century occurred

during the 1980s; in the future, house plans will include shelter from the sun.

TOMORROW'S GARDENS

The garden of the future will be a shade garden, for all kinds of reasons—fiscal, historical, and most of all, environmental. It may not grow overnight—but this is a return to an older notion of landscaping, planting for generations to come. It may require a little extra planning, some more thought, more effort—but the knowledge that this small patch contributes to the health of the planet makes it worthwhile. It may not result in masses of frothy color—but there will be color. Just look again at the plants from the forest's floor: they have so little time to gather light, flower, attract pollinators, and set seed that they pack every precious bit of energy into a few spectacular blossoms. Some may seem more grotesque than showy—the plant's energy may not have been put into something we consider "pretty," but into uniqueness. To me, these are the exotic stars of the plant kingdom, destined to become the stars of tomorrow's gardens as well. And by the end of our walk in the woods, I trust you too will have come to see shade not as a curse, but as a natural opportunity to grow some of the most remarkable botanical wonders of the temperate world.

INCREDIBLE PLANTS GROW IN THE TEMPERATE FORESTS OF THE WORLD SUCH AS,
ABOVE, *the amazing* Smilacina stellata, *star bead.* OPPOSITE: *The easiest North American slipper
orchid to grow,* Cypripedium calceolus *var.* pubescens. OVERLEAF: *Fantastic autumn* Tricyrtis hirta, *toad lily,
and spring* Fritillaria meleagris, *checkered lily.*

THE SHARED COMMUNITY OF THE WOODLAND CAN BE VIEWED IN MICROCOSM IN A
corner of Jean Pope's garden. OPPOSITE: *Working with nature is the goal of the consummate natural gardener. Jim*
and Conni Cross help it along by adding tender fuchsias for color beneath a purple-leaf Acer palmatum *hybrid.*

LIVING
WITH SHADE

The woodland inspires the natural shade garden. You can't completely re-create the environmental harmony of the forest—you have to live in the garden too—but nature supplies advice and makes recommendations. Our job is to make the right choices, and to provide the conditions that will help our plants thrive.

Shady gardens can be quite self-sufficient. They can be as simple as the covering of pine needles and occasional ferns of the forest floor. But that's often not enough. We admire self-sufficiency; our gardens, however, will exhibit design, color combinations, and arrangements of texture and form. That requires planning and maintenance, of course;

no garden is maintenance-free, although that's the desire of the uninitiated. A garden that didn't change and grow wouldn't be a garden at all.

Gardening is a matter of trowel and error. Catalogs make suggestions. Zone maps provide a point of departure. But first-hand experience is the only certain method. Trying something out, finding that it does or doesn't do well, is key to discovering the right plant for the right place. And it is often necessary to observe over a good period of time. One winter, I thought I lived in a comfortable United States Department of Agriculture (USDA) zone 7 (zero degrees to

"SHADE" IS A RELATIVE *term—differing degrees will be found beneath a tall oak or below a Japanese maple,* ABOVE. OPPOSITE: *Light and dark can be used in design. Sunlight beckons from the bright side of Martha Paull's garden gate.*

ten degrees Fahrenheit). The next year I lived in zone 6 (minus ten degrees to zero degrees Fahrenheit). I didn't move; it was just a change in the weather. It takes time, too, to find out just what kind of soil you have, and, most importantly in planning a shade garden, how much light.

DEGREES OF SHADE

People often ask what they can grow in the dark. Mushrooms, I suppose. No plant (excluding some undersea flora, perhaps) will survive without light. But it doesn't have to be twelve hours of direct sunshine, what the nur-

series call "sun," or "full sun."

Sun and shade are not simple matters of black and white. There are degrees of both. If a garden is in sunlight for half the day, say from eight A.M. to one P.M., then it obviously must be in shade for the rest of the daylight hours, maybe one to six P.M. Is this a shade garden? It certainly is a place where shade must be considered.

A purple coneflower, an adaptable prairie dweller, will survive and bloom in six hours of sunlight, and in some situations (good drainage and an open site) do very well. This is what many catalogs call "sun to partial shade," or "sun to part shade." This book focuses on places that receive four hours or less of direct sunlight. A daylily species will bloom quite well in four hours of sun. A hybrid might need four hours in the middle of the day to perform. Both plants will survive with a lot less, but blooming will be reduced, if there are flowers at all, and the foliage will flop and look rather untidy.

Two hours of unobstructed midday sunshine might constitute *partial shade* at its most sunny. A hosta, normally a denizen of the deeper shade, would put on a respectable flower show in such circumstances, although it would probably wilt. Some garden lilies would bloom well in this sunny shade, and their smaller leaves could cope with the heat that follows the cool, shady morning.

Light shade would be an area that basks in morning sun or

IVY GROWS IN DENSE shade under open-riser steps, ABOVE. BELOW: *Jack-in-the-pulpit,* Arisaema triphyllum, *grows in dappled shade.* OPPOSITE: *Filtered light supports* Lamium maculatum *'White Nancy', and a tropical herb,* Parochetus communis, *in a planting by San Franciscan Ron Lutsko.*

afternoon sun—before ten A.M. or after three P.M.—better for the blooming hosta. (Remember, though, that the cool morning sunlight has a different effect than the direct afternoon rays. The combination of afternoon heat with sun acts as if it were stronger sun than morning sun— some plants like it, some don't.)

Filtered light is in the shadow cast by a small-leaved tree, such as a honey locust or mimosa, or perhaps in an area under a light-diffusing material such as a nearly clear fiberglass overhang. This might also be an area under a lath covering in which slats are evenly spaced with openings. It is half in shade, but the sunlight is always moving—passing over the leaves. All too often, these bright situations are what the catalogs call "shade."

In *bright light,* no direct rays come to the garden, but the space is open to the sky, perhaps in a city garden, or on the north side of a house. Often the light is good here because buildings reflect a lot of the light as it bounces from wall to wall and down to the garden below. Many broad-leaved evergreens could do well in this place.

Dappled shade comes from larger-leaved trees. It is true *shade,* but there is light piercing through from the sun above the tree umbrella. Ferns could be selected, and some of the early-spring-blooming woodland wildflowers. The species would be chosen depending on how much competition for moisture exists from the tree, which grows below the soil as well as above.

The final category is *deep shade,* or *dense shade,* beneath the treads of open-riser steps, or close to a north-facing wall in a crowded urban setting. Mosses and ivy might grow there, but there is hope for more.

The catalogs and nurseries must use simplistic references. We have the luxury to delve deeply into the realm of the shady garden. For example, many hours of bright, open light can equal some direct sunlight as "seen" by the cells of a plant. Even artificial light can affect growth. Have you ever noticed how the trees near the streetlights lose their leaves later in the fall than those away from the light?

Sunlight in the far north may not be as intense as noonday sun in Georgia, but it stays light quite a bit later, and dawn is earlier too. (That's one reason plants do so well in England.) A garden I saw recently in the Pacific Northwest was in shade all day, but the plants grew beautifully. Many were ones I would have suspected would need more sunlight, but they were blooming. I think it had a lot to do with the far-north location: more hours of daylight in the summer. Similarly, two or three hours of southern midday sun will be all that's needed for plants that are generally thought of as sun worshipers. Indeed, in the South, just a few hours of sunlight can prohibit the use of our most beloved shade plants. And gardening in the shade there might be the best way *to* garden.

Just as there are different kinds of light, there are different kinds

of shade. One would think that a solid building would cast denser shade than the leaves of a tree, but the place in the shadow of the beech tree can be darker than one in the shade of a house. The garden next to a building is open to the sky, open to bright light even if never in direct sun. Also, the building reflects a good deal of light back to the garden. You can observe this just by standing under a dense tree and beside a house, perhaps on the east side in the afternoon. If the house is painted white (as so many American houses are), the reflected light will be dramatic.

For the gardener all this means is that divisions of light and shade are indistinct—and that shade can be modified. If you have a garden area that gets sun only from ten-thirty to two—less than four hours—it's still the strongest sun of the day. Plants marked for partial shade would do well; you could even try a sun lover. Beds beneath fastigiate or columnar trees (narrow-growing cultivated varieties) could work for partial-shade plants, since the shadow passes in thin bands. Spots on the east side of shrubs or walls could also be considered partial shade.

In the Northern Hemisphere, confined places adjacent to north-facing walls are in shadow —dense shade—for almost all of the year. When walls are painted white, or a pale color, or outdoor mirrors are used, the area directly against the wall can become just "shade" and used for planting.

Over time, you will discover

A NORTH-FACING WALL,
painted white, bounces light to
plants, A B O V E , *as does the*
stuccoed surface that reflects late
afternoon rays to daylily hybrids,
B E L O W . O P P O S I T E : *Many*
spring blooming shrubs and
herbaceous perennials can grow in
light shade.

more about the various kinds of shade around your property, and through experimentation, you'll discover plants that can be nudged into or out of the darkness. Sun lovers planted in the shade will need compensation in the form of excellent air circulation, more moisture perhaps, and maybe more phosphorus from plant food. Flowers may be fewer, but at times they will be bigger and deeper in hue since there is no sun to fade colors. Others, unfortunately, need sun to bring out color—you'll find out. Some sun-loving nursery stock may not transplant that well into the shade, but small seedlings or rooted cuttings of the same plant will adapt. Sowing seeds might be a way to get some of these plants to take hold.

Some stalwart individuals surprise me. In one of the darkest parts of my garden, among the English ivy cultivars, I have a forsythia shrub. It will never flower there. And yet, it performs magnificently as a foliage plant. It isn't even too leggy. Deep green leaves cover this woody shrub from early spring through late fall. Near it is a corkscrew willow (*Salix matsudana* 'Tortuosa'). This tree grows more like a vine in this location —tall and flat up against the fence. It does not support itself well—it kind of weeps. But it is a perfect espalier candidate for the garden fence. A few well-placed staples and string were all it took to have this fascinating tree sprawl across the fence in this darkest of places.

THE UNEDITED FOREST,
RIGHT, *limits the plants of the floor to a few shade-tolerant covers.*
ABOVE: *An arch made by an apple tree frames the view of the flower garden.* BELOW: *Careful removal of lower branches can let in more light. A professional service might be best for pruning a mature tree.*

MODIFYING SHADE

Sometimes, though, there is simply too much shade. You will need a sunnier patch to grow vegetables or roses, or to sit in on a late-spring afternoon. If the shade is cast by a building, there's not much you can do—beyond painting it white, if it's yours. But if it's shade from a tree, you can modify it—usually by pruning.

First, prune for good health, removing any dead or damaged wood and the faded foliage of herbaceous perennials. Next, prune to "thin." When a shrub gets too big or becomes a tangle of twigs, it must be thinned from within—by removing whole stems from their origin at or near ground level. In this way, more light will be let in to the center of the plant and there will be better air circulation.

Large evergreen shrubs should have sections removed from the base, carefully and sparingly. Use your artistic sense: you just want to preserve or re-create the natural form. This may mean trimming away a bit from the top as well, but never crew-cutting with hedge clippers.

If you have a tree casting too much shadow, sometimes the solution is *limbing up*—removing lower branches in their entirety. Trees like beeches, though, are best left alone. Little, if anything, will grow beneath them, so why not delight in their apron of low, leafy branches?

Height is more difficult to control. A tree should rarely be

A PRUNING PRIMER

In general, prune flowering shrubs just after blossoms fade. Prune evergreen shrubs just as new growth appears. For needle evergreens, trim new growth only, and only when necessary.

Take two years to renovate a deciduous shrub. Thin twigs originating from the base, along with half of the very oldest stems in winter. By the following year, sturdy new growth should have come from ground level and the remaining old stems can be removed. The new growth will produce vigorous lateral shoots in its second season.

The best time of year to prune a deciduous tree is in late winter. At the place where a branch flares wide to meet the trunk, there's a distinctive ring or line on the bark called the branch collar. This collar should be left intact after pruning. The best method involves three cuts. First make a cut on the underside of the branch, about a third of the way through and over six inches away from the trunk. Then make a cut from the top down and about half an inch outside the first cut, farther away from the trunk. The branch will fall without tearing the bark from the underside because of the first, scoring cut. Then you can carefully trim the stump down to the branch collar, just beyond the discernible bark seam or ridge at the junction of the trunk and branch. No wound dressing is necessary.

topped—that is, pruned so the tallest growing point, or leader, is a stump. In young trees, the leader will just take a small jog to the side and continue to grow up; in older trees, a ring of water sprouts, very thin vertical twigs, will form around the cut area.

There is a technique called *drop crotching,* in which the highest crotch formed by a scaffold branch and the trunk is removed, or dropped, to a lower one. This does not always work. A vertical leader may still form, and it may also result in weakening branches below. If you attempt drop crotching, cut back most of the branches on the tree at the same time, especially the upper ones.

A SHRUB CAN BE

thinned as it grows. Rubbing off new spring shoots with a gloved hand revealed the beautiful structure of a mature Pieris japonica.
OPPOSITE: *The edited forest allows space and light for azaleas at Winterthur.*

As a last resort, a tree may have to be eliminated entirely. This task must be done carefully. Pulling out several trees by the roots throughout a thick woodland may damage the remaining individuals. If the trees are too big to just cut to the ground, prune them severely in one year and remove them the next, roots and all if you can.

I wouldn't kill a full-grown tree without considerable forethought, or malice. It would take me months to get up the courage. (In some communities across the country the wait is enforced: you need a permit to cut down any tree, even one on private property.)

SHADE GARDEN SOIL

A shade garden's soil must be rich in organic matter—there should be a layer of humus equal to the soil's sand and clay in volume, as there would be on the woodland floor. Assuming you are not lucky enough to have such soil, the best way to add humus is with leaf mold—last year's leaves. Shade-tolerant plants love leaf mold; just think of the litter on the forest floor. Leaf mold holds moisture and nutrients, and contributes plant food itself. It is open and airy and plant roots run through it. It also makes a natural mulch layer that falling leaves will add to year after year. Oak leaves are great because they curl when they drop and this keeps them from matting down and excluding oxygen. They also are acidic, and most of our woodland plants want that too. Five years ago, I might not have suggested adding leaf mold because it was impossible to come by unless you "grew" your own. However, since most municipalities have outlawed leaf burning, the town leaf dump has come into exis-

COOL, MOIST, WELL-drained soil is perfect for plants such as Epimedium, Lathyrus vernus, Pulmonaria, Asarum, Anemone, Dodecatheon, *and* Primula, *seen here at Connecticut's Oliver Nursery.*

TESTING YOUR SOIL

First, you need to know your soil. Take a trowelful of earth and dump it in an empty quart mayonnaise jar. Fill the jar with water, shake it, and let the contents settle completely. Soon you will have a rough but useful idea of your soil's makeup. The largest particles, gravel and small rocks, will sink to the bottom. Next will be the sand. Above that will be the sludgy clay, and floating on top, the organic matter—humus.

Next, you can buy an inexpensive home soil-testing kit to determine the acidity and nutrient content of your medium. Directions are provided. Acidity and alkalinity are measured on the pH scale. Neutral is pH 7, that is, the middle of the scale that runs from 1 to 14. A reading below 7 is more acidic, sometimes called sour; above, more alkaline, sometimes called sweet. A shade medium should have a reading between 6.5 and 5.5: somewhat acidic. Leaf mold and peat moss can acidify soil; lime will "sweeten" it.

High alkalinity may come from unexpected sources. If your planting space is close to the house foundation, cement may leach lime into the soil. You might have to remove the soil and even treat the foundation with "acid." White vinegar, painted on the foundation and then rinsed off, might help.

tence. With a little research, you will find a place in your area that not only composts collected leaves, but gives away the result. When I looked for a source, I found that a nearby town provided free composted leaves and loaded it in bags or a truck at no cost—they can't get rid of the stuff. One would be well advised to compost town-dump leaf mold, or at least store it through the season before using: composting will heat up the leaves and kill most weed seeds and roots.

Humus is the cure for both fast-draining sandy and water-logged clayey soil. Clay and sand are somewhat similar in content: sand has relatively large grains, and clay has microscopic mineral particles. Sand will be made more absorbent; and clay better drained, by adding leaf mold or other sources of humus.

WATERING THE SHADE GARDEN

The soil in the shaded garden should be moist—just damp—all the time. You can buy a house-plant probe and stick it into the earth, about seven inches down, or plunge a trowel into the soil to about the same depth to check the moisture content. Just-moist soil will feel cold. It shouldn't be soggy, just cool to the touch. You can figure that if your garden gets one inch of rain water per week, things should do fairly well; tree leaves deflecting rain-drops, however, can alter the amount of water that actually

OPPOSITE: AN ESSENTIAL nutrient, nitrogen, falls from the sky in raindrops that pool and bead on the leaves of a columbine. Additional food can be provided to plants such as the impatiens, ABOVE, in water, using an organic foliar spray of liquefied seaweed or manure tea.

hits the ground. (An inexpensive rain gauge would be a helpful, if general, guide.) After you feel the soil a few times, you'll get to know when things are the way they should be. Wilted plants are sometimes an indication of soil conditions, but can also result from hot weather following cool, soil-born insects, or disease.

I would not start a new shade garden without including an underground drip-irrigation or soaker hose system. For me, this

began as a labor saver, but now it has become important for conserving water. Delivering water directly to plant roots minimizes loss through runoff or evaporation from above-ground sprinklers. Many diseases are associated with wet flowers and foliage, so keeping plant leaves dry keeps diseases under control. Irrigation systems are available through mail-order catalogs. By saving your time, and in places where you pay for water, by using less, you will save money. Keep an eye on your automated system, and check the battery from time to time.

"FOOD" FOR PLANTS

I used to use my underground drip-irrigation system to deliver a water-soluble commercial plant food, but I stopped doing that because it seemed to drive away the earthworms, who are perhaps the best possible source of extra plant food for the shade garden. You'll get more nutrition from them than you would from fertilizer. Organic fertilizers such as manure tea, liquid seaweed, or compost won't discourage the worms. In fact, they love compost, and they love leaf mold best of all. In spring, I broadcast a light covering of an organic, slow-release 20-20-20 granular fertilizer and for an occasional boost, use a foliar spray. Select a food designed for this purpose such as liquefied seaweed; other plant foods may leave a residue.

THE WOODLAND MULCH

When you mulch, you cover the exposed soil around plants with a thick cover of organic or inorganic material. The mulch keeps the moisture in the soil, keeps the soil cool, and inhibits weed seedlings from sprouting. It's like a nonliving ground cover. You'll want to spread a layer of mulch in the early spring and perhaps a coarser mulch, such as pine boughs, for winter protection. Contrary to popular notion, the winter mulch doesn't keep the soil warm, but cold. It keeps drying winds off the ground and shades it from the sun, so that on warm, sunny days there will be less chance of thawing and subsequent refreezing, which can cause plants to heave right out of the ground. Following the path of our model, the woodland, chopped leaf mold is about the best choice for a shade-garden mulch. Other good organic sources are compost, sawdust, shredded fir bark, pine needles, well-rotted cow manure, and aged grass clippings, not only for their appearance, but also because they all contribute nutrition and humus to the soil as they break down.

Gravel doesn't look natural, least of all if it is quarried white quartz, slate, or red stone. But pea gravel, river-washed little round stones, can have some uses, especially for paths. And because this material is light in color, it can be tried as a means of reflecting light back to plants.

LEAVES MAKE UP THE

indigenous mulch for Trillium grandiflorum, A B O V E, *and the early-spring-blooming* Hepatica acutiloba, B E L O W.

O P P O S I T E: *Chopped fir bark is a perfect foil for cinnamon fern crosiers and white* Phlox divaricata.

One of my favorite mulches to walk on is long pine needles, and they take a long time to break down compared to other leaves. But they're murder on any slope because they are slippery. When you select a mulch, try to pick the most organic one you can find. Small scale tends to look most natural. The giant pine-bark nuggets, readily available, and beloved by landscapers,

make me think, *Honey, I shrunk the plants*. Mini-nuggets are better, and shredded bark, better still. If you use a wood-based mulch, be sure to add a bit more nitrogen to your fertilizer, because the micro-organisms that break down the mulch use nitrogen and will pull it out of the soil. Sprinkle a handful of nitrogenous fertilizer such as composted manure, or mix in some dried lawn clippings with bark when spreading.

The mulch should be as thick as you can make it, about three inches if possible. But try not to bury the crowns of the plants and be sure to keep fresh vegetable waste, such as grass clippings, from touching stems. These mulches can burn plants as they heat up and break down. Also, fungi and bacteria might spread to healthy plant tissue in areas of poor air circulation, an ever-present condition down below in the shade.

It can be rather difficult to spread a three-inch-thick layer of mulch on an existing garden bed. Place handfuls of the material between plants and gently spread it into place so that it remains thicker in the areas between plant crowns. Since most of our shade plants have low, spreading basal foliage, you'll need to mulch early. Before the perennials emerge, place some of the lighter mulches like shredded leaves directly over the bulbs and perennial crowns. As plants emerge, gently scratch some mulch away from the shoots.

PLANNING THE

SHADE GARDEN

DIVERSE SPECIMENS INCLUDING THE FLOWERING ARUNCUS DIOICUS,
rhododendrons, Rodgersias, *and a hosta, share a place in the shade.* RIGHT: *Contrasting foliage forms have endless variation, as in the case of the spiky iris and mounded* Sedum spectabile *flower heads.*

USING NATURE'S DESIGN

The natural style is derived from examples in the wild. Observing and understanding how nature works will give you clues to creating successful gardens in both difficult and not-so-difficult sites. Unlike sun-loving plants, which can flourish in near wastelands, woodland plants need the shadow of others to survive. They live in a balanced community, a shared environment of woody, fleshy, and shrubby landsmen. It's a calm world in which temperature and other environmental extremes are rare, unlike the habitat of the open prairie.

In the sunny places, reproduction is the first order

and flowers are the main attraction. The longer-lived shade plants don't have to pack every ounce of energy into seed production. Of course they flower too, and their blossoms are often as impressive as those of the sun lovers. But as you plunge into shade gardening, you'll probably realize that much of the beauty of these plants comes from their leaves and their mass as a whole. You may not be able to create the color drifts of the sunny perennial border, but thoughtful arrangement of plant forms, textures, and colors can be equally radiant. The effect isn't harder to achieve, but arguably, harder to master. It takes a certain sophis-

IT'S ALMOST IMPOSSIBLE to force formality upon the plants of the shade garden. Even an antique urn filled with Hosta lancifolia *looks delightfully unkempt.* OPPOSITE: *Ruth Levitan's plantings capture nature's informality.*

tication and an artistic eye.

People have always pushed and prodded plants into situations that may or may not suit them. The earliest cultivated plantings were fields of grain, contained and watched, but barely managed. Early gardens were often what we would call formal. They evolved around the irrigation source, like the crops grown in Egypt along trenches dug to carry the Nile's water. Ornamental plantings too grew out of the proximity to the water source: the central well of the cloister's geometric beds eventually led to the tightly controlled Elizabethan knot gardens.

Our notion of glorifying na-

JON ROWEN'S TINY
urban planting is confined by space,
but his imaginative juxtaposition of
plants seems unlimited. ABOVE:
Repeating golden hostas brings the
composition together. BELOW:
The eye comes to rest on the
elephantine Rodgersia tabularis
behind a "sparkling stream" of
variegated pachysandra.

ture with a planting in its image is a romantic ideal that has more to do with sharing an environment than controlling it. A shade garden can have formality forced upon it, I suppose. But the very nature of this environment, and the plants that enjoy it, is informal. That's one reason why naturalistic design is perfect for our conditions. In a small backyard or area where the patio meets the house, architectural elements, such as paving and walls, will impart a flavor of formality, but be hard-pressed to impose it. Elevate a *Hosta lancifolia* to an urn, and you've gone about as formal as possible. But the headdress of green foliage still looks wonderfully shaggy—irresistible. And to me, better than an urnful of red-hot geraniums in the sun.

Isolated as it is, this assemblage still depends on the plants around it. The urn-and-geranium combo would look fairly good at the center of a vegetable garden but the lovely hosta *must* bask in some shade from an overhanging tree and be seen against a background of green shrubs. It is a single component of the secluded, private world of the shade garden—not the star, perhaps, but a principal player in a rather democratic ensemble.

THE
FUNDAMENTALS
OF DESIGN

There are some basics to consider when you design a garden. First, you are dealing with space, physically and aesthetically. Within every planted hori-

THE FINE ART OF PLANTING USES LEAF FORM AND TEXTURE AS SCULPTURAL
elements. Ginny Purviance accomplishes this in a middle-layer mixed border with arching Polygonatum biflorum,
flowering mounds of hydrangea and variegated Daphne x Burkwoodii *'Carol Mackie'*.

zontal swath of green there are various levels or planes. Your decisions involve these planes of landscape and the form and texture of the plants. Form isn't limited to the shape of a bushy shrub or a fastigiate tree; it's also the definition of the edge of a planting bed or the line of a border growing along the garden wall or against the side of a building.

Vertical plants and objects produce points of punctuation that grab attention. Repeating plants can bring a design together; a lime green fern at one side of a planting can have a twin at the other end to connect the planting area. But you will tend to be drawn to asymmetrical constructions, skewing plants to the left or right of center, and then restoring the equilibrium of the arrangement with unlike shapes and masses.

Colors, whether in harmony or contrast, or just in shades and tints of light and dark green, can help make a cohesive garden. The pale green color of a fern could blend gradually toward a deep green plant, through a host of related colors, fading to darkness. Since the foliage outlasts the flowers on all plants, *leaf color* plays an important role. Repeating a purple-leaved plant, such as a barberry, three times through a planting bed gives the scheme movement: the eye goes from point to point. Variety makes the planting stop and go. Sameness, on the other hand, can be soothing, the calm between storms of color—a quiet background for action.

THINK OF YOUR YARD as three areas, defined by use as much as by demarcation: the inner area, the area in-between, ABOVE and CENTER, and the outer area, BELOW.

Your goal will be to create an interesting, uninterrupted scene that flows from plant to plant, garden space to garden space, to emulate the rhythm of nature.

AREAS OF THE GARDEN

Think of the different parts of your landscape. Some are independent and clearly defined, surrounded by lawn or up against the paved driveway. Others gently flow into one another— their perimeters blurred by a consistent surface texture or obscured by dappled shade.

I tend to describe a property in three sections: the inner area, the outer area, and the in-between area. The inner area is the high-traffic space for utility, paths and walks, patios and terraces, and such. This space usually surrounds the house. Durable hard-surface materials underfoot make these places easy to maintain.

The house casts shade on three sides. In the Northern Hemisphere, the north, east, and west sides of buildings cast shadows. Corners and turns made by walls and steps will be in shade for some part of the day. Trees, shrubs, and even vines that grow right up against the house will also cast shade. Yet you will probably want plantings here, in plain view of the house. Shrubs are most common in the planting areas next to the house's foundation, but containers on the patio, herbaceous perennials (non-woody plants that die to the ground each fall and return in

spring), or vines that scale the house walls can also provide color and interest. Color can also come from more unconventional sources—paint and ornament, or even water features and fish.

The in-between area can be "lawn-scape" for recreation or just to gaze upon. There are special lawn-seed mixes for this place if it's in shade. However, this part of the landscape can also support your most ambitious flower plantings. You might choose to have an island of perennials or mixed plantings of shrubs and herbaceous flowering plants. You could have a small tree collection, perhaps a few fruit trees in the sun, or trees with special flowers or fall color. A garden scene can be created by a single tree, or even by the clever use of sculpture and ornament. Flowers are not the only solution. You'll find shaded spots within this area as well, underneath trees and shrubs where shade-tolerant, low maintenance ground covers make the line of lawn more casual, less abrupt.

The outer area, usually surrounding the property, is the most informal. Simple plantings offer privacy, hide undesirable views, provide shelter from wind, and baffle noise. Trees help achieve all these goals, and beneath them is a place that's

STEPPING STONES MAKE
an informal, permanent path
through the inner area of this New
England garden.

perfect for planting. You might want to create a meandering path that features flower-color along its borders. Spring bulbs, woodland wildflowers, and ferns could thrive there. The transitional edge between the outer area's tall trees and the in-between area can be softened by smaller trees and shrubs.

MAKING YOUR BED

Any planting bed, whether an island bed, up against a wall, or out in the woodland, needs planning and preparation. Straight lines look best in formal gardens, so try soft, undulating plantings that will melt into the foreground or drift away into the background. Make the border as wide as possible, around five feet or so, with a narrow, concealed path at the rear for maintenance. Stepping-stones strategically placed in the bed will also be useful when grooming dead leaves or faded flowers, planting new treasures, or dividing colonies that have crept out of bounds. An island bed, accessible from all sides, is usually no wider than twice the height of the tallest plants within.

You can sketch some ideas for the shape of your borders and beds, or "draw" in the landscape itself, using stakes connected with string or a garden hose laid directly on the ground. It helps to view your design from above —either on a ladder, or from an upstairs window.

The bed can ramble, undulate,

THE INNER AREA IS FOR relaxation, ABOVE. OPPOSITE: *The in-between area, which leads to the outer area, can be the place for your most ambitious plantings.*

pour up to a tree, enclose it, and continue on its way. It can rise and fall with the land. It can turn corners and surround a pond, rock, or other landscape element. Plants will have to be chosen to fit the conditions as the bed travels through damp and dry soil, dark and light shade.

One way to build a bed is to have soil dumped directly on the site. This is much easier than digging or double digging—the arduous method of preparing ground. It also means you can give the site the type of soil that will be enjoyed by its future tenants. For acid-loving woodland plants, a mix rich in organic matter could be applied. If topsoil is all that's available, work in some humus such as peat moss and leaf mold, or ground redwood bark on the West Coast.

The result will be a rolling hill or hillock perhaps two feet high at its highest point. The edge will gently smooth down to lawn or mulch. Edging materials can be used: smooth rocks possibly, or granite blocks, redwood benderboard, or even a mowing strip constructed of brick laid for the wheel of a lawn mower to ride over. A bed can also be cut into an existing slope. The resulting terrace would be even with the ground at the back and raised at the sides and front. You could contain the soil with rock edging or by stacking thin logs.

You might also be able to build up a rock-raised planter on top of the root area of one of the moisture-sucking trees. Tread lightly. I'm experimenting with a weed barrier placed over a small area of tree root. This is a woven plastic cloth that lets most of the moisture trickle down and oxygen flow, but stops weeds from coming up and, I hope, stops maple roots from finding their way up to the new planting mix. I've placed some respectable rocks and a thin layer of gravel above the barrier to hold them and ensure circulation and drainage, and filled in the pockets with a very open, humus-rich medium incorporating shredded fir bark. Redwood compost in the West Coast would be an excellent medium.

THE SHADE GARDENER'S MEDIUM IS FOLIAGE, FROM THE FINE FILIGREE OF THE

Polystichum polyplepharum *fern,* ABOVE, *to the sharp blades of the native* Iris versicolor, RIGHT, *whose foliage fans last all season—its flowers come and go in as little as a single day.*

LOOKING
AT LEAVES

As you learn more about gardening in the shade, you will begin to see plants a little differently. You'll be looking more closely at leaves and at the structure of branches and limbs. Volume, shape, texture, proportion, and subtle shadings, rather than simple masses of color, become the shade gardener's means of expression.

It's hard to generalize about plants—harder still to make rules, or speak in absolutes, especially when talking about design, much of which is personal taste. I *can* say that in the shade garden, we are dealing primarily with foliage, and that once you learn to look at leaves you'll discover a world of unlimited diversity and beauty.

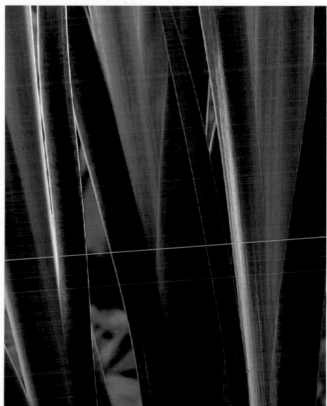

There are simple and compound leaves. Among the simple (not divided or segmented) there are configurations of enormous variety. Leaves can be fan-shaped, spear-shaped, shaped like broad spades, hearts, clubs, or clovers, and in a rare case, like a diamond. *Lanceolate* leaves are shaped like a spear. *Linear* leaves are long and thin, like blades of grass and bulb foliage. *Reniform* leaves are kidney-shaped. *Deltoid* leaves are the spades; *cordate* the hearts. *Spatulate* are shaped, well, like a spatula. Leaves are often *lobed: palmately lobed,* like a maple, or *parted,* like an oak. When a stem comes to the center of the underside of the leaf it is *peltate.* Sometimes peltate leaves are also deeply lobed, like the mayapple's (*Podophyllum peltatum*). And many leaves have serrated edges.

Leaves made up of segments are compound. *Pinnate* leaves are like a feather. *Bipinnate* leaves are arranged in a double row, like fern fronds. Locusts, mimosa, ash, and sumacs have leaves like this, as do *Mahonia* spp., *Sambucus* spp., and the variegated box elder (*Acer negundo* varieties). *Cimicifuga* spp. and *Actaea pachypoda* have segmented leaves that are *biternate. Palmate* and *digitate* leaves are shaped like a hand: *Parthenocissus quinquefolia* (Virginia creeper), *Rodgersia pinnata* and fan palms. *Trifoliate* leaves have three sections, like a cloverleaf.

The size of leaves varies greatly. Evergreen rhododendrons alone have incredible variety, from the tiny leaves of the Kurume hybrid azaleas to the

LEAVES CAN BE SMALL OR large, segmented or whole: Euonymus fortunei *'Kewensis' (*E. f. *'Minima') climbs behind* Bergenia cordifolia *'Bressingham White' at the New York Botanical Garden.* OPPOSITE: *Staghorn sumac's (*Rhus typhina*) pinnate leaves are at their greatest glory in autumn.*

downy, two-foot-long leaves of their subtropical relatives.

Tiny leaves may read as a textured pattern from a short distance. For example, the Japanese holly (*Ilex crenata*) looks a lot like boxwood but is cityproof, hardier, and more shade-tolerant. It creates a textured mound of deep green. But masses of small foliage viewed at once can read as a solid form and are usually used for background. If you are trying to create an effect with a column or mound of leaves, then solid foliage would be useful up front. A light and airy specimen wouldn't have the volume or density to be much more than a flag in the breeze.

Medium-size leaves are large enough to provide impact without dominating: *Heuchera,* geranium, whorls of dark green *Paris polyphylla* leaves, peltate *Podophyllum peltatum,* and evergreen *Bergenia,* for instance. Large leaves, those of cordate *Brunnera, Ligularia,* and *Veratrum* (false hellebore) make powerful statements and are, perhaps, best on their own.

I've heard countless gardening experts claim that broad leaves should always be in front of small ones so their bold effect may be set off by a textured background. But I have seen a group of monochromatic broad, bold leaves, such as those of *Hosta sieboldiana* 'Elegans', appearing as a single mass of deep blue-green and serving as a perfect foil for the delicate warm green filigree leaves and tiny ever-present pink flowers of herb Robert (*Geranium robertianum*).

You can often tell just by looking at a plant whether it will tolerate sun or shade. Consider the plants of the sun, most of which have small leaves, or in the case of cacti, no leaves at all. Their leaves often have either waxy coatings or little hairs, down, or powder—all devices to help them conserve moisture. Shade plants have little or no coating. The holes in the leaves, or *stomata,* rarely have hairs. The stems and leaves usually are not thick like the cacti or succulents, but thin—very thin, in fact—for little water is stored in the leaf areas. The cells in these leaves are large and widely spaced. Most shade plants have leaves that are smooth and shiny. (That's why many are excellent choices for city gardens. They wash clean of soot and grime in every rain shower.)

Some shade plants have evolved larger leaf surfaces to gather as much light as possible. They are often dark in color to absorb light as well. Picture the jungle's philodendron and the woodland's jack-in-the-pulpit.

The leaves can afford to be large because they live in humid environments with ample soil moisture; the leaves won't wilt from evaporation through the leaf surfaces (called transpiration).

If you study these plants, you'll also notice that leaves often overlap. Plants such as twinleaf (*Jeffersonia* spp.) and the wild gingers (*Asarum* spp.) can grow in their own shade. A sun plant would shade itself into oblivion. Their leaf growth is often whorled, so that leaves do not shade each other. On the other hand, the hostas and others have multiple leaves emanating from the base, or crown, not a tall stem and tiny leaves. This density has advantages for the plants. It shades out weed seedlings that would vie for nutrients, moisture and space.

The shade plants are their own living mulches. They aren't in a competitive rampage for moisture and nutrients like the sunny meadow plants. They just amble on, shading out competitors in a slow, deliberate pace that suits their simpler ecology.

SHADE PLANT LEAVES ARE OFTEN LARGE TO HELP THEM GATHER AS MUCH LIGHT AS
possible. A baby toad, no bigger than a pinky nail, rests on a Hosta plantaginea 'Grandiflora' in my garden.
OPPOSITE: Shade plants can often bask in their own shadow, as with twinleaf, Jeffersonia diphylla.

Imagine how the open quality of ferns and other plants with tracery foliage could impart an air of lightness to an area. Feathery foliage in a small garden space would open it up and let the ether flow. Next to a heavy wall they would be as devastating to its solidity as Joshua's trumpets.

Twigs and leaves (whether they are shiny, matte, puckered, or smooth), along with the spaces between them where the light passes freely, become separate parts of the whole when the plant is viewed up close. Consider the scattered arrangement of a corkscrew willow. Its small leaves are turbulently twisted. From far enough away, they combine to create a single mass. But close up, the stems and trunk of this small, fast-growing tree *twirl*. Masses of evergreen yew or podocarpus can form a nearly seamless background for more colorful plantings.

Some plants are so familiar they "read" the same near or far. The bamboo retains a lot of its jagged, grassy texture. An evergreen conifer is always distinctive; it looks like what it is. We're used to recognizing it. From a great distance we know a pine tree by the shape that all the tiny needles together make—the familiar conical Christmas tree.

ENGLISH IVY CLIMBS A
north-facing wall in deep shade.
OPPOSITE: *Arisaema sikokianum*
is an Asian jack-in-the-pulpit to try.

PLANTS TO TRY IN DEEP SHADE

GROUND COVERS

Ajuga repens, bugleweed
Asarum spp., wild ginger
Cornus canadensis, bunchberry
Epimedium spp., bishop's hat
Galax urceolata, galax
Gaultheria procumbens, wintergreen
Goodyera repens, rattlesnake plantain
Hedera spp., ivy
Lamiastrum galeobdolon, yellow
    archangel
Liriope spp., dwarf lilyturf
Lycopodium spp., club moss
Maianthemum canadense, false lily-of-
    the-valley
Mitchella repens, partridgeberry
Mitella diphylla, bishop's-cap
Ophiopogon spp., mondo grass
Pachysandra spp., pachysandra,
    spurge
Phlox stolonifera, creeping phlox
Pulmonaria spp., lungwort
Saxifraga spp., saxifrage, strawberry
    begonia
Vinca minor, vinca

HERBACEOUS PERENNIALS

Arisaema spp., jack-in-the-pulpit
Chimaphila spp., pipsissewa
Clintonia borealis, clintonia
Cypripedium spp., slipper orchids

Dicentra spp., bleeding heart
Dodecatheon spp., shooting star
Eomecon chionantha, snow poppy
Gentiana spp., gentian
Helleborus spp., hellebore
Hosta spp. and cultivars, hosta,
    plantain lily
Impatiens wallerana, impatiens, busy
    Lizzy
Jeffersonia diphylla, twinleaf
Medeola virginiana, Indian cucumber
Mertensia spp., bluebells
Oxalis acetosella, wood sorrel
Paris polyphylla, Paris
Phlox adsurgens, periwinkle phlox
Polemonium spp., Jacob's ladder
Polygonatum spp., Solomon's seal
Pyrola elliptica, shinleaf
Sanguinaria canadensis, bloodroot
Stylophorum diphyllum, celandine
    poppy
Tellima grandiflora, false alumroot,
    foam flower
Tricyrtis spp., toad lily
Trientalis borealis, starflower
Uvularia grandiflora, merrybells,
    bellwort
Uvularia sessilifolia, wild sea oats

FERNS

Adiantum pedatum, maidenhair fern
Asplenium trichomanes, maidenhair
    spleenwort

Athyrium thelypteroides, silvery glade-
    fern
Dryopteris filix-mas, male fern
Dryopteris marginalis, marginal shield
    fern
Hymenophyllum tunbrigensis,
    Tunbridge's filmy fern
Osmunda regalis, royal fern
Polystichum acrostichoides, Christmas
    fern
Polystichum braunii, Braun's holly
    fern
Pteridium aquilinum, bracken fern
Trichomanes petersii, Peter's filmy
    fern

SHRUBS

Aronia arbutifolia, chokeberry
Forsythia spp. and hybrids, forsythia
Ilex aquifolium, English holly
Leucothoe fontanesiana, drooping
    leucothoe
Sarcococca hookerana digyna,
    sarcococca
Taxus spp., yew
Tsuga canadensis, hemlock

VINES

Hedera spp., ivy
Parthenocissus quinquefolia, Virginia
    creeper

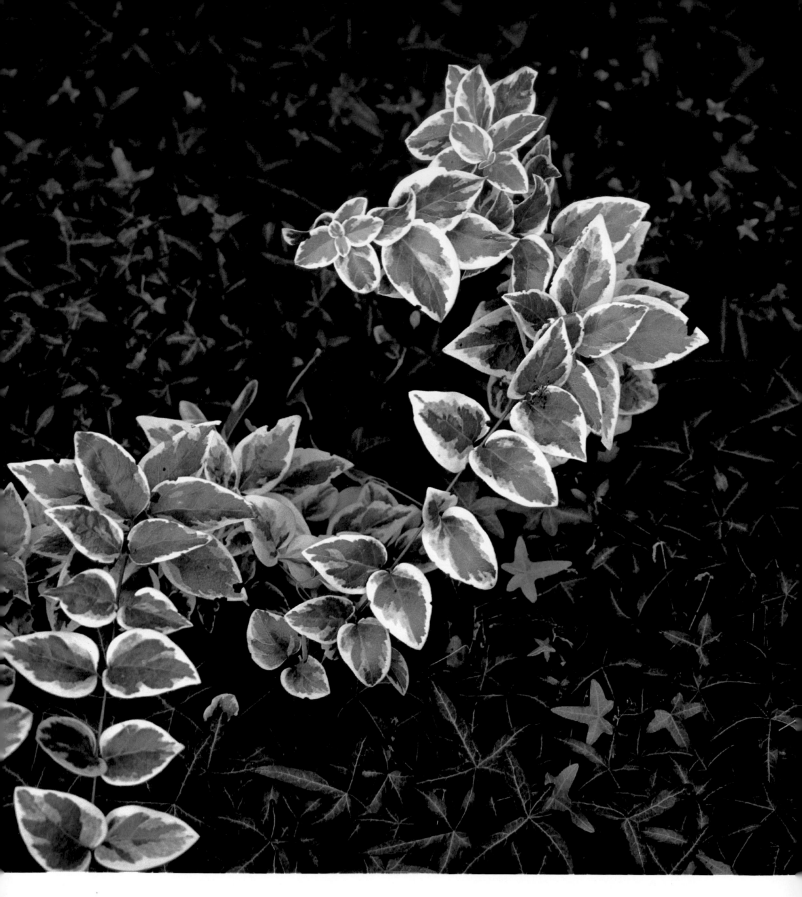

VINCA MAJOR 'VARIEGATA' SCAMPERS OVER A BIRD'S-FOOT IVY, LEAVING LIGHT

trails in the shade. White stands out. Red does, too. OPPOSITE: *A red-flowered azalea appears to jump forward when it blooms; later it recedes into the depths of the shade garden.*

LIGHTING
WITH
PLANTS

By selecting and arranging foliage and flowers for color and tone, you can paint a three-dimensional garden picture and bring "light" into dark areas. Bright color placed in front of deep, dark color jumps out. On the other hand, a dark form in front of a lighter one recedes to suggest the opening to a secluded garden room. Vibrant hues counter subtle tints while related shades harmonize, providing opportunities for variety.

Some colors naturally stand out. Red advances, thereby foreshortening a garden. If you have an element at the rear of a long garden that you would like

to bring closer, plant it (or paint it) red. You'll probably be selecting some evergreen azaleas and tulips for your shade planting; if you choose those with red flowers, be prepared to have a rather narrow garden for about a month in the spring. Bronze-leaved *Ligularia dentata* 'Desdemona', smaller *L. d.* 'Othello', or plum-colored foliage from *Corylus maxima atropurpurea* (purple filbert), *Sambucus nigra* 'Atropurpurea' (elder), or *Berberis thunbergii* 'Atropurpurea' (barberry), or even common coleus are subtle enough to use carefully within a planting, but they still cause the eye to leap from spot to spot of reddish foliage, making other plants blend to solid green.

Carefully placed, white is often a perfect choice for an accent in a colorful flower planting,

SPIRAEA *X* VANHOUTTEI
has lacy white tufts, ABOVE. *A claret-colored coleus casts a mysterious spell,* RIGHT.
Ampelopsis brevipedunculata *'Elegans' is an arresting variegated vine,* FAR RIGHT.

where it can help clashing colors go together—just by refereeing the bout. But even though white goes with every color, it can dominate. It zooms into view. White flowers sprinkled through a planting will grab attention, sometimes at the expense of the entire scheme. By the same token, the perfect planting for the working stiff would be chock-full of white flowers that could be enjoyed well into evening. The pop-out whites would be more than welcome in the moonlight.

Masses of pale-colored foliage behind bolder color has a different effect. Mountains seem to become lighter the farther away they are. Small leaves, reading as a pale tone, will also amplify an illusion of depth.

When you use the fainter tones, you will also have an opportunity to "light" with plants. You can add sparkle to an especially dark place with pale-colored leaves. Take the dark corners—the spots at the end of the path, or under the eaves, or in the shade of a tree—and bring light to them by employing plants and flowers that reflect light back to the viewer. These areas will no longer recede but be brought to the forefront. You can decide when you want to draw attention with tinted shades (and you can also decide when to let some areas fade away).

There are many plants from all over the world that have silver and gray leaves. These would be perfect for lighting, but if you remember that these plants appear to be silver because of their waxy, powdery, or downy coverings, evolved to help them withstand burning sun, then you'll realize that, unfortunately, most are not plants for shade. There are, however, plants with silver splashes, such as *Lamiastrum galeobdolon* and the *Pulmonarias,* and plenty of plants with gray-green glaucous leaves, such as *Corydalis lutea,* hosta, and rue (*Ruta graveolens*). There are also a few "blue" grass and grasslike plants that will tolerate shade— *Carex nigra, Festuca scoparia* 'Pic Carlit'—and some shading— *Helictotrichon sempervirens* and *Panicum virgatum* 'Strictum'. Gold, on the other hand, is less rare in the shaded garden, but no less precious. There are numerous plants with foliage color that is commonly called gold and that ranges from chartreuse to butter yellow.

VARIEGATED PLANTS

Another way to create patches of light in the shade garden is to use variegated foliage. Nearly every beginning gardener says that he or she *hates* variegated

SILVER RUTA

graveolens, TOP; Helictotrichon sempervirens, BOTTOM. Physostegia virginiana *'Variegata',* CENTER *and* OPPOSITE, *lights the garden with other variegated plants.*

plants. We go along quite innocently dismissing striped plants as being vulgar, almost embarrassing—the clowns of the plant world. They seem unnatural, man-made aberrations. Then, one day, experience catches up with us. We encounter a new plant, our first irresistible variegated charmer. It's not just a white-edged hosta. For me, it was a speckled porcelain vine (*Ampelopsis brevipedunculata* 'Elegans'), whose leaves are "broken" into zones of white, gray, lime-milk, khaki, and moss green. In addition, the stems of the new growth are magenta.

Once you've seen a special plant in a friend's planting or at a public garden, the search begins. Quest becomes obsession. Overnight, the formerly silly variegated plants have become priceless variations of uninteresting others. If there is a solid green maidenhair fern, then there might be a variegated version (there is). A collector is born.

When a plant is variegated, it has distinct markings of various colors, usually light on dark, white on green. They often originate as *sports,* side shoots that are naturally occurring mutations. These parts of plants are cut off and rooted, or propagated by other vegetative methods such as modern tissue culture.

Flowers themselves may be variegated, called "bicolor." The striped tulips of seventeenth-century Holland led to "tulipomania," frenzied trading on the stock market and the collapse of the Dutch economy. The magnificent shade-tolerant under-

A COLLECTION OF GOLDEN AND VARIEGATED PLANTS STARS A DIMINUTIVE HOSTA,
H. 'Golden Scepter', ABOVE, along with Epimedium pulmonorium and milium. OPPOSITE: Milium effusum aureum,
a handsome grass, keeps its color in shade and is semievergreen.

SOME PLANTS DISTINGUISHED BY "GOLD" FOLIAGE

SHRUBS

Berberis thunbergii 'Aurea', gold-leaved barberry

Corylus avellana 'Aurea', golden-leaved hazel

Ilex aquifolium 'Flavescens', moonlight holly

Ligustrum ovalifolium 'Aureum', golden privet

Lonicera nitida 'Baggesen's Gold', box-leaf honeysuckle

Physocarpus opulifolius 'Luteus', eastern ninebark

Sambucus racemosa 'Plumosa Aurea', golden elder

HERBACEOUS PERENNIALS

Filipendula ulmaria 'Aurea', golden meadowsweet

Hosta fortunei 'Aurea', hosta, plantain lily

H. 'Gold Edger'

H. 'Golden Scepter'

H. 'Lights Up'

H. 'Little Aurora'

H. 'Midas Touch'

H. 'Piedmont Gold'

H. 'Royalty'

H. 'Sun Power'

H. 'Wogon Gold'

H. 'Zounds'

Lamium maculatum 'Aureum', lamium, dead nettle

Lysimachia nummularia 'Aurea', creeping Jennie

Origanum vulgare 'Aureum', yellow marjoram

GRASS AND GRASSLIKE PLANTS

Carex stricta 'Bowles Golden', Bowles golden grass

Milium effusum aureum, golden grass

Sesleria autumnalis, autumn moor grass

FLOWERS CAN ALSO BE VARIEGATED, OR BICOLOR. THE STURDY SHRUB ENKIANTHUS
campanulatus *produces nodding cream bells with red veins and, later, brilliant fall foliage.* OPPOSITE: *Delicate*
dangling flowers grace Polygonatum odoratum *'Variegatum', one of the best foliage plants for shade.*

story shrub *Enkianthus* spp. has lovely dangling bell-shaped flowers in creamy pink with coral stripes. The incredible flower of *Fritillaria meleagris* (the guinea-hen flower, checkered lily, or snake's-head flower) is actually broken into perfectly square sections of oxblood and creamy mauve variegation.

Some foliage is tricolored. *Ajugas* are trouble-free ground covers whose common name is bugle or bugleweed. They can put on a valiant effort in shade (except for *A. pyramidalis*). In late spring, they send up wonderful spikes lined with deep blue, pink, or white flowers. One of the nicest ajugas is *A. reptans* 'Burgundy Glow', with cream-, green-, and wine-colored leaves in tight basal rosettes. *A. reptans* 'Multicoloris' is bronze, red, white, and yellow.

Physostegia virginiana 'Variegata' is quite shade-tolerant, and through the winter it has tricolored basal rosettes, gray-

green and cream-flushed rose, that resemble those of an ajuga. *Physostegias,* called false dragonheads, are familiar garden favorites typified by square stems and pink flowers lasting a long period in late summer. It's the variegated cultivar's foliage and especially the stripes of gray-green and white along the prominent stems that are remarkable; the flowers are a muted lilac color.

Simple fans of iris foliage become living sculptures in their variegated forms. In spring, the yellow-and-cream blades of *Iris pseudacorus* 'Variegata' shoot up. By summer, they've become solid green but continue to grow, and established plants can have blades five or more feet tall. Yellow flag, as it's commonly called, can stand wet feet, as can *I. laevigata* 'Variegata', an enchanting white-and-green iris for the bog garden. *I. pallida* curses the damp.

Iris foetidissima (sometimes called stinking glad or stinking

iris—charming names, I think) is a familiar standby in English gardens and is particularly adored for its winter effect. It is evergreen and has very ornamental cylindrical seedpods that split open into three sections, revealing scarlet seeds that last through the winter. Brace yourself: there is a variegated form that is at its whitest in shade and at its best in winter. For some reason, this plant is rarely offered for sale in North America.

There are variegated grasses that can also add a strong vertical to a planting. *Glyceria aquatica* 'Variegata' is creamy yellow with green stripes, and easy to grow. *Miscanthus sinensis* 'Variegatus' not only bears color variation on its long, arching leaves, but it is the best of its genus for tolerating partial shade, especially in the South, where it needs shelter from heat.

A light and airy grass, *Phalaris arundinacea* 'Picta' is an old-fashioned garden plant with delightful common names: gardener's-garters and ribbon grass. I have read that this is a plant for sun. It *will* tolerate sun if there is enough moisture, but it does very well in partial shade and will make do in the deep dark. I guess that is why I think of it as floppy —in shade it lies around. And it can spread! But you can easily pull it out, roots and all, so I wouldn't consider it invasive, just a friendly naturalizer. It is terrific for underplanting with bulbs, since its leaves come up in spring to hide fading flower-bulb foliage.

Liriopes are not grasses but grasslike semievergreen peren-

OPPOSITE: CORNUS ALBA *'Sibirica Variegata' lights a hillside,* ABOVE; Berberis thunbergii *'Rose Glow',* BELOW LEFT; *and* Acer negundo *'Variegatum',* BELOW RIGHT. ABOVE, *tulips underplant* Phalaris arundinacea picta.

nials that have strappy foliage. They look a bit like the household spider plant (*Chlorophytum comosum* 'Vittatum', a good choice for subtropical gardens in zones 9–10). The showy variegated liriopes are difficult to use well, because they are incredibly neat and tidy. In formal gardens, there is a tendency to line the walk with them: a nasty habit. I think it's best to cluster them— three little neat mounds among some rocks, perhaps—so that they look like a shaggy little colony that has taken hold between the stones. Liriope is very easy to grow and has varieties that

flower well in shade, pushing hyacinthlike spikes of white or pale to dark violet flowers. Other nongrass plants include sedges such as the *Carex* spp. and acorus (*Acorus calamus* 'Variegatus').

There are several variegated mints. Pineapple mint has fuzzy leaves and is dainty compared to the galloping members of its clan. *Lamium maculatum* varieties, dead nettles, are well-behaved relatives of the mints, typified by square stems. They are necessities for the natural shade garden. These colorful ground covers have wonderful mottled leaves and flowers of white or pink to rose. But beware their black sheep cousin *Lamiastrum galeobdolon*, yellow archangel: You'll be pulling it out everywhere, but still find it beautiful. Fuzzy silver-and-green leaves cover trailing wiry stems, and in spring, stiff ten-inch-tall flower stems bear wonderful yellow blossoms. The solution? Grow it in a container where it can be corralled. *L. g.* 'Herman's Pride', on the other hand, is a very tidy variety that has lost its desire to rove. Someday the taxonomists may give this plant its own species name and take it away from its altogether untidy relative.

Down by the ground is the place for the variegated pachysandra and, if you happen upon it, *Convallaria majalis* 'Variegata', variegated lily of the valley. Search for the variegated vinca (*Vinca minor* 'Variegata').

Brunnera macrophylla has sprinklings of sapphire blue, forget-me-not flowers on airy stems held above the foliage, from midspring to summer. But I love the velvety cordate leaves, and there are white variegated forms, *B. m.* 'Hadspen Cream', *B. m.* 'Langtrees', and *B. m.* 'Variegata'.

When you think of dogwood, you picture the native American tree *Cornus florida*. There are many other members of this genus, which includes trees and shrubs, some as tiny as the *Cornus canadensis,* which is barely eight inches tall. This interesting and varied group includes a host of variegated subjects. The red-twig dogwood, named for the stems, which are bright magenta through the winter—great against the snow after the leaves have fallen—is among the most useful shrubs in its variegated form. *C. alba* 'Sibirica Variegata' (*C. alba* 'Elegantissima') has white-edged, gray-green leaves. *C. alba* 'Spaethii' has gold-and-green leaves.

There are several small dogwood trees with colorful foliage as well: *Cornus florida* and *C. kousa* cultivars (the Asian dogwoods), for example. New varieties are introduced all the time. *C. mas* 'Variegata', a form of the native cornelian cherry, has silver variegations and very early, tiny yellow ribbonlike flowers, like those of a witch hazel, followed by edible red fruits. *C. alternifolia* 'Variegata' (pagoda dogwood) and *C. controversa* 'Variegata' (wedding cake tree) have wide-spreading branches.

Daphnes can be a bit temperamental, but one of the best and easiest to grow not only has pale-edged foliage, but wonderfully fragrant pink flowers as well. *Daphne* x *burkwoodii* 'Carol

Mackie' has gray-green leaves with white banding and is semi-evergreen. *D. odora* 'Variegata' is a choice for the West Coast.

Familiar plants often have variegated offspring. *Pieris japonica,* Japanese andromeda, and euonymus are good examples. The only possible drawback to the latter is that some are susceptible to scale insects. But try *E. fortunei* (*E. radicans*), wintercreeper, an evergreen shrub that ranges by variety from quite miniature to medium-sized, and offers several choices such as *E. f.* 'Emerald Gaiety', *E. f.* 'Silver Queen', *E. f.* 'Sunshine', and *E. f.* 'Variegatus'. All will tolerate shade, but the golds may lose some of their shading there. *E. japonicus* is also evergreen, and generally a bit larger. Varieties include *E. j.* 'Albomarginata', *E. j.* 'Aureopicta', *E. j.* 'Macrophylla Alba', *E. j.* 'Microphylla Pulchella' ('Microphylla Aurea'), the very tiny *E. j.* 'Microphylla Variegata', and *E. j.* 'Ovatus Aureus'.

In warmer climes, where the temperature rarely dips into the twenties, consider variegated *Pittosporum tenuifolium* and *P. tobira* with orange-blossom-scented flowers. *Osmanthus heterophyllus* 'Variegatus' is a holly look-alike for areas that do not drop below fifteen degrees Fahrenheit.

Fortunately, the variegated hollies (*Ilex* spp.) are much more plentiful. You'll probably be able to find some at your nursery or garden center. Look for *I.* x *altaclarensis* 'Golden King', *I. aquifolium* 'Ferox Argentea', *I. a.* 'Golden Milkboy', *I. a.* 'Golden Queen', *I. a.* 'Handsworth New Silver', and *I. a.* 'Silver Queen'.

Kerrias are among my favorite deciduous shrubs for shade. Their Kodak-yellow pompons wouldn't be so special if they were out in the blazing sun in the middle of summer, but on a spring-blooming plant in the shade, they're miraculous. The other nice thing about *Kerria japonica* 'Pleniflora' is its arresting grass-green canes, lasting throughout winter. The single-flowered, butter-yellow kerria is much more refined, and the daintiest of all is variegated, *K. j.* 'Variegata', with single flowers in spring and sporadically throughout the growing season.

The thrill of discovering and finding variegated plants is enough to justify their use. However, the greatest test of the artist in the shade garden is knowing how they go together. Plant association is the horticultural equivalent of combinations of color, fabric, and furniture in a room, light and dark in a painting, form and mass in architecture. It's an art.

VARIEGATED PLANTS, FROM LEFT TO RIGHT, TOP ROW TO BOTTOM ROW:

Pittosporum tobira *'Variegata'*; Hydrangea macrophylla *'Variegata'*; Euonymus fortunei *'Silver Queen'*; Pachysandra terminalis *'Variegata'*; Tsuga canadensis *'Albospica'*; Tovara virginianum *'Variegata'*; Disporum sessile *'Variegatum'*; Euonymus fortunei *'Emerald Gaiety' (winter color)*; Lamiastrum galeobdolon *'Herman's Pride'*; Pulmonaria saccharata *'Mrs. Moon'*; Daphne x Burkwoodii *'Carol Mackie'*; Tsuga canadensis *'Gentsch White'*.

OPPOSITE: Lamiastrum galeobdolon, *controlled in a container.*

PLANTS AND

PLANTINGS

THE PLANTS THAT SPREAD ACROSS THE WOODLAND OR GARDEN "FLOOR" ARE THE
ground covers. Here elegant wild ginger, Asarum canadense, *forms a thick blanket.* OPPOSITE: *Another native, red-
and yellow-flowered* Aquilegia canadense, *columbine, brightens light shade, along with phlox and geraniums.*

THE GARDEN FLOOR

The forest is made up of plants arranged in horizontal layers. The top layer is the forest canopy, where the tall deciduous hardwoods or evergreens live intertwined with the occasional vine. The middle layer is the home of the small trees, shrubs, and tall herbaceous perennials. The lowest layer is the forest floor. This is a simplification, of course, and there is no solid line of demarcation. The lower branches of the taller trees bend down to touch the tops of the middle-layer trees. The shrubs blend with the lower herbaceous perennial plants, and they in turn meld into the creeping ground covers. But examine this layer system because it will be a guide to plants and planting in the shade garden.

GROUND COVERS

Everyone knows what a tree is. Shrubs too, and vines. But what is a ground cover? Can it be a low-growing shrub, herbaceous perennial, vine, grass? It usually is one of these. Any plant that spreads to cloak the soil can be used as a ground cover. Most often, these are low-growing plants that hug the earth, but a hosta, even a good-sized hosta, can be used as a ground cover. Since the definition of a ground cover means just that, you can use tall plants in some situations. A mass planting of evergreen azaleas might be considered a ground cover. Or even tall, naturalized foxgloves (*Digitalis* spp.), or meadow rue (*Thalictrum* spp.), which tops out at five feet. For the most part, though, it's the little plants—those that tend to grow horizontally more than vertically—with which we are now concerned.

The low ground covers spread by means of underground stems, or runners, self-sowing, under- or aboveground stolons that root along the stems at leaf nodes, spreading branches, or simply from ever-expanding clumps. Lawn grass is *stoloniferous*: its rhizomes, modified horizontal stems, travel just below the surface, rooting and sprouting. Many ferns spread that way, too. Ivy can form roots anywhere along the stems. Clumps of *Dicentra* spp. (bleeding hearts) just grow bigger each season. Plants that self-sow can naturalize to become ground covers, such as

forget-me-nots (*Myosotis* spp.). And many annuals can be sown for a similar effect. Hardy annuals, those whose seeds survive the winter, could be used for cover; they return like the biennial forget-me-nots, but new each year from self-sown seed.

I would be lax if I didn't mention the most famous ground cover of them all: grass lawn. No other living plant can stand so much foot traffic. But there are problems with lawn. Besides the fact that it has to be mowed often, fertilized endlessly, watered, weeded, and mowed again, it doesn't like shade very much. Grass prefers to bask in the hot sun of the open golf course.

Lawn is a "gross-feeder," as they say in the trade: it perishes not only from lack of light, but also from insufficient nutrition. So it is definitely not the cover of choice under a low-branched or shallow-rooted tree. Grass also likes an alkaline environment—unsuitable for the shade plants that come from the forest, where leaf litter keeps the soil pH neutral-to-acid.

*GROUND COVERS CAN BE shrubs (*Leucothoe fontanesiana*), ABOVE; biennials (*Myosotis sylvatica*), CENTER; or tiny evergreens such as the shiny European wild ginger,* Asarum europaeum, *shown with a* Rhododendron yakusimanum *seedling,* BELOW. OPPOSITE: *Another ginger,* A. virginicum.

As I traveled preparing this book, I asked everyone about their favorite grass seed for lawn in the shade. Most people admitted that they just planted a commercially prepared shade mixture and the plants that could tolerate shade most were the ones that lived on to be there today. A simple Darwinian process of elimination.

Plan to reseed once or twice. In these difficult situations, you will rarely get it good from the start. If the grass fails to grow altogether, it's time to let some of the other ground-covering plants take over. If the lawn grass fades in a shaggy roundish haze, you might want to mark and cut this zone into a defined circular bed. The negative space abutting the lawn could become a shady-garden planting bed for perennials, shrubs, and the low ground covers.

I often see queries to gardening columns that read, "I have moss on the ground under trees where I would like to grow grass. What can I do to get rid of this?" And then there's the one about "unsightly" lichen on a wall. (I even know of a gardener in Great Britain who washes her trees with bleach to keep the moss from growing on the trunks. Deliver me.) I love these lowest of covers. If you are blessed with moss, enjoy it. I've met one gardener who gave up trying to keep a lawn in the shade and let his soil go to moss. He was very surprised to find that it kept up quite well, even under teenagers and touch football.

THE MOST FAMILIAR GROUND COVER IS LAWN.
Some grass varieties will survive in partial shade. In places
where lawn won't grow (acidic soil, too much moisture, and shade),
the no-mow mosses, OPPOSITE, *make a velvety cover,*
and some can even stand foot traffic.

ENTHUSIASTS HAVE THEIR OWN RECIPES FOR ESTABLISHING MOSS, FROM DARK BEER
*to manure tea, or a cocktail of both mixed with some moss in a blender. At the John P. Humes Japanese Stroll Garden
in Mill Neck, New York,* ABOVE, *water and buttermilk, eight parts to one, is sprayed three times a year.*

There are hundreds of matting plants we lump together under the name *moss*. Most insist on an acidic environment, some even like it somewhat putrefied. Most mosses require moisture, if not in the ground, then plenty in the air. If you have a little bit of moss, there's your beginning: encourage it by keeping leaf litter off the plants and attempt small transplanting experiments.

There are some so-called lawn alternatives for shade. These are plants that can take some traffic. Dichondra (*Dichondra micrantha*) is a familiar lawn plant for warm climates. Ajuga can take traffic, as can white- or purple-flowered mazus (*Mazus reptans*), but the latter is not always reliably hardy, although included in lists for zone 5. *Sagina subulata* (Irish and Scotch moss) is great to spread among stepping-stones, provided there is good drainage and light. Vinca, *Phlox subulata* (moss pink), and *Lysimachia nummularia* (moneywort) will take occasional traffic.

Dry, dense shade—the place under low-limbed, shallow-rooted trees like beeches and maples—presents the most difficult problem for the ground covers, or any underplanting for that matter. These places may have to be left for nonliving ground covers: mulches. Organic mulches such as shredded pine bark, salt marsh hay, buckwheat hulls and one of my favorites, pine needles, can be very attractive. If you like crushed white gravel, then you may find you're reading the wrong book.

THERE ARE HUNDREDS OF moss varieties (detail BELOW*). Generally moss grows where it likes to grow, which occasionally is not where it's wanted. It can also be included in a garden's design, as with these moss steps created by Fletcher Steele for Helen Stoddard.*

THE MANY WILD GINGERS

range from deciduous plants to low

evergreens, ABOVE. BELOW:

Pachysandra *is an ubiquitous ground*

cover; here P. t. *'Variegata' grows*

with the native bulb, Allium tricoccum,

called ramp or wild leek.

Select from the limited number of dry-shade-tolerant ground covers to plant under high-limbed trees where there is more light. Ivy springs to mind, along with the two other most popular covers for shade, Japanese pachysandra and vinca. Epimediums, variegated *Aegopodium, Galium,* and annuals such as fibrous-rooted begonias (*Begonia semperflorens*) are worth trying. *Vancouveria hexandra,* from California, Oregon, and Washington, is hardy to zone 5, despite its origins. It is a light and airy alternative to so many of the leatherleaf subshrubs. It has trilobed, ovate, one- to two-inch light green leaflets that make it look like a maidenhair fern. Flying above these are panicles of up to thirty white flowers.

Vancouveria planipetala also has a bevy of common names, including American barrenwort, redwood ivy, and inside-out flower. It is also a native to the Northwest, but it is not as quick to colonize, nor is it as hardy (zones 6–9, as opposed to 5–9). But it is wonderful combined with epimediums and ferns.

When there is adequate moisture, you can grow interesting fruit- or berry-bearing ground covers. Bunchberry is the tiniest dogwood, *Cornus canadensis.* Its typical white dogwood flower bracts surround insignificant flowers that when fertilized yield bright red berries.

There are evergreen and deciduous cotoneasters. Most have red berries. Many tolerate shade. The low kinds have long arching

AJUGA REPTANS *IS A VIGOROUS GROUND COVER FOR MOIST OR DRY LOCATIONS.*
Grown between paving stones, it can be walked on. Some hybrids, such as A. r. *'Burgundy Glow', are much less*
aggressive. This flowering one grows on the rocks by the pool.

stems and are wonderful cascading over a wall. But please don't use them as some landscape architects do, in a mass planting with nothing else—they tend to look bristly and artificial that way, unnatural.

Cowberry is one of the native cranberries (*Vaccinium vitisidaea*). Mountain cranberry (*V. v. i. minus*) has smaller fruits and leaves, but is hardier. *V. angustifolium laevifolium* is the lowbush blueberry—prized for its beautiful red fall foliage.

Creeping snowberry (*Gaultheria hispidula*) is also called wintergreen—both the fruits and the foliage of this native plant have a wintergreen flavor. It makes a good cover once established in acid, moist soil. Bell-shaped white flowers lead to white pearl-like fruits nestled among the shiny green leaves of this three-inch-tall plant. Oregon holly grape, *Mahonia aquifolium,* is another berried native plant. It has hollylike leaves and bright yellow flowers followed by blue-black, glaucous fruits. Partridgeberry, *Mitchella repens,* is a wonderful woodland plant. The leaves are veined in white, and fragrant white or pink flowers precede and often bloom with the red fruits. But this can be a difficult plant to establish, even though it creeps naturally from Massachusetts to Minnesota and down to Texas.

Mock strawberry, *Duchesnea indica,* has little blossoms like its namesake's, but yellow, and fruits like gumdrops. This wiry runner is definitely invasive, and

EVERGREEN COVER

Pachysandra terminalis, TOP, *and*

natives Asarum shuttleworthii,

CENTER, *and* A. arifolium,

BELOW. OPPOSITE: *Grasslike*

Liriope muscari '*Variegata*'.

if you fall for its spell, beware. Use it where you can keep it from invading plantings—near a paved area, perhaps.

Many of the ground covers are evergreen, including Oregon holly grape, pachysandra, partridgeberry, wintergreen, galax, vinca, certain cotoneaster species, and some ferns. Drooping leucothoe (*Leucothoe catesbaei*) is a graceful broad-leaf evergreen available in various foliage colors. Mountain andromeda (*Pieris floribunda*) is a tallish shrub for cover, while bog rosemary (*Andromeda polifolia*) is low. This true andromeda is beautiful. Blue foliage sparkles in spring with nodding pink urn-shaped flowers that fade to white. But note one of the common names, *bog* rosemary: this plant likes a moist location for its spreading underground roots; and it does resemble rosemary a bit in leaf. Although it is much hardier than *Rosmarinus* spp., it can be damaged by temperature extremes through the winter.

European wild ginger (*Asarum europaeum*) is evergreen. It has the most magnificent round leaves and there are several varieties and related small species. Our larger native ginger (*Asarum canadense*) is deciduous, but unrivaled in a mass planting under trees. Its soft leaves in dull green look mysterious. The flowers from all gingers are very unusual, but hard to see, as they grow facing the ground. Our native American pachysandra (*Pachysandra procumbens,* called Alleghany pachysandra or Alleghany spurge) is

rarely seen in gardens. Like *Asarum canadense,* it has a soft green color and matte finish, but is evergreen for the most part. It makes a wonderful break from Japanese shiny-leaved *Pachysandra terminalis,* and looks much less like plastic.

The liriopes are evergreen perennials that resemble tufts of ornamental grass. These plants, which have several species and varieties, come in both variegated and solid forms. All flower quite well in shade. Check the hardiness of the different kinds for your zone.

There are quite a few flowering plants that make good ground covers for shade. The

BEAUTIFUL FLOWERS ARE a bonus from some of the ground covers. Epimedium flowers come in many colors, including the double white E. *x* youngianum *'Niveum'.*

OPPOSITE: *Lavender plumes adorn one of the smallest astilbes,* A. chinensis pumila.

ajugas all bloom, adding a bonus to their impressive foliage. Astilbes make great ground covers, although most of them are taller than eighteen inches in flower. Some are remarkable when they are just emerging in spring, with bronzy-red ferny foliage hugging the ground. *Astilbe chinensis pumila* is about the best choice for a short one; it has lavender-colored flowers in summer, about one foot high.

Sometimes called green-and-gold or golden star, *Chrysogonum virginianum* is nearly everblooming. Small yellow flowers that look like a cross between coreopsis and rudbeckia grow along the trailing stems that are covered

VERONICA *IS CONSIDERED A CREEPING WEED BY MOST LAWN LOVERS, BUT IT DOES*
have its beautiful side (even in the lawn): tiny bluish spring flowers on a prostrate, spreading plant. Natural gardeners
are not so quick to get out the herbicide.

with dark green leaves. It grows only six inches tall and is semievergreen.

Epimediums are semievergreen—actually, last season's foliage lasts through winter. New growth replaces the old in early spring and can be magnificent. Often the leaves are green edged in red. But don't forget the flowers. Epimediums, depending on species and variety, bloom in white, yellow, orange, pink, grape, rose, or cream, single or double. These are supposedly called barrenwort or bishop's hat, but everyone calls them epimediums. Look for *E. album*, *E. alpinum*, *E. grandiflorum*, *E. pinnatum*, *E. purpurea*, *E.* x *rubrum*, *E. youngianum* and varieties. I've seen these long-lived, easy-to-grow perennials naturalizing in dry shade, even under maple trees, where few plants flourish.

Galax, already mentioned for its evergreen foliage, has a lovely floral spike covered with fuzzy white flowers not unlike those of foamflower (*Tiarella cordifolia*). *Galium odoratum*, still found under its former name, *Asperula odorata*, is sweet woodruff. The wilted leaves and white flowers of this easy, spreading herb, used for flavoring May wine, smell somewhat like raisins, or hay. It is fast-growing when it finds a home it likes (and it's not too picky about that either). The tiny white star-shaped blossoms appear in late spring.

The bluets appear in great masses in spring. Only two inches tall, they are covered with white-to-blue flowers in moist areas of open woodland or

THE STIFF LEAVES OF THE native woodlander Shortia galacifolia, A B O V E, *which requires a woodsy soil, are similar to the galax.* Gaultheria procumbens, *wintergreen,* B E L O W, *is an evergreen with flowers that bloom along with red fruits formed from earlier flowers.*

shaded meadow. *Houstonia caeru-lea* doesn't seem to be grown intentionally very often. *H. ser-pyllifolia* is a creeping variety that does well with less moisture and can be used between stepping-stones. Creeping speedwell (*Veronica repens*) is similar in appearance and habit to the bluets, but mention this plant to a lawn enthusiast, and he or she will run for the herbicide. Within bounds, it makes a wonderful plant among the pavers in fil-tered light. Another species, *V. filiformis,* is nearly evergreen and also welcome in the stepping-stones of the shaded path, though reviled in the lawn. It has bright blue flowers in spring, and makes a wonderful underplant-ing for primroses or bulbs. *V. ar-mena* has lacy evergreen foliage and brilliant blue flowers and will enjoy popping out from a rock crevice or between bricks in shaded patios.

Lawn lovers are usually violet haters, if you can imagine such a thing. The easiest violets to grow, and the ones that perform brilliantly in the shade, are inva-sive weeds if growing where they are not wanted. In shade they can be quite tall, ten inches or so, and the flowers, although longer lasting, will be fewer. The dangerous species are *Viola cucul-lata* and, especially, *V. papiliona-cea* (*V. soraria*), marsh blue violet and woolly blue violet, respec-tively (although the latter may be white or white striped with blue). *V. cucullata* is in the trade, as it were: there are varieties. 'Princeana', often called confed-

NATIVE PHLOX

divaricata *and* Iris cristata, BELOW, *show their violet colors. True violets,* TOP, *though despised by lawn enthusiasts, are beautiful.*
OPPOSITE: Viola cucullata *'Freckles' is one of the better behaved hybrids.*

erate violet, may actually be a hybrid of *V. papilionacea*, but is usually listed under *V. cucullata*, perhaps to keep the weed-wary from being frightened away. It has magnificent white blossoms with a purple center and yellow eye. *V. odorata* is supposed to be the fragrant violet, but I can de-tect very little scent in most of the plants offered as hybrids in catalogs. It is possible the *V. odorata* hybrids of merit, such as 'White Czar', which has a white flower with a yellow throat striped brown, and 'Red Giant', with rose red flowers, are ac-tually *V. cucullatas*. The shim-mering 'Freckles', white covered with deep purple flecks, is a *V. cucullata* hybrid and must be grown to be believed.

Viola canadensis is one of the best natives for deep shade. Wine-colored flowers have yel-low throats on plants about twelve to eighteen inches high. *V. labradorica* is native to the northeastern United States and up to Greenland; however, it is a fine plant for warm southern shade gardens and spreads well. *V. l. purpurea* has wonderfully deep purple leaves and is branch-ing, unlike the familiar lawn in-vaders. The flowers are mauve and purple and appear en masse in spring and then sporadically throughout the season.

The violet color range is also found in the flowers of many na-tives noted as ground covers. *Iris cristata* (crested iris) likes partial shade and can stand some sun. The thick, fleshy rhizomes creep along the soil, the fans of foliage

are only about six inches tall. *I. tectorum,* Japanese roof iris, has leaves that arch toward the light and white or violet flowers in spring. It is the best iris for shade in dry soil.

The low-growing phloxes also have lavender-colored flowers. *Phlox divaricata,* wild blue phlox, or wild sweet William, grows to about a foot. The flowers are fantastic to interplant with tulips, and equally at home in the woodland garden. *P. stolonifera* is creeping blue phlox. It grows five to ten inches high and blooms in midspring. Neither of these plants are rampant growers, more's the pity.

I've written about *Lamium* and *Pulmonaria* in the section on variegated plants. Keep them in mind for ground covers; they are among the best.

Caltha palustris, Doronicum plantagineum, and *Anemone nemorosa* are magnificent ground covers that spread (in the case of *Caltha,* rapidly). But these plants become dormant in summer, so they might not be the preferred choice for every situation. The *Caltha* (marsh marigold) departs almost as soon as the flowers fade. It might be a good choice among hostas that are late to emerge, as the *Caltha* blooms along with the daffodils. Left behind, you'll find little tubers like pine nuts on the soil surface. These can be collected and scattered to increase the size and scope of the stand or to introduce the plants to another site. Because they are so early, they will do very well under a deciduous tree. They are called marsh plants, but I've found them to be quite tolerant of dry conditions. There are also double varieties to try, *Caltha palustris* 'Flore-Pleno' (*C. p.* 'Monstruosa'), and a white cultivar, *C. p.* 'Alba'.

Calthas are members of an enormous family called *Ranunculaceae.* Other members are clematis and columbine, but there are also some ground covers that are *Ranunculus,* widely known as buttercups. They have finely dissected palmate leaves. Some of the ones that do best in shade are horrible brutes, and should be avoided. Gardening friends might offer you some common buttercups or creeping buttercups (*R. acris, R. repens*—aliens, by the way), which just might be the easiest plant to grow. They're just trying to thin their mess with as little guilt as possible. Politely decline, and direct their attention to a certain plant of which you would like a division; perhaps *Tiarella cordifolia,* foamflower, a semievergreen wildflower that makes a good ground cover and is much better behaved.

I have seen hardy cyclamen growing under shallow rooted rhododendrons and maples, especially the late-summer-blooming *C. hederifolium* or *C. neapolitanum.* Little pink or white flowers are followed by ivy-shaped leaves mottled with silver, purple, or gray on deep blue-green. The leaves usually disappear in spring. (Hardy cyclamen bulbs have been known to be harvested from the wild, so query your source.)

GROUND COVERS, FROM LEFT TO RIGHT, TOP ROW TO BOTTOM ROW: AJUGA
reptans 'Burgundy Glow'; Vinca minor; Convallaria majalis (lily-of-the-valley); Pachysandra procumbens;
Alchemilla mollis; Symphytum grandiflorum. OPPOSITE: Viola labradorica grows in gardens from its native
Greenland south to Georgia.

BULBS AMONG
GROUND COVERS

Many spring-flowering bulbs can grow with ground covers or low woodland plants. Those that want sun will get enough to ripen their foliage and food-storing bulbs before the trees fully leaf out in midspring. Some bulbs, such as tulips, may or may not be able to get enough light, but they will flower the first year from the previous year's field-grown conditions of light and fertilizer. These plants can be treated as decorative annuals. Therefore, these and most bulbs can be used in very dense shade, left in the ground, or dug up and discarded. If they do blossom the following year it's a bonus.

Allium moly, lily leek
A. tricoccum, ramp
A. triquetrum
A. ursinum, ramsons
Anemone blanda, windflower
Brimeura amethystinus (*Hyacinthus amethystinus*), Roman hyacinth
Camassia leichtlinii, cammasia
Cyclamen spp., cyclamen
C. repandum, cyclamen
Endymion hispanicus (*Scilla campanulata, Hyacinthoides hispanica*), Spanish squill
E. non-scriptus (*hyacinthoides nonscriptus*), scilla, English bluebells
Eranthis cilicica, winter aconite

E. hyemalis, winter aconite
E. x tubergenii, winter aconite
Erythronium spp., dogtooth violet, pagoda lily
Fritillaria meleagris, checkered lily, guinea-hen flower
F. persica, Persian fritillary
F. verticillata, fritillary
Galanthus nivalis, snowdrop
Hyacinthus orientalis var. *albulus,* Roman hyacinth
Leucojum aestivum, snowflake
L. vernum, snowflake
Narcissus spp., daffodils
Puschkinia scilloides, puschkinia
Scilla siberica, scilla
Tulipa spp., tulips

CYCLAMEN HEDERIFOLIUM, *TOP RIGHT,*

is an endangered exotic that, fortunately, is

being propagated widely by conscientious nurseries. It

naturalizes freely and blooms in late summer. Other

species bloom in spring. Erythronium spp., *dog tooth violets,*

C E N T E R , *are so-called for the shape of their bulbs.*

Blue Scilla siberica, B E L O W , *is easy to grow.*

O P P O S I T E : Anemone blanda, *windflower, looks like a daisy.*

Soak tubers in warm water before planting in the fall.

PLANTING ABOVE TREE ROOTS

Be very careful if you decide to put soil above tree roots to create an environment for ground covers. I've seen trees killed with the addition of only twelve inches of topsoil spread on their roots. Some books suggest excavating around a tree to a depth of twelve inches or more to make planting beds that go up to the trunk. I can't agree with this advice. (I have seen tulips and other bulbs, however, plugged into the ground directly under deciduous trees with little apparent damage, but I wouldn't experiment on an aged and important tree.)

Carefully prepared *shallow* raised beds can be made on part of a tree's root area. Use a coarse planting medium, one that allows a lot of air to get through and is fast draining. You could use loam with gravel and shredded bark or very coarse peat moss over a two-inch layer of gravel. You'll have to irrigate diligently. A line of rocks could be used on the outside of the area as a small retaining wall, so that no cutting of roots would be necessary.

RIGHT: THE SMALL,
shallow-rooted native orchid,
Goodyera pubescens, *rattlesnake*
plantain, poses no threat to a
venerable tree's roots. Its flower
spikes are a foot tall.

FERNS

There are several ferns that can spread to make a substantial cover. Three are notable for their tenacity: hay-scented fern, New York fern, and lady fern. *Dennstaedtia punctilobula* (hay-scented, named for the fragrance of its leaves when crushed) is one of the best choices for a ground cover —and cover it will. New York fern (*Thelypteris noveboracensis*) prefers a damp, slightly acid woodland mulch, and an open site. Don't tell this to my plants, however, which grow throughout my garden with average soil and quite a bit of shade. They may flop a bit in the densest shade, but I find them quite drought-tolerant, and the rhizomes are very easy to transplant. They are brittle, however, and fall apart when touched, so locate them where they will be out of harm's way. The lanceolate pinnate leaves are one to two feet long and three to six inches wide.

Athyrium filix-femina is the lady fern, one of the easiest ferns to grow. It will do well in dry soil and even in some sun, but it spreads more rapidly in somewhat moist locations. The fronds are eighteen to thirty-six inches long and light lime green.

OSMUNDA

claytoniana, *interrupted fern,* TOP;
O. cinnamomea, *cinnamon fern,*
CENTER. OPPOSITE: Athyrium
nipponicum *'Pictum'* (A.
goeringianum), *Japanese painted*
fern, in Cathy Heyes's garden.

THE BROAD LEAVES OF ONOCLEA SENSIBILIS, SENSITIVE
fern, combine well with flowering perennials such as these astilbes.

Taller ferns can be used by the foundation of a house. The cinnamon fern (*Osmunda cinnamomea*), so called for its brown, spore-laden fertile fronds, makes a strong statement for a group planting under the eaves, or as a specimen in the woodland by a rock outcropping. These tall ferns can be terrific in front of understory shrubs to conceal the leggy, empty growth that tends to be the norm among the shrubs of the shaded woodland, such as buttonbush or the acid-loving rhododendrons. Rugged relatives, the royal fern (*O. regalis*) and the interrupted fern (*O. claytoniana*), named for its unusual tiered spring growth, are also useful for this purpose. The cinnamon fern likes a touch of sun. Their magnificent fiddleheads, or crosiers, are among the most welcome signs of spring.

The royal fern doesn't have as finely dissected foliage as the more familiar cinnamon fern, but I think it is among the most lovely and useful landscape plants. It needs a bit more moisture and a bit less sunlight. Though it doesn't spread rapidly, it does become quite large.

The fronds of the shield ferns (*Dryopteris* spp.) grow from crowns in typical fern fashion. Marginal shield fern (*D. marginalis*) has dark evergreen fronds, one to two feet long and about six inches wide. It is native to much of the United States, throughout the East and west to Oklahoma. Goldie's wood fern (*D. goldiana*) can grow to four feet high or more. The male fern (*D. filix-mas*) is one of the crested ferns, which forms frayed feathers along the outside of the frond edges. It can tolerate shade to dense shade, and might be one to try in the depths. But this is a rare plant in its range from Newfoundland to the Rocky Mountains and should never be removed from the wild. There are plants available for sale, though, and even some cultivated varieties.

Christmas fern (*Polystichum acrostichoides*) is ubiquitous in the eastern and central United States. It is one of our best hardy evergreen ferns, and certainly one for the woodland garden. I saw one recently planted at the base of an outdoor staircase, where the whorled leaves ended the descending glide with perfect circular punctuation.

The ostrich fern is deciduous. *Matteuccia pensylvanica* forms a large vase and the fronds do look a lot like ostrich feathers. Japanese painted fern has become enormously popular. Its incredible colors are finding their way

FERNS, FROM LEFT TO RIGHT, TOP ROW TO BOTTOM ROW: BLECHNUM SPICANT,
deer-foot fern; Polystichum braunii, *Braun's holly fern;* Osmunda regalis, *royal fern;* Athyrium filix-femina, *lady fern;*
Thelypteris noveboracensis, *New York fern;* Osmunda claytoniana, *interrupted fern;* Polystichum acrostichoides,
Christmas fern; Dryopteris dilatata *'Grandiceps';* Adiantum pedatum, *northern maidenhair;* Asplenium
daucifolium; Polystichum setiferum *'Plumoso-divisolobum';* Dryopteris filix-mas *'Cristata', crested male fern.*

out of the woodland and into the shaded perennial border. *Athyrium goeringianum* 'Pictum' (*A. iseanum*) lies low to the ground, and once established, puts forth many fronds of bronze, silver, and metallic green. It is the Asian relative of our lady fern.

Perhaps the most beautiful of all the woodland ferns, and one for which you must make a place, is the hardy northern maidenhair (*Adiantum pedatum*). This is a relative of the indoor plant, *A. capillus-veneris,* which could be grown in subtropical regions and north to Virginia, its native habitat. The northern one, however, grows palmate whorls that are like birds' feet. *Pedatum* is descriptive of this. It is so delicate and airy that the slightest breeze makes it dance. I have found that although it does grow in ordinary garden soil, it will not create a large colony unless the soil is loose, woodsy, and damp.

Although most of the ferns are known for acid soil and lots of moisture, there are some that grow along limestone ridges and are good choices for rock gardens. Bulblet fern (*Cystopteris bulbifera*) spreads by little bulbils that form in the axils of the undersides of the leaves and drop down to take root among the limestone rocks. *Cystopteris fragilis* is called bladder fern or brittle fern: perfect for rock gardens.

Surprisingly, there are also quite a few choices for dry locations. *Asplenium platyneuron,* ebony spleenwort, is a good choice among stones. It even thrives in sandy and clayey soil.

There are sterile and fertile fronds—the sterile being ever-green. *Athyrium thelypteroides,* silvery glade-fern, is also easy to grow. The tall, finely divided fronds start out bright green, deepen to darker green, and finish the season by turning red-brown in autumn.

Pteridium aquilinum var. *latius-culum,* bracken, is quite invasive and eager to spread. Leathery deep green leaves can grow to five feet long. It might be a choice for a very large area in a large garden. If you can locate some, you might try it in a dry spot, where it would be slowed by drought.

Onoclea sensibilis, the sensitive fern, is one of my favorites. The unusual undivided fronds are terrific for a tall ground cover (twelve to thirty inches tall). This plant will tolerate sun if there is an abundance of moisture (or else it wilts), but it does very well in shade with moderate moisture, and even dry soil. It is very easy to grow and propagate from sections of rhizome. But it tends to look bad toward the end of the growing season and is devastated by frost (hence "sensitive"). However, the fertile "fronds," which look like espresso-colored beads on a stalk, persist through the winter. It spreads, but is easy to pull out, and worthwhile. It's a wonderful plant for all parts of the shade garden.

TALL DRYOPTERIS

goldiana, *Goldie's wood fern, in the late afternoon sun.*

THE SHRUBS ARE THE PLANTS OF THE GARDEN AT EYE LEVEL. THEY FLOWER IN TURN
and contribute lasting foliage interest. White Hydrangea paniculata blooms in partial shade next to Weigela florida
'Variegata'. OPPOSITE: A mixed planting designed by Conni Cross features variegated kerria and astilbes.

THE MIDDLE LAYER

A garden makes its strongest impression in the middle layer—between the ground covers and the trees. It's where the eye naturally comes to rest. So, it's an area that requires special consideration. This is home ground to the herbaceous perennials and the flowering shrubs. The shrubs create a framework for your plantings with year-round form and texture and set the stage for the perennials to light the garden with color. Choosing plants from the woodland and the edges of the forest, and carefully selecting and preparing their new home, will be your mission. Subtle and alluring, these enchanting specimens captivate the visitor to the gardens in the shaded understory.

HERBACEOUS PERENNIALS

The flowering herbaceous perennials for the middle layer are culled from the woods and the edges of the woodland, but they blossom later than the small spring wildflowers, or have a longer season of bloom. Often, these plants are tall, with floriferous spires to inspire. They do not usually grow from basal foliage, with the exception of the hosta, so they should not be covered up by other plants, or they will be shaded out and rot.

The *Actaeas,* or baneberries, sprout early and blossom with foamy flowers resembling those of the *Cimicifugas* (bugbane). Later, beautiful ornamental berries form—white on *Actaea pachypoda,* and red on *A. rubra* (*A. p. rubrocarpa*). The white form is sometimes called doll's-eyes, because each berry has a black spot at the blossom end. This is a plant to try in dense shade in zones 2–9. (*Actaea* berries are poisonous, but, as with monkshood, only if ingested. Although I rarely eat the border, it is best to know.)

A few *Cimicifugas* are natives, but there are others from Asia. If you collect carefully you can have blossoming bugbane (black cohosh, or black snakeroot, as they are variously called) from late spring to fall. These plants tend to colonize and look marvelous in drifts, where their blossoms shoot up into tall spikes covered with fuzzy flowers. I think the buds that precede the flowers are as nice. The foliage of

FRUITING ACTAEA

pachypoda, *doll's-eyes,* ABOVE, *and* A. rubra, *snakeberry,* BELOW, *along with* Cimicifuga *spp., bugbanes, have foamy flowers on spikes above biternate foliage.*
OPPOSITE: Cimicifuga racemosa, *known as snakeroot or cohosh, blooms in late summer. Species can be selected to bloom from spring to fall.*

the plants is handsome, especially that of the species and varieties of *C. simplex ramosa* 'Atropurpurea' and 'Brunette'. (The cognoscenti claim this to be one and the same plant, but my 'Brunette' seems to have deeper maroon foliage—more light, more color, I think.) The species include *C. racemosa* from America and *C. simplex* from China. *C. simplex* 'The Pearl' has large flowers.

Aruncus are tall, four to seven feet, with fuzzy flowers, usually white to cream. Commonly called goatsbeard, it is a trouble-free native of the roadside, where it likes some sun.

The *Astilbes,* or false spiraeas (a name I have heard only once), are probably the most important flowering plants for shaded gardens. (A bonus is their bronze or green foliage.) There are so many to choose from, especially among the *A.* x *arendsii* hybrids, that you can just go for the colors. Some, especially among the reds, are nearly as ornamental when they go to seed as they were in flower, and the faded spire lasts for months. There is a lot of variety among the whites, and they should be used for different effects. The "dirty" white can be used well in an informal planting. The bright, clear whites are like bed-linens hung to dry—brilliant, but perhaps for a different situation.

A. x *a.* 'Cattleya' is nearly the same color as the ground-covering *A. chinensis* 'Pumila'; they look sensational grown together. In back of them, you could use the tallest of all, *A. taquetii* 'Superba'. It blooms with

PREVIOUS PAGES: ACONITUM CARMICHAELII *IS A LATE-SUMMER PERENNIAL FOR* partial shade. It must be staked to stand tall. ABOVE: Aquilegia x hybrida, *also for partial shade, is a short-lived perennial that self-sows to create unbelievable colors.*

the late astilbes and continues well after the last ones have faded. It forms good-size colonies in short order, but is not invasive. The flower spikes are tall and not delicate, nor are the leaves, which are a bit coarse. But it is stalwart and dependable. It may need staking, especially if the area is windy and exposed, for the flower heads are huge and become heavy in the rain or when seeds form. (I tied a line of green hemp from stake to stake to corral the entire group.) This is a must-grow plant if your garden is in zones 4–8.

Filipendula purpurea, meadowsweet, is a foamy flower that looks good with the astilbes. Its more widely available giant American cousin, the queen of the prairie (*F. rubra*), is an excellent plant with handsome palmate foliage and buff pink plumes for use in a bit more sun. *F. ulmaria* 'Aurea' and 'Variegata' are plants with outstanding golden and variegated foliage, respectively.

Some *Thalictrums,* meadow rues, also have frothy flowers, especially *T. aquilegifolium,* which blooms early for the genus, with lavender tufts. They are tall plants, for the most part, up to six feet, including my favorite, *T. rochebrunianum,* which has breezy panicles of dancing purple flowers with white and yellow. Most of these plants have glaucous, nearly blue leaves reminiscent of columbines (*Aquilegia* spp.)—hence *aquilegifolium.* The true columbines can all take some shade, but few will tolerate deep shade, and most want some

TALL AND DELICATE
Thalictrum rochebrunianum,
lavender mist, A B O V E , *can reach*
six feet. Ferny foliage is a bonus of
Dicentra formosa *'Alba',* B E L O W
—a hardy, white bleeding heart
from the West Coast.

CORYDALIS LUTEA, *A*
dicentra relative, has silvery foliage
and blooms longer than almost any
other perennial. It flowers from
April to November in my garden.

OPPOSITE: *An effective*
combination in Charles Cresson's
third-generation garden is Filipendula
purpurea *and feathery* Astilbe *x*
arendsii *'Ostrich Plume'.*

sun. Among the best are two of our natives, *A. caerulea,* a blue-and-white flower, and red *A. canadensis,* which I think is the easiest and most forgiving. These are generally not long-lived plants. If you dead-head them, they will bloom longer, but you must let a few seed heads form, since they often return from seed, even when the plants prove not to be persistently perennial.

The American *Dicentras* include plants for the woodland, such as spring-blooming *D. cucullaria* (Dutchman's-breeches), *D. canadensis* (squirrel corn), and the long-blooming eastern *D. eximia* and western *D. formosa.* The last two are good for flower gar-

dens, and look for their hybrids, especially *D. e.* 'Alba' and *D.* 'Luxuriant'. But the tall, spring-blooming Asian bleeding heart, *D. spectabilis,* is the familiar one. It only blooms once, but for a long time, and it is a vision. *D. s.* 'Alba' is even more beautiful. It is not a fragile plant, despite its delicate appearance, but the stems are brittle. Although it does not need staking, it's best to place it where it will not be damaged by passersby.

A plant that resembles, and is related to, the dicentras, *Corydalis lutea,* can grow just about anywhere. The glaucous, grayish foliage on this twelve-to-fifteen-inch mound is welcome, but surpassed by yellow flowers over an astonishing period. Although hardy (zones 5–10), I noticed that my plant, usually quite evergreen, looked bad one winter so I ordered more (at around $2.50 each). By the time they arrived, self-sown seedlings from last year's plant were up throughout the area.

To extend the season, include some of the Christmas roses, the hellebores. It is rare to see these plants in bloom in the snow, although catalogs often make that claim. They are really just early and long lasting. Corsican hellebore (*Helleborus argutifolius, H. corsicus, H. lividus corsicus*) makes voluptuous clumps two feet high by three feet wide with pale green flowers. In mild climates, blooming does begin in winter, and flowers persist, sometimes into summer. And it self-sows, though plants take years to bloom. It is not for the deep shade. Better in the shade of the woodland garden are *H. foetidus* (stinking hellebore), *H. niger* (Christmas rose), and *H. orientalis* (Lenten rose). The last two resemble each other to a great extent, but *H. orientalis* might be the easiest to grow.

There are several plants from the woodland to include in beds and borders for their long season of interest. False Solomon's seal, *Smilacina racemosa,* has delicately airy flowers in spring, leaves reminiscent of its pseudonymous namesake, and, later, equally interesting berries. The real Solomon's seal, like *Polygonatum biflorum,* and the giant Solomon's seal, *P. commutatum,* are useful

SMILACINA RACEMOSA *FLOWER BUDS WITH VIOLET*

Geranium maculatum, A B O V E , *and summer berries,* B E L O W .

O P P O S I T E : Kirengeshoma palmata's *flower buds last for months, finally opening into nodding, creamy yellow flowers in late summer.*

for foliage and black fruits. Keep your eye out for some new-to-the-market relatives, *P. humile,* an incredible foot-tall plant with layers of pleated leaves, and the variegated import, *P.* x *hybridum* 'Variegatum', all white, closed flowers at the leaf nodes.

Kirengeshoma palmata and *Macleaya cordata* (plume poppy) are love-it-or-hate-it plants. Both are tall—the *Macleayas* grow to eight feet or more. The *Kirengeshoma*'s flower buds last for months. In early fall they finally open, if you can call it that, into nodding lemon-ivory bells. The plant has maplelike palmately lobed leaves and rich aubergine stems. The flower buds are like peas or beads, and I like them as much as the flowers. It has a lot of class for a shrubby "thug," as author Fred McGourty calls it.

HELLEBORUS ORIENTALIS,

ABOVE, *is a woodlander for*
flower beds. RIGHT: Tradescantia
species tend to invade, but hybrids
*(*T. *x* andersoniana*), with*
blossoms ranging from white to
near-blue, behave.

A plant that is considered to be a thug by many is the native *Tradescantia virginiana,* called spiderwort. I must recommend that you not grow the purple-flowered native, which blooms only in the morning and runs like crazy, but seek out the hybrids. Fortunately there are many available and their flower colors are wonderful. The plants themselves hybridize and self-sow like crazy, so if you have the space, you'll have flowers in white to shades of purple-blue. If you've got a moist spot and crave true-blue flowers, as we all do, look to the various *Gentiana* species, the gentians.

Other tall plants include foxgloves (*Digitalis* spp.); not all are perennial. The most familiar, *D. purpurea,* is a biennial. It can be outstanding as a naturalized cover in the shaded woodland. After the biennials become established, the two-year-old plants will bloom consistently enough to provide the effect of perennials. However, *D. ferruginea* is perennial, and tall—not too similar to the smaller yellow perennial ones or the crushed-strawberry-colored *D.* x *mertonensis.* It likes some sun, the more the better, as shade plants go. The effect in a mass planting where height is desired is spectacular. The shorter ones, *D. grandiflora, D. lanata,* and *D. lutea,* are useful shade plants. These smaller, yellowish foxgloves, believed to be native, are actually alien. They seed freely.

Turtlehead, *Chelone lyonii,* often tops out at four feet. This plant from the southern United

States is good for the waterside, and it blooms from late summer into fall, when flowers are needed. The various Japanese anemones are also late-blooming. If you're willing to experiment, try some of the tall ones. I would love to say that they grow in shade, but they must have some sunlight, I think. They can take a long time to bloom from young plants, and you might be better off beginning with more than a beginner. *Anemone hupehensis,* about two feet tall, has typical beadlike buds held on long stems above palmately lobed foliage. *A.* x *hybrida,* often called either *A. hupehensis* or *A. vitifolia* in the trade, is taller, the better to reach for the sunlight. There are many hybrids available. *A. vitifolia* has more deeply lobed foliage that really does resemble its namesake, the grape. *A. tomentosa* is very similar but blooms earliest of these late-flowering gems. All have breathtaking flowers in white or various shades of pink. They will need staking in the shade, and should be isolated a bit from the crowd so their beautiful foliage can be admired.

Some *Tricyrtis* species are very late indeed, blooming up to frost. These wonderful plants, called toad lilies, have long arching stems with alternate lanceolate foliage that can be appreciated while waiting for the

TALL DIGITALIS

ferruginea, ABOVE. OPPOSITE: Tricyrtis latifolia. Ligularia stenocephala '*The Rocket*', BELOW.

blossoms. The flowers are not very large, and do not make much of a show as a whole, so be sure to place them where they can arch over to the path or the front of the planting. The fuzzy orchidlike flowers can be white with purple spots, white and pink, or yellow, depending on the species. They all will tolerate shade, often dense shade. Seek out *T. flava* (yellow toad lily), *T. formosana, T. f. stolonifera, T. hirta* (hairy toad lily) and its hybrid, *T. h.* 'Alba', and *T. macranthopsis,* a plant for deep shade.

For multiple seasons, sedums are useful. Sometimes called showy stonecrop, these plants might be thought of as sun lovers only, since they are succulents. But *Sedum spectabile, S. purpureum, S. acre,* 'Ruby Glow', and others have worked for me in shade. *S. p.* 'Autumn Joy', made famous by Ohme/van Sweden & Associates, landscape architects, is a must-own plant, for it performs in every season of the year. In spring, little hens and chicks form at the base. They grow up quickly and by summer form the flower buds in what is called the broccoli stage. Soon the flowers open and color to pink, then red, then they begin to dry to the rusty red for which they are best known. They remain standing all winter while new round buds form for spring.

Some *Euphorbias* are shade-tolerant. Among the best, one that will truly blossom in dry shade, *Euphorbia characias,* is from the Mediterranean; it is reputed to be hardy in zones 8–10, but I think it could be pushed

THERE ARE A FEW succulents for our gardens. Sedum *x* 'Ruby Glow', A B O V E, *likes sun but tolerates partial shade. Yellow cushion spurge,* Euphorbia polychroma, B E L O W, *blooms in early spring.* O P P O S I T E: *Amazing* Euphorbia characias *grows among trees in dry soil in southern Europe and is naturalized in northern California.*

into the cold, especially in a protected spot. I've seen its very close relative *E. c. wulfenii* in an open, windy, chilly site. *E. amygdaloides* var. *robbiae* can stand deep shade in zones 8–10. *E. palustris* is also shade-tolerant and increases zone range to 7. Its lookalike is the familiar cushion spurge, *E. polychroma,* which forms a compact mound with yellow-green flowers for a long period in spring. It can be grown in zones 3–9, but needs some sunlight.

Adenophora confusa confuses me. From a distance its flowers look like a hosta's, while close up it resembles a campanula (another good genus for shade plants). Ladybells, as they're called, are easy to grow from seed, and look best in masses. One plant would appear spindly, but naturalized they contribute a wonderful cool blue.

There are many members of the *Lysimachia* genus for our garden. By the waterside is the creeping *Lysimachia nummularia,* but up above there are several with yellow flowers, and the especially interesting white gooseneck loosestrife, *L. clethroides.* It has very unusual pointed, arching, and twisting racemes covered with tiny pure white flowers. Look also for *L. punctata,* a nice fuzzy plant with vivid yellow flowers in late spring to early summer, and delicate-looking but extra tough fringed loosestrife, *L. ciliata.* I pull out nearly all I see of the latter after flowering, and the next year there are plenty left. There is one with wine red foliage, which I

HERBACEOUS PERENNIALS, FROM LEFT TO RIGHT, TOP ROW TO BOTTOM ROW:

Helleborus argutifolius; Aster novi-belgii; Astilbe *x* arendsii *'White Gloria'*; Anemone *x* hybrida *'Honorine Jobert'*; Doronicum caucasicum; Lysimachia ciliata; Lysimachia punctata; Lysimachia clethroides; Geranium ibericum *'Johnson's Blue'*; Echinops ritro; Astilbe taquetii *'Superba'*; Chasmanthium latifolium.

am cultivating as I cull the other.

I give the same treatment to the common yellow evening primrose or sundrop, *Oenothera tetragona* (*O. fruticosa*). The flowers open each evening and remain until the following afternoon. It is a delightful and very easy-to-grow plant. It doesn't bloom as many weeks as I wish, and dead-heading seems to do no good, but the plants spread thickly from underground runners. I casually pull out nearly all of them after they bloom—next year, there's just enough, again.

Some summer-flowering bulbs can be grown right along with herbaceous perennials. Many garden lilies (*Lilium* spp. and hybrids), especially the Asiatic hybrids, fare well in shade. Select natives as well, such as *L. canadense* (Canada lily), *L. superbum* (Turk's-cap lily), and the naturalized citizens such as *L. tigrinum* (tiger lily). The lilies also contribute wonderful foliage—spiky leaves arranged in whorls along the stem. *Allium tuberosum* (garlic chive, or Chinese chive) is an ornamental edible. It grows to about two feet tall and blooms in late summer. White starlike flowers in umbels quickly turn into green fruits containing black seeds. The plant will self-sow, but normally just expands by increasing the number of bulbs and does not become a nuisance.

SUMMER BULBS: ALLIUM

tuberosum, *garlic chive;* Lilium

canadense, *Canada lily;* L.

superbum, *Turk's-cap lily.*

Aconitum spp., monkshood
Adenophora confusa, ladybells
Alchemilla mollis, lady's mantle
Anemone hybrids, anemone
Aster spp. (selected American native
   species), aster
Astilbe spp. and hybrids, false
   spiraea
Chasmanthium latifolia, northern sea
   oats
Cimicifuga spp., bugbane
Corydalis lutea, yellow fumatory
Dicentra spp., bleeding-heart
Doronicum spp., leopard's bane
Euphorbia polychroma, (*E. epithy-
   moides*), cushion spurge
Geranium spp., garden geranium
Hemerocallis spp., daylily
Heuchera spp., coralbells, alumroot
Iris pseudacorus, yellow flag
Kirengeshoma palmata, kirengeshoma
Ligularia spp., ligularia
Lysimachia spp., loosestrife
Macleaya cordata, plume poppy
Oenothera fruticosa, evening prim-
   rose
Phlox divaricata, wild sweet William
Polemonium spp., Jacob's ladder
Polygonatum spp., Solomon's seal
Sedum spp., selected varieties of
   stonecrop
Smilacina spp., false Solomon's seal
Stylophorum diphyllum, celandine
   poppy
Thalictrum aquilegifolium, meadow
   rue
Tradescantia hybrids, spiderwort
Tricyrtis spp., toad lily

═══════════════════════

HOSTAS

Hostas are essential for the natural shade garden. The original species from the Asian woodland have led to hybrids that range in size from tiny miniatures with familiar deltoid leaves to giants with leaves of green, gold, or variegated combinations. *H.* 'Thumb Nail' is a small *venusta* variety with one-inch leaves in a typical hosta shape and color. The famous *H. sieboldiana* 'Elegans', on the other hand, is a blue-whale of a plant, several feet across with fourteen-inch-long, spade-shape leaves. But both—and all in between—will thrive in the shade.

It's remarkable to find hostas in vogue. Not very long ago, they were considered all-too-common shade perennials: what's so special about something that anyone can grow? Of course, the hostas looked down upon were commonplace among the genus: those big green things, kind of full-figured and terribly conspicuous—the Ethel Mermans of the garden bed.

Still, there were gems among those humdrum hostas. In the 1920s few gardens were without *H. undulata.* Other old favorites, *H. plantaginea,* and *H. p.* 'Grandiflora', the August, or peace, lily, produce huge flowers late in the gardening season, when you need them most, and they are as intoxicatingly fragrant as any fancy garden lily. *H.* 'Honeybells' is currently the popular choice for perfume, but *H.* 'Fragrant Bouquet' has more, prettier flat-faced flowers over a longer period of time.

I have many clumps of the ubiquitous *H. lancifolia,* the familiar narrow-leaved species. They were among the begged and borrowed garden plants that inhabited the backyard jumble that came with my 120-year-old house. I would throw them away, but they are so useful. They look great draping over the pond edge, and I can fill in anywhere with a piece or two. It seems that no matter the size of the division, each section equals the size of the parent after a single season.

John Elsley, director of horticulture for Wayside Gardens Nursery, calls hostas "perfect perennials." And they are excellent companions for a host of shade-tolerant perennials such as astilbe, *Heuchera, Dicentra,* daylilies, iris, *Rodgersia,* vinca, *Anemone, Galium,* and ferns of all kinds. Depending on their size, hostas can be background plants, ground covers, choices for edging a planting, rock-garden candidates, floral highlights, or specimen plants. Fred McGourty adds that they make an acceptable spinach substitute. What more could you want? Exceptional foliage variation? Hostas have it.

Now we're looking at hostas in a new light. They are no longer limited to the two or three gathered green growers. The foliage colors, flower forms, fragrance, texture, size, and adaptability are making them eminently collectible. You can add some of the thousands of varieties to your early selections. A new introduction may cost up to

GOLDEN HOSTA 'ZOUNDS', ABOVE, *echoes the pale yellow foliage of* Iris pseudacorus 'Variegata'. H. montana *'Aurea Marginata' is one of the first hostas to emerge in spring,* BELOW. OPPOSITE: *For flowers, H. 'Blue Cadet' is sensational and likes as much sun as it can get. (H. 'Sum and Substance, beyond).*

three hundred dollars, but after the plant proves gardenworthy and easy to propagate, supplies increase and prices drop. *H. undulata* 'Albo Marginata', a stalwart beauty that also inhabited my inherited garden, can be found for as little as $3.50.

Each year, the American Hosta Society publishes a list of over fifty of its members' favorites. Kurt Tramposch, the owner of the wholesale Weir Meadow Nursery in Wayland, Massachusetts, made a smaller list of suggestions based on sales to professional gardeners. The diminutive *H.* 'Allan P. Mc-Connell' is the best ground-covering hosta and makes an excellent edging plant as well. *H.* 'Antioch' is always on everyone's "best" list. It has light green leaves with wide, creamy white edges, and is a medium size, twelve to twenty-four inches tall. *H.* 'Louisa' has a narrow leaf, delicately edged in white, and is good in the foreground of a mixed planting. Mr. Tramposch recommends *H.* 'Blue Cadet', with its medium-size round blue leaves, for the rock garden, and I think it would be welcome in a flower garden as well. *H.* 'Golden Tiara' is a fine variegated edging plant that is light green with golden edges, and it holds the color throughout the growing season. *H.* 'Francee' is a deep green with a fine white line around the edges of its five-inch-long leaves. *H. montana* 'Aurea Marginata' (*H. m.* 'Aureomarginata') knows the way to my heart: it sprouts early in the spring. Once up, the leaves un-

WHEN PLANNING A design, consider foreground, middle ground, and background planes. Large-leafed hostas, ABOVE *and* OPPOSITE, *placed in the front of a planting, accentuate depth and distance.*

furl to be very large, light green with irregular yellow edges. This showstopper is best grown as an individual clump so that it can show off. *H.* 'Big Daddy' makes the list (at the expense of *H.* 'Big Mama'). Large, deep blue, puckered leaves grow about nine inches wide and eleven inches long. It's a perfect background hosta. *H.* 'Frances Williams' may be the most popular hosta today. Very large puckered blue-green leaves have irregular margins of clear primrose yellow. It blooms early with pale lavender flowers and is slug free.

H. 'Gold Standard' has leaves the reverse of *H.* 'Frances Wil-

liams'. I grow them together for a great negative/positive combination. Both plants vary considerably in color depending on the amount of light they get. As with most hostas, there are fewer leaves—and no flowers—in deepest shade, but the leaves are often larger.

In general, golden-leaved hostas become green in too much shade, while blue-leaved hostas green up in too much sunlight. Admirable chartreuse-to-yellow-gold cultivars include: *H.* 'Midas Touch', *H.* 'Piedmont Gold', *H.* 'Royal Standard', *H.* 'Royalty', *H.* 'Sun Power' (a sun worshiper among hostas), and *H.* 'Yellow-gold'. Among the best of the blues are: *H.* 'Blue Angel', *H.* 'Blue Moon', *H.* 'Blue Mammoth', *H.* 'Blue Wedgwood', *H.* 'Hadspen Blue', *H.* 'Love Pat', *H.* 'Halcyon', and *H.* 'True Blue'.

Most catalogs describe the size of a plant at maturity, about four years old. This information rarely includes the height of the flower spike, which can be considerable. *H.* 'Krosa Regal' has a flower-covered shoot that can soar to six feet, something to be reckoned with. Regardless of ultimate size, what you get from a mail-order supplier is probably going to be a small division with perhaps only one *eye,* or growing point, at the crown. The immature hostas, depending on the cultivar, can take quite a while to get going. Take heart; once they do catch on, they grow rapidly. You can often find larger, older plants at garden centers or local growers and nurseries.

Water early in the day so that the leaves will be dry before noon, if possible. Use a gentle spray, especially with blue hostas, whose color may come from *indumentum,* the powdery "frost" covering the leaves. In a moderately protected location with plenty of light and good air circulation, hostas will require about an inch of water per week.

Hostas never really need dividing, but if you decide to make new plants, it's best to do so in spring, before the shoots get too tall. You can actually divide them any time throughout the growing year—even in summers—as long as you compensate for root loss by trimming the leaves and supplying adequate moisture.

Catalogs claim that hostas are pest-free. But hostas play host to a few denizens that prefer nothing better on which to dine: snails and slugs. With their tonguelike *radulae,* covered with tens of thousands of rasping "teeth," slugs can tear through a hosta leaf overnight.

There are many ways of dealing with this problem. You've probably heard of burying cat-food cans to their rims and filling them with beer. The slugs crawl into the cans to have an intoxicating fatal fling. But who wants a garden full of slug-filled cat-food tins? There are commercial slug motels to hold beer and hide bodies. They are usu-

ally bright green, someone's idea of camouflage.

For angry gardeners willing to resort to poison, slug pellets are effective. But the pellets look just like rabbit food and are attractive to children, dogs, and bunnies. (If you spray them with water they turn to mush and still remain effective, but less appealing to pets and children.) The active ingredient metaldehyde dehydrates slugs, as does table salt, which can be sprinkled across slug highways, indicated by slime trails.

Since I have frogs and toads I don't use any poison, for fear that they might consume a tainted "slimer." I'm an enthusiastic hosta collector, and we've had some very rainy springs in the East recently, yet my garden is nearly slug-free. Answer: amphibians? I can think of no other explanation.

Another environmentally conscious alternative is diatomaceous earth, a white powder containing the ground fossilized ectoskeletons of primitive sea creatures. Sprinkled around a hosta, its microscopic razor-sharp particles will slice up the slug on its way to dinner. You must not inhale this dust, as it can irritate your lungs. Diatomaceous earth is nonselective; it will kill any small creature that crosses its path, including beneficial insects. And it's ugly! I'll stick to frogs.

HOSTAS FROM LEFT TO RIGHT, TOP TO BOTTOM ROW: H. 'BLUE WEDGWOOD';

H. lancifolia *'Kabitan'*; H. undulata *'Variegata'*; H. *'Decorata'*; H. undulata erromena; *H. 'Wogon Gold'*; H. *'Zounds'*;

H. *'Blue Angel'*; H. *'Big Daddy'*; H. *'Halcyon'*; H. *'Gold Standard'*; H. fortunei *'Albo Marginata'*. OPPOSITE:

Flowers of H. *'Royalty'*.

ANNUALS FOR THE SHADE GARDEN

Impatiens is a most useful and important flowering plant for the shade. It is actually a herbaceous perennial plant, but not hardy. It will be killed by frost. But until death, impatiens plants will flower their heads off. Some people insist on setting impatiens in the sun, where they wilt and gasp for moisture. Although they tolerate heat quite well, they do not like the midday sun.

I think that some impatiens are a little out of keeping with the shade plantings. They can overpower. The flowers are a little too big, and in some colors, too bright. I think it is difficult to successfully integrate these plants with others in the ground. They may look best in containers. Bedding-out in the shaded areas looks ridiculous to me; it ruins the naturalism of the natural shade garden.

Unlike some annuals, impatiens will bloom all summer without *dead-heading,* that is, removing the faded flowers. New softer shades such as lavender and mauve will soon be in garden centers. These subtler tones, approaching blue, might appear less brilliant among other plants. There are also dwarf plants, and be on the lookout for the new miniature-flowered kinds (sometimes called Hawaiian impatiens), which will be coming to the nurseries in the future (if I have anything to do with it).

ANNUALS INCLUDE miniature Hawaiian impatiens, ABOVE, *and double impatiens,* OPPOSITE. *Johnny-jump-up,* Viola tricolor, BELOW, *is a short-lived perennial that self-sows and returns as if it were a hardy annual.*

These plants look more like drifts of color and less like polka dots.

Several tender (nonhardy) bulbs, such as caladiums and tuberous begonias, can be used to similar effect in partial shade. These will have to be lifted from the garden and brought indoors in the fall, or if grown in pots, simply brought to a dry, dark location for over-wintering. Caladiums are grown for their foliage. Small-leaved examples and those with subtle colors, perhaps just white and green, look better than the Christmas-color combinations too often seen. You can also set the tubers directly into the garden, but they will get a good head start if they are potted, watered, and begun indoors in a sunny window in March.

Tuberous begonias do very well for some people. The most important ingredient is a cool temperature in the summer, something not too many of us have. That's why these plants are terrific in New England, the Pacific Northwest, and Canada.

The new small-flowered, colorful calla lilies seem to like sun, but I have seen many of the large-flowered ones growing in dense shade. These tender bulbs, *Zantedeschia aethiopica,* have to be stored indoors, best in pots, for the winter in cold climates. But they do very well in zones 9–10 outdoors year-round.

Torenia (wishbone flower, *T. fournieri*) has an interesting cream, violet, and white flower that blooms in profusion. There are hybrids now that range from

white to pink. The familiar species looks a bit like Johnny-jump-ups, quasi-perennial violas (*Viola tricolor*) that so readily self-sow they can be treated as a hardy annual. They will quickly come up and bloom from seeds sown as late as midspring. Sometimes they cross-pollinate to develop amazing colors besides the yellow-violet-white of the most familiar one, *V. t.* 'Helen Mount'. *Browallia* will flower with limited sun, and four-o'clocks (*Mirabilis jalapa*) do well with afternoon sun. In fact, since the flowers do not open until the afternoon, those from the previous evening will remain open if they are in morning shade.

Many flowering tender woody plants, including such fragrant favorites as gardenia, heliotrope, and jasmine, can be used in shade. Fuchsias will often bloom in low light, though some of the voluptuous hanging-basket types want a bit of sun and lots of water. Pot-bound they flower their heads off, but may dry out every day.

Nearly all begonias will do well outside in partial-to-dense shade. Flowering will increase with some sun. Wax begonias (*Begonia semperflorens*) will scorch in full sun, but are still used as a bedding plant there, even in hot, dry climates. This same plant will become a lush, full plant for a hanging container in shade.

Other options for varying degrees of shade are biennials such as pansies (*Viola* x *wittrockiana*), forget-me-nots (*Myosotis sylva-*

TENDER BULBS CAN ADD interest to the summertime garden. Some will have to be started indoors in winter and be lifted in fall, or be grown in frost-free zones.
ABOVE, *the giant calla* Zantedeschia aethiopica *'Green Goddess';* BELOW, *a tuberous begonia hybrid.*

BIENNIALS BLOSSOM AND SET SEED IN THEIR SECOND GROWING SEASON.

These naturalized Digitalis purpurea, *foxgloves, self-sow freely enough so that after a few years, there will be some blooming each and every spring.*

tica), and money plants (*Lunaria annua*, also called honesty, moonwort, satinpod, satinflower, silver dollar). Money plant grows quickly in its second spring to be topped by fragrant violet-to-white velvety flowers that are typical of all members of the mustard family. Shortly thereafter, green, flat, ornamental seedpods form, and if you peel

KERRIA JAPONICA

'Variegata' and daffodils, ABOVE.

Cephalanthus occidentalis,

buttonbush, RIGHT.

OPPOSITE: Camellia japonica *hybrid.*

the sheaths back, they reveal their shimmering contents. And try tall, large-leaved mulleins (*Verbascum* hybrids) in partial shade.

SHRUBS

The "permanent" features of the forest understory, the middle layer, are the shrubs. Shrubs can be tiny spreading ground covers, the one-inch-tall partridgeberry, pachysandra, and vinca, or the skyscraping Himalayan rhodies. All are perennials; all are multi-stemmed woody plants with branches emanating from

CLETHRA ALNIFOLIA 'ROSEA', ABOVE; ROSA
rubrifolia (R. glauca), BELOW. OPPOSITE: Rubus odoratus *is a*
blackberry relative with pink flowers; Hypericum kalmianum
has yellow tufts.

ground level, or nearly ground level—that's how the adjective *bushy* became irrevocably linked to the shrubs (synonymous to some). There's a fuzzy distinction between the tall shrubs and the small trees that reside beneath the forest's canopy of towering oaks and ash. A mature *Stewartia* is a tall shrub because it tends to branch low on the trunk. But a dogwood of the same height is a small tree; it tends to have a single trunk for its first five feet or so. To me, it is only this branching that distinguishes them. I prefer to think of all these woody plants as members of a shared community.

Shrubs are like sculptures that blossom. The beautiful camellia's shiny green leaves are enough to please, but when its winter "roses" unfurl, staid grandeur becomes perfection. *Corylopsis* shoos winter away with pendant yellow racemes. *Kerria* flowers with the daffodils, and is as dependable. Olympian evergreen rhododendrons, the flesh and blood of every shade planting, also bear fragrance and color for months. The *Skimmia* spp. and hollies produce small white flowers but add fall berries to an already impressive presence. Flowering viburnums frequently have a fruitful bounty. And there are enough hydrangeas to satisfy every greedy gardener. These plants, especially the ones between three and ten feet tall, are the bones of the garden, and the ones that provide riveting attraction. Shrubs are often the plants on which designs depend.

THE LARGE GENUS HYDRANGEA PRESENTS MANY SHRUB CANDIDATES FOR GARDENS
in various degrees of shade. Hydrangea macrophylla *'Blue Wave', the lacecap hydrangea, with its tiny blue fertile beads surrounded by flat, sterile bee landing pads, is a favorite.*

There is a reason for chauvinism for indigenous plants, but many of the shrub genera have traveled well over millennia. The hibiscus clan is endemic to temperate and tropical climes. So the rose of Sharon (*Hibiscus syriacus*) grows in Brooklyn. It's kind of a messy shrub, but it blooms so well in late summer that it must be forgiven its faded-blossom hangers-on. And it is being hybridized and cultivated. Now we have 'Bluebird', the closest to blue, and a better white, 'Diana', which is nearly self-cleaning.

You can make an all-shrub shady border for flowers with hydrangeas and even the wonderful *Rosa rubrifolia,* with single, little "dog" roses and foliage that is glaucous and powder-covered like an Italian plum. Often listed as *Rosa glauca,* the name it was given in the nineteenth century, it can take more shade than just about any rose.

Fragrance is not in short supply. Most of the understory shrubs rely on scent to attract pollinators. Many bloom in spring, such as the very fragrant viburnums and the daphnes. Others carry fragrance through the seasons. *Calycanthus floridus* (Carolina allspice) blooms throughout the summer and smells to me like the inside of a whiskey barrel, nice, but not at all like the catalogs' claims of fresh strawberries. *Hydrangea quercifolia* (oakleaf hydrangea) has the hot smell of summer, much like honey. And I think it is just about the best all-around shrub on earth. Huge panicles last for

THE VIGOROUS DOUBLE-flowered Kerria japonica *'Pleniflora' has sturdy grass-green canes that provide welcome color in winter,* ABOVE, *and cadmium yellow pompon flowers in spring and sporadically through summer. The large shrub* Stewartia pseudocamellia, BELOW, *has exfoliating bark that looks like camouflage.*

weeks—first white, then shading to pink, rose, and then finally chestnut brown as they remain until the following spring. The foliage too is magnificent. Huge leaves turn purple and bronze in the fall, and in mild winters will stay that way until spring's new growth pushes them to the garden floor. It is a good choice for the naturalist's garden, where shrubs could be collected to attract some of the more acceptable animals, the butterflies and the bees. *Clethra alnifolia* (summer sweet, sweet pepperbush) has upright slender panicles of fluffy white flowers that look like fireworks when dusk turns to night. But if I could have only one, I would go for the pink hybrid, *C. a.* 'Rosea', or the newer *C. a.* 'Pink Spire'. All of these, along with *Clerodendron trichotomum*, are bee favorites.

There are few plants to grow for food that don't need full sun, but wineberry (*Rubus phoenicolasius*) is a native relative of the raspberry that will take to shade and bear glistening amber red fruits sheathed in fuzzy pods. Ornamental *Rubus* spp. are familiar in Great Britain, and although offered in catalogs here, have not been discovered by many. *Rubus* x *tridel* is a favorite. It has a giant blackberry flower that looks like a single rose—its very close relative. Our native one, *R. odoratus,* has large pink flowers in early summer, thornless stems, and large felty palmate leaves that color up in autumn. Blueberries like some shade, although not too much. You'll

≡══════════════════════════════≡

FLOWERING SHRUBS FOR PARTIAL SHADE

DECIDUOUS

Abelia x *grandiflora*, glossy abelia
Abeliophyllum distichum, white forsythia
Calycanthus floridus, sweet shrub
Clethra alnifolia, sweet pepperbush
Cornus alba (C. sibirica), red-twig dogwood
Corylopsis spp., winter hazel
Daphne x *burkwoodii* 'Carol Mackie', Burkwood's daphne
Enkianthus campanulatus, enkianthus
Fothergilla major, large fothergilla
Hamamelis spp., witch hazel
Hibiscus syriacus, rose of Sharon
Hydrangea arborescens 'Annabelle', tree hydrangea
H. aspera, rough-leaved hydrangea
H. quercifolia, oakleaf hydrangea
Kerria japonica 'Pleniflora', double-flowered kerria
Magnolia stellata, star magnolia
Rhododendron spp., azaleas
Spiraea x *Bumalda,* spirea
S. x *Vanhouttei,* bridal wreath
Viburnum spp., viburnum

EVERGREEN

Camellia japonica, camellia
Kalmia latifolia, mountain laurel
Pieris spp., andromeda
Rhododendron spp., rhododendron, rosebay
Viburnum spp., viburnum

≡══════════════════════════════≡

need more than one variety for good pollination, and acid soil—perfect for the woodland edge.

Sarcococca hookerana digyna, sometimes called sweet box, fragrant sarcococca, or Himalayan sarcococca, is a three- to four-foot-tall evergreen with lanceolate leaves that thrives in dense shade in zones 6–10. The fragrant flowers bloom in late winter and are followed by black berries. *S. hookerana humilis* is a dwarf kind, only about 1½ feet tall, best for our purposes, and it's hardier (zones 5–10).

Paxistima canbyi is a dwarf evergreen that resembles one of the most useful of all the evergreen shrub families, the wintercreepers, *Euonymus* spp. There are deciduous species and upright evergreen *Euonymus* varieties too; most come from Asia. Look especially for *E. fortunei (E. radicans)* and its hybrids. Some have golden foliage and many are variegated (*E. f.* 'Variegatus' among several); others turn purple in the winter (*E. f.* 'Coloratus'). The leaf size varies from about one-eighth of an inch to just over an inch long. Most of these are low, dense, spreading plants. Winged euonymus (*E. alatus*) is also called burning bush for its brilliant fall color. It is a taller shrub, deciduous, and usually seen in sun, but it will perform admirably in shade. There it weeps and spreads; although fall color is not as sensational, this open habit makes it more useful for a cover on a hillside or embankment. The branches have papery fins—hence the former common name.

SHRUBS, FROM LEFT TO RIGHT, TOP ROW TO BOTTOM ROW: HYDRANGEA
quercifolia; Paeonia suffruticosa *hybrid;* Leucothoe fontanesiana *(winter color);* Corylopsis spicata; Calycanthus floridus;
Kerria japonica; Deutzia gracillimis; Leucothoe fontanesiana *'Girard's Rainbow'; edible* Rubus phoenicolasius; Aucuba
japonica *hybrids;* Hibiscus syriacus *'Diana';* Acer japonicum *'Aureum'.*

RHODODENDRONS

There was a time when young lads dreamed of plant hunting in Nepal. In the British Empire's heyday, horticulture and botany inspired voyages in search of the *Bounty*'s breadfruit. Exotica from all over the world were brought to England. The herbaria at Kew Gardens were filled with literally millions of twigs and leaves and, most of all, flowers pressed between the pages of volume after volume. Plant collectors dreamed of fortunes made from botanical dyes, foods—and medicines. (Even now, a quarter of all the medicines we know are derived from plants. Who's to know what curatives of tomorrow are being destroyed along with the world's endangered rain forests?) But more than anything, plants were gathered and valued as ornamentals.

Explorers to the Himalayas came back with tales of snowy peaks, aquamarine glaciers, and towering tree-size rhododendrons. These exotic shrubs were destined to become the most popular ornamental plants discovered. Whole gardens were developed from seeds and plants sent back by Sir Joseph Dalton Hooker. But the craze was not limited to the Himalayan discoveries. One hundred years ago, the great English garden designer Gertrude Jekyll wrote of her hardiest wild species from the far-off United States.

Consider this enormous genus, whose ancestors survived the breakup of Pangaea to travel throughout the Northern Hemi-

RHODODENDRONS COME
in many shapes and sizes and all
colors but true blue. R. 'Nova
Zembla', ABOVE; R. catawbiense
'Borsault', BELOW.
OPPOSITE: R. *'Janet Blair'.*

sphere and settle in places like Borneo, India, and the Carolinas. This may be the most numerous and diverse group of ornamental shrubs. There are at least eight hundred known deciduous (azalea) and evergreen (rhododendron) species. The species' name comes from the Greek: *rhodon* for rose and *dendron* for tree. The *rose* refers to the incredible flowers, held above the foliage in huge clusters, usually from late spring to early summer. (Did you know that there is an American species that blooms in late summer? The plum-leaved *R. prunifolium* has flowers that are the deepest coral pink.) Each blossom has five petals. The evergreens have frilly bells; the deciduous, trumpetlike flowers. They come in nearly every color. There are many warm-temperate species that feature yellow flowers—somewhat elusive among the hardier evergreen kind.

Hundreds of deciduous varieties have been bred abroad from American natives, but unfortunately, they do not always make the trip back in good stead. Our hot summers wreak havoc in the form of mildew and rust on many of the 'Exbury' and 'Knaphill' hybrids. We can take our revenge with the evergreen azaleas—stalwart specimens that laugh off our summer's heat and humidity. There are many (besides the all-too-familiar Kurume azaleas, originally from Japan), such as the "Gables," hybridized by J. B. Gable in the United States, and the "Indian azaleas," bred from what used to be called *Azalea indica* (*R. indicum, R. sim-*

sii). Often overused, these ubiquitous shrubs with flowers of bright orange, magenta, and red are the suburbanite's nadir.

Fortunately, some new and wonderfully colored hybrids are coming. The flowers of *Azalea* 'Winterthur' are a haunting lavender. There are some remarkable miniature and dwarf rhododendrons. *R.* 'Purple Gem' (*R. fastigiatum* x *carolinianum*) is one of the best. *R. impeditum* is a foot-tall cushion-forming miniature whose leaves smell like cinnamon when brushed. It has lovely, nearly blue flowers and is a terrific rock-garden or alpine subject. (But do note that this plant has really tiny leaves and needs some sun. I wish I had.)

R. carolinianum, the Carolina rhododendron, comes from the Blue Ridge Mountains. It is very compact and floriferous. It can be grown in zones 6–8. At maturity it forms a perfect mound six feet high and seven feet wide. There have been many introductions since this plant came into cultivation in 1815, too many to list here, but keep in mind that various colors exist. Look for the variety called 'P. J. M.'. Named for Peter John Mezitt of Weston Nurseries in Hopkinton, Massachusetts, 'P. J. M.' is hardier than the species, and presents its bright lavender blossoms in midspring, ahead of most of the *R. carolinianums*. 'P. J. M.' doesn't set seed often, so it directs its en-

THE HYBRID

Rhododendron *'Winterthur' has*

unusual violet flowers.

ergy toward flower-bud production and is a profuse bloomer. A white one is on the way.

R. catawbiense is sometimes called catawba rhododendron, mountain rosebay, or purple laurel. *R. catawbiense* is remarkably drought-resistant. Dead-heading will increase flowers and each place you pinch will sprout more new shoots for the flower buds that form above the stem and foliage buds. Because it is so sturdy (zones 5–8; 4 with protection), it has been bred extensively since it ventured beyond its native West Virginia, Virginia, Alabama, and Georgia in 1809. Look for *R. c. compactum,* a dense, slow-growing dwarf, and the 'Catawbiense' hybrids, especially the "ironclad" group.

R. macrophyllum (California rosebay) is native from Northern California to British Columbia, and to the West is what catawba is to the East. *R. maximum* (rosebay rhododendron) is another southeastern American. It flowers from late spring to early summer. In cultivation since 1736, it has been popular because it adapts better to deeper shade than most.

Among the best of the Asian members of the genus is *R. fortunei.* The hybrids of this species are magnificent for flower lovers. The individual flowers can be up to 3½ inches wide in trusses of up to twelve. The flowers are usually pink to lilac, sometimes with streaks of white or yellow. The species likes warmth. Floridian gardeners take heart: this is one of the best for zones 8 and 9. Nevertheless, it

The large-leaved rhododendrons are the kings of the shaded understory and the variety from which to choose is colossal. Rhododendrons don't like temperatures in the extreme and are not always successful in the north-central portions of the United States. They dislike soil alkalinity, another aspect of the hardpan clay and limestone soil often found there.

They are incredibly tolerant of air pollution, and because of their shallow roots, they transplant well. They benefit from being placed among other plants, as long as there is little root competition. Mulch is a must and should be coarse-textured, like shredded pine bark; too fine a mulch might encourage roots to grow up as they search for moisture.

Most available rhododendrons are field-grown in open sun with regular irrigation. You may buy a very compact, densely branched specimen that will grow into a loose informal shrub in the shaded garden.

When planting, incorporate a good deal of organic matter, especially into the top foot of soil, where much of the root system will live. Dig a hole as deep and twice as wide as the container or burlap-covered root ball. Enrich the excavated soil with compost, well-rotted cow manure, leaf

mold, or the ever-available peat moss. Moisten this amalgam.

Place some of the mixed medium in the hole, and then the root ball. (If your specimen is in a plastic or metal container, remove it before planting and break up the root ball.) Lower the root ball into the ground and place a stick across the hole to make sure that the crown—the place where the roots meet the stem, usually discolored by soil stains—is growing at the soil level or just below. Check that it is symmetrical and not leaning to one side. Carefully cut away all the burlap and discard. Old practice recommended leaving the burlap in the hole to disintegrate, but I've seen plants with bits of burlap showing above the soil surface, which can act as a wick to remove moisture. Also, a lot of "burlap" nowadays is made from a plastic material that will never decompose.

Fill the hole about halfway up and water well. Then fill the hole all the way and press down firmly. Stepping lightly around the new soil should be just fine. Then water again.

In dry locations, red spider mites might visit. Safer's insecticidal soap works, but you'll need to apply it more than once. A humid atmosphere is not only a deterrent, but a cure. These mites will not survive in moist air.

does just fine north to zone 6, and the hybrids are often hardier. Perhaps the most wonderful is 'Scintillation', an incredibly dependable, hardy subject whose colorful flowers capture a sunset.

Many of the deciduous rhododendrons, all called azaleas, come from North America. Although they are certainly useful, shade-tolerant foliage plants in the growing season, they are really floral performers and would like more sun. (I have an 'Exbury' hybrid that blooms in nearly total shade, but it grows very slowly.) Many are fragrant, and some have incredible flower structures with long spidery stamens. Yellow shades and tints are not uncommon in these plants—from flame orange to primrose yellow. They have fall foliage color as well.

Rhododendron vaseyi is the pink-

A RHODODENDRON cultivar, ABOVE, R. *x*. grandavense plenum *'Rosea Plenum'*, BELOW. OPPOSITE, from top: *Summer-blooming* R. prunifolium; R. doricum *x* carolinianum *'P.J.M.'*; R. *cultivar;* R. 'Purple Gem'.

shell azalea, a fine subject for lower light. This native of the North Carolina swamps is remarkably adaptable, even to a dry location. Deep green five-inch-long leaves will turn brilliant crimson in most years, especially in places with cool summers. In midspring, before the foliage appears, unscented gossamer blossoms of pale pink to rose with rusty brown speckles appear. The spicy, clove fragrance of the swamp azalea, *R. viscosum,* is wonderful. Trumpet flowers in pale pink to white come in early summer—July in zone 6, the middle of its range. Among the naturalized citizens and hybrids that fall into this deciduous group I must mention the breathtaking *R. schlippenbachii,* a native of Manchuria, Korea, and Japan. It looks natural everywhere.

ONE OF THE BEST VINES FOR FOLIAGE AND FRUIT IS VARIEGATED PORCELAIN BERRY,
Ampelopsis brevipedunculata *'Elegans'*. OPPOSITE: *Shiny, deep green leaves and white flowers in early summer*
make the climbing hydrangea, Hydrangea anomala petiolaris, *a garden necessity.*

REACHING THE TOP

I f ground covers are the bottom, vines are the top. But there seems to be some question when it comes to finding vines for shady gardens. There are many vines for partial shade or filtered light, but few flowering ones for shade to dense shade. And yet, think about this: A vine's roots may very often be in the densest shade and need it, but up above, where the flowers form, there's quite a bit of light and even sunshine. Most of the vines have evolved for just such conditions. They're rooted in the cool, moist forest floor, but twine up to spread across the tree-tops and bloom above the forest canopy in the unob-scured rays of the sun.

VINES

In the idealized garden, lovely flowering vines (what the Brits call climbers) scamper over the cottage garden door, adorning the threshold with romantic blossoms. Now stop for a moment and picture a Tarzan movie. Vines evolved in the forests and jungles to climb up to the light—hitching a ride on the trunks of trees and even on other vines as they went. These opportunists need trellises, wires, strings, houses, walls, fences, and so forth upon which to rest their weak stems or attach their botanical devices. It's easy to become attached to them.

The vines work in various ways. Some twine like wisteria. Whenever these fast-growing stems come in contact with anything, a hormonal signal goes off, and cells on one side of the stem begin to grow rapidly. You can almost see this happening with annuals such as scarlet runner beans. The twining stems turn either clockwise or counterclockwise, and if you are trying to help a vine take hold, take note. If you twirl a vine around a support the wrong way, it will struggle to untwine itself.

Tendrils are little side stems that usually appear at the leaf axils. The tendrils are often branched at the ends. They reach out straight into space until they

HYDRANGEA ANOMALA

petiolaris, ABOVE, and

Schizophragma hydrangeoides,

CENTER and BELOW.

come in contact with something. Then they wrap around it and, in many plants, corkscrew to bring the main vine closer to the support. This twirling spring also acts like a shock absorber to help keep the delicate stem from being damaged in wind. Grape vines have obvious and beautiful tendrils. The clematis's leaves act similarly to the tendrils. The leaf stems themselves will twist around a support.

Some plants form little suckers at the ends of their nontwining tendrils. These disks attach to surfaces as if they were suction cups. Other vines merely drape over neighboring plants. Rambling and climbing roses just lie about, sometimes calling upon a thorn to catch onto something nearby. Jungle vines have aerial roots that plunge down to earth or find nooks and crannies in rocks or tree bark to gather water and nutrients. (You may have seen these on large philodendron houseplants.) Tiny aerial rootlets less than a half-inch long are the means by which several vines cling, *Hedera* and climbing hydrangea among them. The *Euonymus fortunei* and *E. f. radicans* varieties we know as ground covers are also useful vines that use rootlets to cling to bark or brick.

Often fast-growing vines shoot up into the trees and, when they hit the light, branch in every di-

OPPOSITE: AMERICA'S

favorite clematis, C. x jackmanii,

blossoms in shade but produces fewer

flowers there.

rection to form an umbrella that just spreads across the treetops for support. In England, much more than here, gardeners encourage climbers such as clematis to grow up through the darkness inside a shrub to reach the light at the top, where they add flowers to foliage plants. (Consider planning for the effect of all-flowering vines when viewed from upper-story windows.)

Climbing hydrangea, *Hydrangea anomala petiolaris,* is a deciduous vine that clings with rootlets in sun or shade. It has marvelous panicles of white sterile and fertile flowers, and will attach to a tree trunk. *Schizophragma hydrangeoides* is the climbing hydrangea's look-alike, but it blooms slightly later, and the sterile

WISTERIA SINENSIS, ABOVE, *from China, produces flowers before foliage.* OPPOSITE: Lonicera *x* heckrottii, *gold flame honeysuckle, blooms longer than most varieties.*

flowers are a bit different. I think they make marvelous companions. When grown together, the result is an extended period of bloom. Some catalogs and books recommend these vines for full sun, and yet they bloom well when climbing the trunks of deciduous trees.

Wisteria is a full-sun plant, or so the experts say. It blooms for me with only a few hours of sun. It grows atop my Arts-

and-Crafts-style post-and-lintel arbor. It was a naked eight-foot-long twig and root rescued from painter Robert Goldstrom's backyard when he gave me a three-minute warning, machete in hand. I coiled the three-foot-long root section and placed it under my bluestone patio, letting the stem come up through a space between the pavers. The leafless stem was about three quarters of an inch in diameter.

In order to generate flowers, wisteria should be under stress. Many plants flower and fruit best when they "think" they must produce progeny. That's why pot-bound houseplants bloom well, and sometimes spring-flowering trees and shrubs are wonderful the year following a

dry, hot summer. Give wisteria everything it wants, and it will send you a postcard from the next county. I never feed mine.

When I planted my stick in June, I let the nub of the single leader sprout grow its long, lanky shoots until they were the length I needed to cover the structure. Then I pinched the ends of all six or seven branches. They immediately sent out side shoots, which I diligently shortened to four leaf nodes from the main covering branches. I pruned the hell out of it persistently through the growing season and was rewarded with blossoms the next year. If my approach seems daunting, just prune once in the spring, after blossoms fall, and once in midsummer.

Sometimes there's a fine line between a plant that covers quickly and a garden monster; the very nature of "covering" has this built-in hazard. *Polygonum aubertii* (silver-lace vine or fleece vine) is one of the quickest climbers. Like many of its nonvining polygonum relatives (commonly called knotweed), it can go wild.

But if you need quick cover, choose the vining silver-lace. It can easily grow twenty feet in a season. Restrict it to an isolated area if you can, perhaps over a trellis or against a fire escape. Many people love it, I must add, and it does have nice flowers in late summer—racemes of white, some in shade, many more in full to partial sun.

Campsis radicans, trumpet vine or trumpet creeper, is another

POTENTIALLY RAMPANT
Campsis radicans *'Flava' is the yellow trumpet vine,* ABOVE, *in sun, and,* OPPOSITE, *in more shade. Another garden "monster" is* Polygonum aubertii, BELOW, *best for a controlled space.*

monster of merit. A member of the prestigious *Bignoniaceae* family, it climbs by little rootlets like the ivies and hydrangea. It can become a nuisance not only for its rampant growth above ground, but because it sends up little plants from the surrounding ground, even if the parent has been torn out in a rage. Nonetheless, this vine, a favorite of hummingbirds, will bloom in shade. I like *Campsis radicans* 'Flava', which, unlike the orange-red species, has yellow flowers. In sun they are honey yellow, but in shade, they become creamy apricot. I've decided their beauty

is worth the danger—for now. Mine grow up and through the honey locust trees and droop down inside where most of the blossoms occur from new growth in summer, for months.

There are two Akebias, *A. trifoliata* and *A. quinata.* They are called chocolate vines for the fragrant maroon-brown flowers that appear in pendant racemes in late spring, followed with some irregularity by purple sausage fruits. Of course, I love them: I think both the flowers and the fruits are beautiful (others think they're Barnum relics, and should be lumped with the *Rhodochiton, Aristolochia* and *Ceropegia*). If you have to choose between the two, take the fast-growing *A. quinata;* it has five distinct leaflets in a whorl and is semievergreen.

Akebias are fine for sun or shade, and the foliage is enough to recommend them. Mine is growing well in the darkest part of my garden, in dense shade. The foliage effect is airy and pleasant, and this would be a good vine to use on a trellis where it could be viewed close up, perhaps by the bench under the eaves of the porch. Watch out though—it can be invasive.

I raved about *Ampelopsis* as a variegated vine; though the non-variegated invasive one has prettier berries it should be avoided. The common name is porcelain vine, so called for the berries, which can be blue, aqua, white, black, or purple, at the same time on the same plant; the flowers are insignificant. *A. brevipedunculata* 'Elegans' is the one I grow on top

SCHISANDRA CHINENSIS, *MAGNOLIA VINE, HAS SHOWY FRUITS HERE IN THE SHADE*

of a mature yew. OPPOSITE: *Aristolochia durior,* Dutchman's-pipe, *can be grown in partial shade, or used for making shade. It has giant, deep green leaves that overlap like heart-shaped shingles.*

of the fence under my neighbor's dreaded Norway maple. I also have a potted plant I believe to be *A. heterophylla* 'Variegata', smuggled in from Britain (papers in order, actually). There are other species, but I have never seen them offered in the United States.

Aristolochia spp. are tropical climbers for the most part. *A. durior* is very hardy. It not only can grow in shade, it can be used to make shade with its very dark green and overlapping shingle-like leaves. It will flower in shade, but the little inflorescence that gives it its common name, Dutchman's-pipe, pales in comparison to tropical members of the genus.

Schisandra chinensis (magnolia vine) is a woody deciduous climber with little, fragrant white flowers in mid-spring followed by pendant red fruits. There is a great deal of it at Willowwood Arboretum in Glad-

stone, New Jersey, growing through an ancient yew hedge.

Catalogs often recommend clematis for partial shade, especially the *C.* x *jackmanii* hybrid. But *C.* x *jackmanii* will look like it does in the catalogs only if it is grown in lots of sun. In partial shade it has a nice blend of foliage and flowers that I think looks more natural anyway. I haven't had terrific success with this purple-flowered hybrid, which might be the best known clematis in America. For me, *C.* 'Nelly Moser', introduced in 1897, is more dependable. A friend of mine refers to it as *"Clematis putanesca"* for its wanton abandon. "She" never fails to deliver her five-inch-wide, pale-rose-colored blossoms with a slightly darker broad stripe in each petal. Most of the bloom is in spring, with sporadic flowers throughout the season, but glorious seed heads persist until fall.

C. virginiana, virgin's bower, a native northeastern vine of the woodlands, will do quite well in limited light. In the wild, it's found scrambling over and under brush along the path and road-side. C. maximowicziana (C. paniculata), sweet autumn clematis, resembles the former and does fairly well in shade. The parts of the plant that climb up into the light will bloom profusely. It has wonderful fuzzy flowers that are intensely fragrant. C. x jouiniana 'Praecox' is somewhere between a low-growing vine and a lanky, woody deciduous shrub; it certainly likes to drape across shrubs in the shade garden. It is something of a mess, and I would banish it but for the fact that it blooms all summer with fleshy one-inch blue-and-white flowers that look like Delft china.

There are several evergreen clematis. C. armandii is the hardiest and perhaps the most beautiful. This is a foliage plant really, and for that reason, its lovely long lanceolate leaves, leathery and deep green, are wonderful down below. Some clematis have fine threadlike stems—easily tangled and torn. This one has telephone cables. And you might have to cut great hunks away from time to time. Nevertheless, creamy white flowers are a bonus, and varieties come in colors. This plant is not as hardy as

some, although I believe it can be pushed beyond conventional claims: the southern parts of zone 7, perhaps. It is very important to prune it instantly after flowering, so that new foliage has plenty of time to harden off before winter. You'll want to remove browned leaves and some of its growth from time to time at any rate.

Clematis montana (montana means mountain; this one's from the Himalayas) is a tall-growing species that also runs. It clambers up to the top of a tree, explodes in every direction, and has one glorious moment of mid-spring bloom. It is reputed to be easy; as British clematis expert Barry Fretwell says, "It can be an embarrassment." In the right place, it is magnificent. This is one to choose if you have an eyesore to conceal: the unfortunate little garden ruin, somebody's idea of a storage shed, or the back of your neighbor's garage. As with all the vining clematis, it will need a support on which to grow. C. m. 'Rubens' is a pink-flowered variety. The montanas have a strong vanilla scent, and must not be pruned except immediately after flowering, if necessary, or you'll sacrifice next year's bloom.

When you plan to have a light-textured vine go up to the top of a tree, plant it a bit away from

CLEMATIS VARIETIES TO GROW IN PARTIAL SHADE INCLUDE DELICATE C. VITICELLA, ABOVE, *the shrubby* C. x jouiniana *'Praecox' with delft blue flowers,* CENTER, *and* C. maximowicziana, *sweet autumn clematis,* BELOW. OPPOSITE: *One of the easiest clematises to grow is* C. *'Nelly Moser', but the fleeting pink and violet flowers are eclipsed by the golden seed heads that last until fall.*

the base of the trunk (of a deep-rooted tree). Then carefully encourage it to grow toward the tree. This two-foot-long trip can be treacherous. I failed my first time out: I wanted to have my *C. montana* cover a cluster of trees in my garden. But I planted it too close to the trunk of one of them, and the competition proved unbearable. For my redo, I prepared the planting site and built little rock walls on either side of the traveling vine to protect it from accidental injury. You may not lose the plant but if the stem is damaged at the bottom, it has to start all over again. Many vines can regenerate vigorously when cut down. A secret to the success of sweet autumn clematis, for example, may be severe pruning—nearly to the ground.

The pruning schedules of the various clematis species and variety types is complex, to say the least. Planting needs for the more delicate vines should be reiterated: the roots must be kept cool and moist—just like in the forest and jungle habitat. For clematis, the soil should be rich, moisture-retentive, and have good drain-

age. (Wet feet in winter means death to the clematis.) I cover the root area of mine with a flat rock, which seems to help keep them cool and moist down under. They also like a "sweet," or alkaline, environment, so lime should be added to the deep planting hole. Nearly all the clematis will do something in shade as long as their roots have adequate moisture. Here again, you'll have to experiment to see how much flowering you'll get in how much shade. (You might want to start with Ms. Moser and her kin.)

Among the choice flowering vines for the natural shade garden are the honeysuckles. Don't grow the rampant Hall's honeysuckle, *Lonicera japonica* 'Halliana'. There are plenty of better-

CLEMATIS ARMANDII,

FAR LEFT, *is an evergreen species that should be pruned after flowering in spring.* LEFT, *scarlet* Lonicera sempervirens *is a familiar native.* L. s. 'Sulphurea', ABOVE, *is the yellow-flowered version.*

behaved hybrids and a host of natives that do well in shade. Our American vine is *Lonicera sempervirens* (*sempervirens* means "evergreen," but this one is just as often leafless in winter). The leaves are like broad saucers and a lovely glaucous blue-green. The flowers are rich orange-red tubes that are open on the ends and reveal yellow inside, and they come forth in whorls at the ends of the stems; again, fewer in deeper shade. There is a wonderful yellow one, *L. s.* 'Sulphurea', that is nearly everblooming, and superior to *L. flava,* a kind that is more often offered. (*L.* x *brownii* 'Dropmore Scarlet' has scarlet flowers like our native and is pre-

THE EXQUISITE FLOWERS

of Lonicera periclymenum *'Serotina Florida', Dutch honeysuckle, are followed by translucent red berries.*

OPPOSITE: Parthenocissus tricuspidata, *Boston ivy,* ABOVE, *and* P. quinquefolia, *Virginia creeper,* BELOW *with sumac, are ubiquitous garden climbers.*

ferred by some for performance.)

L. tragophylla has very large flowers and is hardy to zone 6. Bright yellow three-inch-long blossoms form in clusters of one to two dozen in summer, and the leaves are blue-green. This honeysuckle doesn't just tolerate shade, it demands shade! *L.* x *tellmanniana* is another honeysuckle that will flower well in shade—not partial shade, but full shade. The flowers are small and bright yellow with a copper blush.

L. periclymenum 'Serotina Florida' is called Dutch honeysuckle. Crimson flaring flowers that open cream are followed by translucent red berries. It is a

steady grower and blooms in partial shade. Semievergreen, it is hardy in zones 5–9. My favorite twiner is a plant that resembles Dutch honeysuckle, *Lonicera* x *heckrottii* (goldflame honeysuckle). This plant combines the best aspects of them all. It is semievergreen, perfectly hardy (zones 5–9) and in bloom for me from May through November, in profusion for the month of June. Some gardeners prefer *L.* x *americana,* which may have contributed to the questionable ancestry of this cultivated variety. *L.* x *heckrottii* has a problem that never fails to raise the ire of the plant snobs: it is too easy to grow.

My plant climbs with ease up a hundred-pound-test monofilament fishing line with no help from me. The line is tied to a brick set in tar on the flat roof of my house's addition, with the other end looped onto a hook set in the brick about a foot above the ground.

The word *ivy* is synonymous with climbing plants. But there are many different plants called by this name besides the genus *Hedera.* There are Boston ivy (*Parthenocissus tricuspidata*) and its cousin, Virginia creeper (*P. quinquefolia*), for example—terrific vines for shade. These are not evergreen like the *Hederas,* although in some winters they will hold a bit of their leaves. They

LEFT: ENGLISH IVY
climbs sheer rock in deep shade.
OPPOSITE: H. canariensis
'Variegata' and H. colchica
'Variegata'.

do have spectacular autumn foliage color, a device to attract birds to their inconspicuous black berries. The fall color changes from year to year depending on the heat and moisture of the summer season and ranges from bright orange-yellow to bronzy black. Boston ivy has a leaf that is somewhat like a duck's foot, and Virginia creeper is palmately lobed like a hand. But these leaf shapes also vary, depending on the plant's maturity. There are other species and varieties, especially of *P. tricuspidata,* which, despite its common name, comes from Japan. Look for ones such as *P. t.* 'Lowii', with tiny frilly leaves, and *P. t.* 'Veitchii'.

Depending upon who you talk to, there are between five and fifteen *Hedera* species. Your choice could depend on where you live. In warm climates, you'll be able to grow the magnificent *H. canariensis* (Canary ivy, Algerian ivy) and its varieties. These are huge-leaved evergreen plants, ubiquitous on the West Coast and in Florida. *H. c.* 'Gloire de Marengo' has silver variegations, *H. c.* 'Ravensholst' is good for ground cover.

H. colchica is called Persian ivy and also has huge leaves, up to ten inches long. It is thought to be subtropical, but I've seen it growing happily in Charles Cresson's third-generation garden near Philadelphia (zone 7). *H. c.* 'Dentata' is an evergreen self-climber called elephant's ears because of its huge drooping leaves. *H. c.* 'Dentata Variegata' has creamy yellow striped fo-

ENGLISH IVY (HEDERA helix), BELOW, *and colorful varieties 'Goldheart',* ABOVE, *and 'Buttercup',* OPPOSITE.

liage. Mr. Cresson also grows a rather unique vine, or perhaps lanky shrub, that is a cross between two genera, *Fatsia* (a Japanese subtropical shrub) and *Hedera,* and so is called x *Fatshedera.* It looks like a giant ivy, and although one of the parents is tender, the result is hardy to zone 7. It is interesting and lends a tropical air to a planting, perfect for the sheltered terrace where houseplants summer.

H. rhombea is Japanese ivy. It is reputed to be hardy to zone 8, but I think it could be pushed into the cold, especially if it were in a protected location. The leaves are diamond-shaped and not lobed. *H. pastuchovii* has shield-shaped shiny foliage and doesn't do as a ground cover.

The *Hedera helix* varieties are the English ivies, and this is where we take off. There are hundreds, many of which are hardy, and all are fascinating. Of the gray-green and white varieties, *H. h.* 'Glacier' seems very hardy and totally evergreen in zone 6. *H. h.* 'Goldheart' has a pat of butter at the center of every dark green leaf. *H. h.* 'Buttercup' is a sensation. The leaves, especially the new growth, are clear yellow, and make this plant shine like a beacon in the shade. *H. h.* 'Atropurpurea' has deep maroon leaves in winter, veined in bright green. *H. h.* 'Pedata' is the bird's-foot ivy. *H. h.* var. *hibernica* makes English ivy Irish.

There has always been a controversy about letting ivy grow up trees. I have heard from experts that it is detrimental, and I have heard from experts that it's harmless. In my own experience, I haven't noticed any serious damage from ivy or other vines that use rootlets or "hold-fasts" as a means of climbing. The short modified roots found on ivy and climbing hydrangea, for example, and Boston ivy's and Virginia creeper's little discs, seem to cause no harm. If the plants become very large and there is a possibility of damage from weight, then they could be removed or cut back. This isn't impossible to do—just cut them off at the ground.

CREATING SHADE

There are reasons to create shade. You might want to provide an environment that favors woodland wildings. Or you might become tired of sun worshiping and want to find a cool place in the shade for yourself. Or you might have a design idea —for a covered arbor, or an allée of trees—that involves shade. And you might consider the future of the giant trees for a moment. Years ago, estate gardens always included stately trees such as European weeping and copper beeches. These trees live about one hundred to one hundred and fifty years here, and soon, all over North America, the giant trees of the city parks and homes will die. No one has been planting these trees for years. There are none to take their places as they die. So think about planting a few trees for our grandchildren and their children.

If you are choosing trees to create shade, start with the deep-rooted oaks. English oak, *Quercus robur,* and nearly all of our deciduous American oaks are deep-rooted beauties. The Americans often have beautiful red fall foliage, especially the scarlet oak (*Q. coccinea*), a large tree not planted enough. The English oak and the pin oak (*Q. palustris*) have leaves that turn brown and persist through the winter, a look liked by some

people, and admittedly quite useful as contrast for evergreen shrubs and trees.

Fastigiate varieties of familiar trees like maples and beeches will cast less shade and still contribute to a forest canopy. The purple cut-leaf beech in its fastigiate form is beautiful and seems to have a narrow root spread.

Birches can be wonderful. Their bark will shine in the shade below. But consider alternatives to the most familiar European clump birch, *Betula pendula* (*B. alba*), which is plagued by disfiguring insects called leaf miners that tunnel through the foliage, and disease. We now have a new river birch variety, *B. nigra* 'Heritage', which is incredibly disease-resistant. Still and all, birches are short-lived trees. Fifty years or so, and that's it.

There are many smaller trees for the foreground of the understory, some of which will tolerate shade. Magnolias, crab apples, and cherries, *Amelanchier canadensis* and *Styrax japonica* (Japanese snowbell) are often choices. And remember to include trees with small leaves, such as the honey locusts (*Gleditsia triacanthos*) and the mountain ashes (*Sorbus* spp.), to create light, pale shade below.

SHADE MADE WITH A structure, ABOVE; *trees,* CENTER; *and shrubs,* BELOW *(the hemlock walk at Old Westbury Gardens).* OPPOSITE: *Trees provide shade and elegant bark* (Betula papyrifera)

SPECIAL GARDENS

IN THE SHADE

A CLUSTER OF LOVELY CONTAINERS UNDER SUZANNE AND CARTER BALES'S SHADY
porch provides color from annuals and houseplants such as impatiens, ivy, begonia, and coleus. OPPOSITE: *Cut*
garden flowers are a way to bring temporary color to the deepest shade.

THE SHADE GARDEN CONTAINED

You probably have the beginnings of a container garden in your own home—houseplants to summer out of doors. Houseplants benefit from a season in the humidity and bright light of the shade garden. A potted plant that demands direct sun indoors often does very well with bright light outdoors, because the hours of daylight are much longer and window glass diffuses much of the available sunlight. Plus, almost all plants love to have the rain or hose wash their leaves clean. Hairy-leaved plants and succulents might be exceptions.

Don't just plunk these plants outside—create a special "room" for them. Victor Nelson's mostly shaded garden is entirely planted in containers of varying sizes and shapes, from tiny flowerpots to planter boxes and faux terracotta urns—plastic pots made from the same molds as their clay counterparts. His terrace is actually a roof garden built over the top of a two-story addition.

Flowering and foliage plants in containers are an important part of every garden in the shade. If, for example, you've tried everything to get some plants and color above the roots of a giant maple, plant some containers, and root competition will cease to be a problem. There is a bit of decorating to container planting, but it is gardening nonetheless. You are simply making smaller plantings. Fill containers with scented geraniums, and the old standby, impatiens, every spring or make permanent plantings with selections like hosta, heuchera, astilbe, and ivy.

Planters do not have the benefit of earth all around them, so if you are not planning to move them to a sheltered place for the winter, a word of advice. Containers not only freeze down from the top, like the ground, but in from the sides as well. Also, plants can be exposed to more wind when they are elevated. As a general rule of thumb, I select perennials from one zone colder than their intended home. That is, if you live in USDA zone 6, collect plants that can tolerate zone 5 winters or colder.

A SINGLE ENORMOUS impatiens plant in a half whiskey barrel, ABOVE; *scented geraniums,* BELOW. OPPOSITE: *Roof-eye view of a container garden.*

You can't leave terra-cotta containers outdoors in cold climates because they will crack. It's the water expanding when it freezes that does it. I know of one gardener who covers her pots with plastic bonnets so that no water enters them from the top, and they do not break. This works if you're just storing soil or for annuals that have to be replaced anyway. I found that tilting the containers on their sides worked well too. Half whiskey barrels are inexpensive and indestructible containers for plants, and available virtually everywhere. But this might not be the look for you.

One mistake people make that shortens the life of the containers and plants and detracts from their appearance is to set them directly on the ground or patio surface. They always look better slightly elevated. They also look "lighter." The easiest way to raise the containers is simply to set them on three bricks spaced evenly. Every container for plants must have drainage holes; in the case of the half whiskey barrels, that means they must be drilled into the bottoms. Drill ten or so half-inch holes.

In my old container garden on a SoHo roof in New York City, I didn't use any soil. I blended peat moss with perlite, about three parts to one—more perlite for plants that enjoyed fast-draining medium, and less for moisture lovers. This mix holds more moisture than garden loam, but more important is that it weighs less than a fifth as much. There was no container that I was not able to move about. In the shade garden this can be useful for continuous color because you can rotate plants into deep shade as they flower. (When they fade, return them to the light until they blossom again.)

Being the ultimate tinkerer, I had to have an automated drip-watering system. It isn't a neces-

THE PLANTS IN VICTOR NELSON'S GARDEN GROW IN CONTAINERS THAT REST ON A
deck built above a two-story addition. There, in the treetops, annuals, perennials, tender and hardy bulbs, shrubs, and small trees share space with summering houseplants.

sity for a few containers in the shade, but I had over a hundred in full sun and wind. When I started irrigating my SoHo garden, I had to adapt a commercial orchard system with timers and valves designed for lawn sprinkling. Today, kits come ready to hook up, and it can be easily done in an afternoon.

Bring cut flowers to the most shaded areas as well. It might seem odd to display cut flowers out of doors, but in the cool shade they will last quite a while and bring color to the darkest setting. You can pick some from another part of the garden, or even bring a plant purchased in flower, such as a rhododendron, into the shade to be added later to a planting in more light.

Hostas are naturals for urns, especially the mop tops of the smaller varieties. *H.* 'Golden Sceptor' looks sensational draping over the rim of a particularly beautiful container. Astilbes do very well in containers and flower their heads off. Just be sure to keep the soil well watered —not soggy, but evenly moist. Usually the top of the medium should feel cold to the touch. A moisture meter, the kind with a long probe designed for indoor plants, can be helpful for testing container medium outdoors.

You could create an all-white-flowered container garden in a sheltered spot, which would bring light to an otherwise impossible site. Impatiens and fibrous-rooted begonias would be wonderful mixed with variegated geranium foliage and perhaps even Madonna lilies.

ANNUALS SUCH AS A subtle green coleus and double-flowered impatiens provide continuous color while herbaceous perennials and shrubs go in and out of bloom, ABOVE. *Birch tree trunks add structure to the wild-like scene viewed from the living room,* BELOW.

VIOLA LABRADORICA *IS AN EASY-TO-GROW VIOLET SPECIES WITH RICH, DEEP-*
colored foliage. It increases from runners that creep among the rocks to start new plants. OPPOSITE: *Rocks themselves*
can be used as colorful focal points in the garden.

GARDENS
OF STONE

Most rock gardens are fashioned after the sunny, open, alpine areas above the timberline. Our rock gardens are in the shade, of course, and that makes for a very different style with different plantings. Reduced sunlight and increased moisture make choices dissimilar. Also, rock-garden plants are often lime lovers—they like the alkaline soil caused by the presence of minerals leached from the rocks. We will have humus-loving specimens that want a neutral-to-acid pH.

Shade plants have the habit of lying about, flopping over one another, quite unlike the tight little alpines of the tundra. Your plants might smother one another, so rather than aiming for the blowsy,

natural shade garden look, you'll have to go slow, and be reserved, so as not to overplant. Select a few small plants and wait to see what happens.

Since this is the natural approach, you will be enhancing an existing rock outcropping as often as creating a new one. But rocks are in themselves beautiful additions to the garden, providing interesting texture and scale, and changing levels; you may want to import some, just as you will bring in plants, or sculpture, or furniture. And rocks can also improve the immediate environment for some plants. Properly positioned, rocks will direct rainwater to plants that need moisture and keep soil around them cool, too. Of course, many plants look exquisite with a perfectly chosen rock.

Most of the rocks you find will be recently broken. When freshly unearthed these rocks don't look right. They are pointed and shiny. They have to "age." Fortunately, rocks take on a weathered appearance much faster in the shade than they do in the sun. In the shade they will grow moss and algae and the sun won't reflect off the shiny particles of mica that make them look brand-new and too noticeable.

"New" rocks can be purchased from stone suppliers, but some of the best rocks you can

BENCHES MADE FROM

rocks and stones, at Blithewold, TOP, *and by Barry Bishop,* CENTER.

find are rounded ones that are already covered with some growth. Look for some with natural crevices to fill with soil and plant a common polypody (*Polypodium vulgare*), ajuga, *Maianthemum canadense* (false lily-of-the-valley, Canada mayflower), crested iris (*Iris cristata*), Kenilworth ivy (*Cymbalaria muralis*), or similar creeper. If you are lucky, you might locate a rock with a depression large enough to hold a bit of water to reflect the sky.

Look again to the wild. Find out something about the plants that hug the rocks in the woodland. You'll see mosses and little ferns. Look at the old stone walls along the country roads. In the days before machinery, farmers piled rocks that were too large to bury into dry walls. Their constructions could inspire the rock gardener.

Fallen trees show the way as well. You might want to take a piece of a fallen log home to install in your shaded rock garden or woodland. A section of log will hold an elaborate community of fern spores and baby ferns (*prothallia*), mosses, and fungi.

Lichen, the symbiotic plant-and-fungal community first analyzed by Beatrix Potter, is one of the most beautiful things in nature. And few lichens look the same. There are threadlike tall

EVERGREENS ON THE

rocks: Skimmia japonica, LEFT, *and* Galax urceolata, OPPOSITE.

ones (one-half inch high) of cela-don green, and others that look like rust. Transplanting lichens is next to impossible. I have had some luck by just bringing a rock already covered in lichen to my garden and attempting to set it up pretty much as it "grew" in the wild. You should note the humidity in the original setting, exposure to light, and perhaps even relation to magnetic north. I treasure the lichen.

As for establishing mosses, if the humidity is high, or the moisture source constant, you can try one of several recipes. Manure and dark beer, yogurt,

ROCK WALLS CAN BE

places to tuck little plants. Vines that creep along the rock face and root-in where they can find moisture are sometimes good choices. Kenilworth ivy, Cymbalaria muralis, *has tiny orchidlike flowers from spring to fall.*

buttermilk, a blended cocktail of live moss and beer, manure tea (the liquid strained off from cow manure steeped in water), and cow urine (although I'm not exactly sure how to collect it) have all been painted on rocks and ornaments to get the process going. And everyone swears by his or her recipe. Moss wants to grow where moss wants to grow, I think.

Mushrooms and fungi are the "fruiting" parts of organisms that are mostly threadlike myce-lia. Fungi in the soil are beneficial for many plants, and for some woodland species like the or-

chids, necessary. If you have a few beautiful mushrooms, enjoy them. Many will dry on wood and last for years. If you have too many, just remove them by weeding them out. Grab an inside-out plastic bag and slip it over the toadstool or mushroom cap as you prepare to snap it off at the base. If it is ripe, this will keep the spores from being released in the air and spreading. Don't eat any.

The mosses, mushrooms, and delicate woodlanders grow among the rocks in the moist northern rain forests. Unless there are large pockets of humus

THE NATIVE OXALIS violacea *grows with other wildings in a rock crevice. Whole, moistened sphagnum moss can be a useful planting medium here. Pack it into the opening with your fingers or a dowel and create a pocket for the plant or bulb.*

and soil trapped among your rocks, you won't see larger moisture lovers. But in your own setting, you can modify the situations. You might assemble a few rocks around a larger one and fill the pocket thus formed with humus-based medium. Then, miniature hostas—often *H. venusta* and its hybrids—*Shortia,* Christmas fern, *Galax,* gingers, and phloxes can join the moss and lichen.

If there are a lot of rocks in your soil, it doesn't mean you have a rock garden: you just have rocky soil. If the idea of digging and removing all the rocks seems

impossible, this might be a good place to *install* a rock garden. You can build up the arrangement on top of this less-than-perfect soil in the shade. It's a raised bed contained by rocks.

Moving rocks is no light task, and each and every one will have to be moved more than once. You have to set the rock, stand back, adjust it, and then adjust it again after considering its relationship to the rocks around it. Most should be buried to some extent, often up to fifty percent.

If you are building up with layers of rock and soil, be sure to position the stones so that water will run toward the plants and not down the rock faces. Also, set rocks so that the inherent patterns in the stone align. Many rocks have veins; keep them parallel. Consider the arrangement from a distance as well as close up. If your rocky area will be seen from the house, line them up so you can see between the open ridges and keep choice plants in view.

SOME OF THE ROCK PLANTS NEED AS MUCH LIGHT AS THE SHADE GARDENER CAN
*supply, and the leaves must not overlap as do many of the more usual shade plants. Two plants that need good air
circulation are* Primula vialii, O P P O S I T E, *and* Aquilegia flabellata *'Nana'*, A B O V E.

SPRING-BLOOMING

Anemone nemorosa,
  European anemone
Aquilegia spp., columbine
Asarum europaeum,
  European wild ginger
Claytonia virginica,
  claytonia, spring beauty*
Cornus canadensis,
  bunchberry
Dicentra canadensis, squirrel
  corn*
D. cucullaria, Dutchman's
  breeches*
Dodecatheon meadia and
  spp., shooting star*
Hepatica americana,
  hepatica*
Maianthemum canadense,
  Canada mayflower, false
  lily-of-the-valley*
Mertensia virginica, Virginia
  bluebells*
Omphalodes verna, blue-
  eyed Mary, creeping
  forget-me-not
Phlox divaricata, wild sweet
  William
P. stolonifera, creeping
  phlox
Polygonatum humile,
  Japanese Solomon's seal
Primula spp., primrose
Pulmonaria spp., lungwort
Sanguinaria canadensis,
  bloodroot
Shortia spp., shortia
Viola pedata, bird's-foot
  violet

SPRING-TO-SUMMER

Dicentra formosa, western
  bleeding heart
Polemonium reptans, Jacob's
  ladder

Saxifraga stolonifera,
  strawberry begonia
Saxifraga spp., selected
  alpines for shade
Tiarella cordifolia,
  foamflower
Veronica repens, creeping
  speedwell
Viola spp., violets

SPRING-TO-FALL

Chrysogonum virginianum,
  goldenstar, green-and-
  gold
Corydalis lutea and spp.,
  corydalis, yellow
  fumatory
Cymbalaria muralis,
  Kenilworth ivy
Geranium robertianum, herb
  Robert
Lysimachia nummularia,
  moneywort
Mazus reptans, mazus
Polygala paucifolia and spp.,
  milkworts

SUMMER-BLOOMING

Aegopodium podagraria
  'Variegatum', goutweed
Astilbe chinensis 'Pumila',
  astilbe
Goodyera spp., rattlesnake
  plantain
Heuchera villosa, *H.
  americana*, and spp.,
  heuchera, hairy alumroot
Sedum spp. (a few creepers
  for shade, such as *S. acre*,
  S. rosea)

SUMMER-TO-FALL

Ceratostigma plumbaginoides,
  leadwort

Hosta venusta and other
  dwarf species and
  hybrids, hosta
Liriope spp., dwarf lilyturf

FERNS

Asplenium spp.,
  spleenworts
Camptosorus rhizophyllus,
  walking fern
Cryptogramma crispa,
  parsley fern
Dryopteris fragrans, fragrant
  fern
Phyllitis scolopendrium,
  hart's-tongue fern
Polypodium vulgare,
  common polypody
Woodsia spp., woodsia

SMALL SHRUBS

Arctostaphylos spp.,
  bearberry
Cotoneaster spp.,
  cotoneaster (prostrate,
  deciduous dwarf types)
Gaultheria hispidula,
  creeping snowberry
G. procumbens, wintergreen
Juniperus procumbens
  'Nana', creeping juniper
Mitchella repens,
  partridgeberry
Pachysandra procumbens,
  Alleghany spurge
Pieris dwarf cultivars,
  Japanese andromeda
Spiraea bullata 'Nana',
  dwarf bridal veil
Vaccinium spp., dwarf
  blueberry

* may go dormant in summer

PACHYSANDRA
procumbens *(Alleghany spurge)*,
A B O V E . Corydalis cheilanthus,
R I G H T . O P P O S I T E : *Although
it can be difficult to make colorful*
Impatiens wallerana *look "natural,"
they seem to blend well with these
moss-covered rocks*, A B O V E .
Thought of as a sun plant, Juniperus
procumbens *'Nana*, C E N T E R ,
*grows well for me in shade. A
"new" plant from Japan*,
Polygonatum humile, B E L O W .

A SMALL POOL DESIGNED AND PLANTED IN MASSACHUSETTS BY MARTHA PAULL
captures the appearance and atmosphere of a deep lagoon in miniature. OPPOSITE: *A tiny corner by my pool's edge provides space for growing a complex mixture of shade-tolerant rock garden plants.*

THE WATER GARDEN

ater features belong in every garden. There may be a tiny bubbling fountain, or a pond in a woodland clearing. Moving water is a blessing in the shade garden: light reflecting upon the water sparkles in the shadows and attracts attention.

You will want to create an informal water feature for the natural shade garden, and that usually means that it will have a free-form shape. You might consider making a series of small pool areas linked by a "stream." Pools should be at least eighteen inches deep for plants and fish. The area must be level; nothing looks more unnatural than a pool with one side at water level, while six inches of the other side is exposed. The edge of the pool should blend into

the surroundings with naturally placed rocks and pockets for waterside plantings. Many of the bog plants can be grown in pots of soil or pond muck lowered directly into the pond or pool. Cover the medium with pebbles so that it doesn't float up and cloud the water. You must also provide that no runoff from high ground can enter and foul the water; rock edging might be the answer. The soil around the pool should also be well drained so that water cannot accumulate and shift a rigid pool shell or lift a plastic sheet liner.

You'll need electricity and a water source for the pond. These elements should be planned for and installed when the pool goes in. Be sure to use a GFI, ground fault interrupter, for all outside power. This is a very sensitive outlet switch that will trip if the slightest bit of moisture enters the plug or there is a problem on the line. It also makes it easy to switch off the electricity for maintenance tasks.

I would advise against installing an in-ground pond or pools if you have young children who play near or visit the garden. It would be best to wait, or make a raised water feature in a tub or elevated fiberglass pool. I've seen beautiful Chinese hundred-year-old egg pots filled with fish and water under the shade of porch eaves. (That setup in sun would be hellish: hot water, algae, and so on.)

A garden pool can be made of concrete, but leak-resistant liners made of PVC (polyvinyl chloride), butyl rubber, and rigid fi-

MOVING WATER BRINGS light, sound, and birds to the garden. OPPOSITE: *Consider planning an island for trees or shrubs if you have the opportunity to make a new pond.*

berglass are much easier to install and maintain (and less expensive, too). A heavy PVC liner will last from ten to twenty years, especially if it is not exposed to sunlight above the water. Small punctures can be repaired. The rubber liner can last forty years.

The catalogs claim it is easy to build a pool with a plastic liner; what they don't tell you is how hard it can be to dig the hole. When I made my small pool, about eight feet long, four feet wide, and two feet deep, I came up against the terminal moraine that passed through here during the last ice age. I brought up enough rocks to edge, hold, and disguise the liner's rim, build the waterfall and rock garden, and fill an area in the center of the "tree house" at the rear of the garden. It was a lot of work. The companies also don't tell you how difficult it can be to smooth the liner and fold the edges. You have to do a lot of overlapping and pleating to get the sheet to lie flat. It is not a job to tackle alone.

Today, my water garden gets more attention than any other part of my natural shade garden. However, all I do is feed the fish once a day and clean the filter once or twice a week. That's only about fifteen minutes—compare that to mowing a lawn. Most of the water-garden chores involve the animals who live in it.

My "pool" has a footbridge crossing it, and a waterfall powered by an electric pump. The pump sucks up water through a plastic-foam material and deliv-

ers it clean and clear down carefully arranged rocks .set in concrete. (Now, there are biological filters to try.) I like the water clear, so I'm into filters, but in the beginning, I simply had a very well-balanced pool. I started with some underwater plants, called oxygenators, a few tadpoles, small fish, and pots of plants that grow out of the water but with their containers submerged. The water stayed very clear. But the fish grew; they're about fifteen inches long now. As I added more, I threw the pool out of balance. So, I installed the filters.

Informal pools in the shade can have another maintenance problem if they are located directly under trees. Decomposing leaves rob oxygen from the water and produce potentially lethal gases, so they must be kept out of the small pond, or cleaned out of the bottom if you miss them and they sink—not the easiest chore. Tree flowers must be skimmed off for the same reasons. Fortunately, the flower drop lasts only a couple of days and removal is easy; leaves only fall for a few weeks. You can spread a garden net over the tree-shaded pond for the duration or just skim the surface every other day. As wonderful as it may seem to have a sheltered garden pond under the spreading branches of a dense maple tree, you should know of these drawbacks at the outset. Yet, a small pool under a tree, especially in a raised container, with a fountain and such, might be a brilliant solution for a too-dark area.

PLANTS FOR THE WATERSIDE INCLUDE HOSTAS
and brilliant-flowered Japanese iris. OPPOSITE: *An exotic denizen of
the shaded waterside is* Arisaema sikokianum, *a relative of our familiar
jack-in-the-pulpit.*

Mosquitoes might be a problem unless the pool is small with rapidly moving clean water, or stocked. I opted for the latter. Seven Japanese imperial *koi,* or *"nishikigoi,"* which means colored carp, live in my pool. When I first got *koi,* they had an unpleasant habit of jumping out of the pond (something no catalogs warn you about). I learned to cover the pond with netting until the fish settled down. Each subsequent introduction just follows the lead of the existing school and stays put, sans net.

Most of the fish came through the mail (once delivered to the wrong address, to two very surprised teenage girls). In Japan, and other parts of the world, *koi* are bred and exhibited and sold at shows. A prize fish in particularly wonderful colors and patterns (all of which have specific names) can fetch a hefty prize— twenty thousand dollars or so. These fish can live about sixty years, and one, "Hanako," was said to have lived two hundred years. These carp relatives can reach three feet in length.

I've gone on about the *koi* because *they* are the source of color in my shady garden pool, where water lilies and lotus will not thrive. But for insect control, even twenty-five-cent goldfish will do. Today we also have *Bacillus thuringiensis israelensis,*

CAPTURING EVERY BIT OF the sun's rays by the edge of the woodland marsh is Joe-pye weed, Eupatorium purpureum.

186

an environmentally acceptable bacterium-based treatment that kills mosquito larvae and does no harm to anything else.

THE BOG GARDEN

You might think of a bog as an enormous marshy area, but it can be small, as little as three feet by three feet, and of course it is an excellent adjunct to a water garden. A larger bog can contain islands or hummocks where acid- and moisture-loving shrubs, and even trees, such as blueberries, pussy willow, *Clethra, Sambucus,* shrub dogwoods, paperbark maple and *Oxydendron arboreum,* can rise above the wet area.

The homemade bog is a mixture of sand and acidic humus with a touch of soil and water. But the water is generally not on the surface of the medium but just a few inches below. If you have an area that collects runoff from rain, is spring-fed, or has a little stream, the bog can be constructed there. If this area is subject to flooding, however, the garden could be washed away.

The simplest method is to excavate a depression in the ground, about eighteen inches deep and as large as you want. Smooth this area carefully so that no sharp rocks protrude from the dug surface. If the soil in the area is nearly pure clay, you may not have to line the depression at all, but in most cases some kind of seal will be required. You can line the area with the same PVC liner used for a fish pond, or you can use polyethylene film in a heavy grade, or even roofing paper. But be sure that the plastic film is not exposed to light, as it breaks down quickly. The edge of the liner is folded down to ground level and held in place with rocks—quite like the pool. The rocks are not cemented but lie close together so that the bog material will stay in place even if there is a heavy rain. Water must be able to drain over the edge of the plastic, through the spaces in the rocks, and into the surrounding ground. The medium should be made of three parts acidic humus, such as peat moss or oak leaves, to two parts sand, to one part loam—good topsoil. It will be hard to mix these materials once they are inside the liner, so blend them in a wheelbarrow, or on a tarpaulin next to the excavation. This is one situation in which dry peat moss might be a blessing. It will be light, and it can be moistened after it's inside the lined area. Run a hose into the bowl of man-made muck. If the peat moss was dry, the sand will help it absorb water, but some will float. Add as much water as you can, wait overnight, and then add more the next day.

Even if your bog is naturally fed, you might have to add water weekly during hot spells and/or drought. But I wouldn't recommend making a bog garden in Arizona. If you are in an area of only moderate rainfall, limit the size of your bog, as it will have to be watered frequently. You should avoid abusing the water source, even if it is inexpensive and plentiful in your area.

AMERICAN AND JAPANESE *skunk cabbages.* ABOVE, Lysichiton americanum, L. camtschatcense. *Giant* Petasites japonicus, BELOW. OPPOSITE: *The leaves of another American skunk cabbage,* Symplocarpus foetidus, *are more familiar.*

If you are planting trees and shrubs in the peat-bog planting, remember that you will be *creating* shade, and root competition. These larger plants should be relegated to the mounded hummocks at the center, or better, the north edge of the crafted bog.

Many marsh plants do want sun, but there are others well known to natural shade gardeners that will do well. *Helleborus* spp., mayapple (*Podophyllum peltatum*), *Rodgersia* species and hybrids, bloodroot (*Sanguinaria canadensis*), and trilliums are among the shaded peat-bog-garden plants.

The jack-in-the-pulpit (*Arisaema triphyllum*) is another. In midspring, the familiar spathe appears just as the leaves unfurl, and lasts quite a while. These plants have the ability to change gender from year to year, so in some seasons individual spathes will be followed by showy red berries. The American jacks, or jills, as the case may be, are not scarce, and typically send up little plants around the original bulb-like tuber.

Another aroid that likes moisture and the acidity of the peat bog is the arum (*Arum creticum, A. italicum,* and cultivars), whose calla-like blossoms are only part of the attraction. Small or large arrow-shaped leaves appear in the fall, last through the winter, and then disappear after flowering in spring. Green-leaved *A. creticum* has a pretty, creamy yellow spathe, while cultivars of *A. italicum,* such as 'Pictum', have marvelous silver veins on the foliage, making this plant more

FOLIAGE SHAPES AND SIZES ABOUND FOR
waterside plantings. Rodgersia pinnata *leaves,* ABOVE, *and flowers,*
BELOW. OPPOSITE: *The nonhardy tuberous* Colocasia esculenta,
elephant ear, or taro, has three-foot-long leaves.

useful than it would be for fleeting flowers alone. All of the arums have showy red berries, not unlike a jack-in-the-pulpit.

A related spathe-forming plant for the shaded bog is the golden club, *Orontium aquaticum,* only its spathe is tiny. The spadix, the flower-bearing inside structure, is usually covered by the spathe in the aroid family, but that of the golden club is in full view, and *very* ornamental. This native has a white poker that seems to have been dipped in yellow paint where the tiny golden flowers bloom in spring. The spear-shaped leaves are waxy, so raindrops bead up into pearls of quicksilver that spin off the leaves.

The skunk cabbages are favorites of mine. I can't believe that everyone doesn't love them. Just picture a woodland where the stream runs filled with the incredible glowing green rosettes of cabbage copycats. The most familiar, *Symplocarpus foetidus,* is known for its leaves alone, but just after the snows melt away, look by the waterside for low, thick purple-brown spathes that envelop the flowering spadix. I don't know where you can buy this plant; no one stoops to sell it. I'm certain, though, that anyone with a wet woodland would be pleased to share some. As these plants are unpleasantly musky when disturbed, dig some very early, when the pointy leaf shoots appear. They are easily mutilated when the leaves are fully unfurled, and since they must have moisture in the leaves, be sure to get a good-sized chunk of the rootstock.

If you have time and patience you can grow two of the most magnificent of all the polecat plants. I had to go to Beth Chatto's garden in England to see our native *Lysichiton americanum,* a huge skunk cabbage with enormous yellow spathes, and its Japanese counterpart, *L. camtschatcense,* with elegant white spathes of the same size and shape. One of the few books to list and show them is *The Natural Garden.* Yet these are sensational bog plants if you have ample room for their three-foot-tall lanceolate leaves.

Plants with huge leaves look tropical in the water garden and tremendously picturesque. *Colocasia esculenta* and varieties *are* tropical. Called elephant's ears, taro, or giant caladiums, they grow from edible tubers that must be stored over winter in a cool dry place, such as the basement. They are easy to grow, best in containers. In mid- to late spring, as soon as the air is warm, bring the dormant tubers, already in their pots, outside. The pots can be set into water, or sunk by the water's edge. In fall, before it gets too cold, the foliage yellows and they should be removed from the pond or pool, pot and all, to be stored over winter again. These plants are susceptible to red spider mites, but only if they are in a dry environment; they won't get them in or near the water. As specimens on their own, they make a memorable impression, especially the red-stemmed taro, *C. e.* 'Fontanesii'.

PINK-FLOWERING

Chelone lyonii, *turtlehead, in late summer,* TOP. Petasites japonicus, CENTER, *and* Peltiphyllum peltatum, BELOW. OPPOSITE: *The tranquil, shaded water garden.*

While on the subject of the big and the beautiful, no plant can touch *Gunnera manicata* for formidability. It's a plant with gargantuan leaves, easily six feet across or more, and up to eight feet tall. It's not usual to see gunnera growing away from water, but more unusual to see it in the shade, as it is almost always used to dominate a sunny pond's edge. However, gunnera will grow in a somewhat shaded spot in gardens up to southern New Jersey.

Not many of us have the space for this colossus; there are several gunnera imitators that are a bit more dainty: Magilla Gorillas if not King Kongs. The rodgersias top the list. Hardly hulking, *R. tabularis* looks like a miniature gunnera—"small" leaves a foot wide and about two feet tall. This plant has fragrant flowers in late spring to early summer. Others have more ornamental flowers and eye-catching foliage. *R. pinnata* is my current favorite. It has pinnate leaves and a buff-pink fuzzy inflorescence. There are cultivars with very large, showy pink flowers, such as *R. p.* 'Superba'. *R. aesculifolia*'s leaves resemble the horse chestnut tree (*Aesculus hippocastanum*), hence the species name. The leaves are similar to those of *R. pinnata,* but palmate and scalloped at the ends.

You can easily divide your plants every other year to keep them in balance with your chosen site (and make esteemed gifts). When the leaves emerge in spring, I plunge my trusty serrated bread knife into the ground

ABOVE: LATHYRUS

vernus *has purple flowers that turn sapphire blue.* BELOW: *Emerging plants show diverse textures in spring.* OPPOSITE: Caltha palustris *'Plena', double-marsh marigold,* ABOVE, *has tufted flowers;* Orontium aquaticum, *golden club,* BELOW, *has chrome yellow and white flowers.*

and cut up the rhizomatous root-stock into pie sections, lifting the wedges with soil intact. Each division quickly becomes a handsome specimen. The earlier the act, the quicker the recovery. My *R. pinnata* didn't seem to miss a beat, and now grows in moist spots in friends' gardens.

The western *Peltiphyllum peltatum* (*Darmera peltatum*) has a lot going for it. Pink flowers are followed by wide scalloped leaves that rise on hairy stalks from the thick rhizomes. Later, there is wonderful fall color, russet red with yellow veins. This gunnera look-alike is aptly called the umbrella plant, and likes more sun than some. *Petasites* spp. (butter-burs) have large, flat leaves. The skyward foliage of *P.* x *hybridus,* bog rhubarb, may reach three feet across; the stiff-leaved *P. japonicus giganteus* (Fuki) grows larger. They love moist bog settings but are tenacious enough to grow in poor soil, and will naturalize. Robust *P.* x *hybridus* has spread in the Northeast, although it hails from Europe and Asia. Thought of as plants for the "waste" places, they are magnificent in massive stands.

I have to note *Ligularia dentata,* but accept it under protest. The leaves of the hybrid *L. d.* 'Desdemona' and its junior, 'Othello', are magnificent burgundy-green. However, this plant is slug bait, pure and simple. In summer, tall spikes bearing lurid yellow-orange rays of striplike wilted-daisy petals rise above the round foliage. You might want to try this plant out. If you love nature enough to suffer Swiss-cheese

foliage, endure until you see the flowers, and judge for yourself; I would cut them off.

You usually find *L. stenocephala,* 'The Rocket', listed as *L. przewalskii* 'The Rocket'. *L. stenocephala* is a good plant, with afternoon shade essential for the fringed, heart-shaped leaves. *L. przewalskii* has deeply lobed toothed leaves and dark stems, and otherwise behaves similarly, including wilting in sunshine. 'The Rocket' is a spectacular plant for partial shade, and is rarely plagued by slugs or snails. If you want to try one ligularia, this is it. The yellow flowers grow on ebony spikes and bloom earlier and longer than most of the genus. Its diffusion of paler lemon yellow stars along the vertical raceme is more pleasant than *L. dentata*'s saffron yellow spiders. However, it is not one of our gunneralike plants, for the reason that leaves come from the stem and not directly from the soil-level basal clump.

Caltha palustris, the marsh marigold, obviously likes wet feet. Look for the double flowered variety (*C. p.* 'Flore-Pleno') too. Flowers look like bright yellow tufts. There is also a white variety, *C. p.* 'Alba'. These plants disappear by summer.

Chelone spp. (turtlehead) are tall plants for moist places. Planted in groups, they make a quintessential wet meadow. The name comes from the individual one-inch flowers, which resemble, well, turtles' heads. *C. lyonii* might be the best choice for the shade; it will wilt in full sun, even when the soil is moist.

Lovely pink flowers on sturdy plants look wonderful at the water's edge.

There are several irises that not only like it wet, but can grow with their roots in water. Our native *Iris versicolor,* blue iris or blue flag, is often found in the wet meadow or bog. The flowers are blue to violet and often have yellow blotches, veined purple on the falls—the part of the flower that curves down. As with most of the iris species and varieties, individual flowers are fleeting, but *I. versicolor* can form a good-size community.

Reference books used to say that Japanese irises had to be grown in water, but I've seen them do very well in borders. Try *I. ensata* (formerly, *I. kaempferi*) in filtered light in the bog; it might need more sunlight. The flowers are very late for the iris family, early to midsummer, and huge, up to five inches across their flat blossoms. Plants range in stature depending on variety, from eighteen inches to about four feet tall.

Again, you'll have to play around a bit with the amount of light and sun the irises need. Some suggest *Iris pseudacorus* for full sun. I have one that blooms very well under an oakleaf hy-

MANY MEMBERS OF THE IRIS GENUS WILL GROW IN various amounts of moisture. Iris sibirica, TOP LEFT, *can tolerate just about anything.* I. Kaempferi, ABOVE, *needs more sunlight.*

drangea. Others, in more sun, have grown taller with thicker blades, but they don't have more flowers. The latter have formed a heroic covey among the rocks above the pool.

Yellow flag, as *I. pseudacorus* is called, will do well in standing water or any garden soil. This is the ancient European strain that was the inspiration for the French *fleur-de-lis*. There is a double variety (*I. p.* 'Flora Plena') and a variegated variety (*I. p.* 'Variegata') that shows wonderful lemon-cream striped blades in spring, though they darken with time to match the solid green of the species.

The Siberian irises (*I. sibirica*) are indestructible, in or out of water. They have beautiful grassy foliage that will flop a bit in wind and shade, but bloom they will in bright light, more in some sun. These wonderful plants suggest a flock of butterflies alighting. The many varieties offer flower colors from white to sky blue to indigo. They are smaller than the German bearded types, but, I think, nicer for that reason alone.

There are other plants with distinctly vertical foliage. *Acorus calamus* is the sweet flag, whose foliage looks pretty much like

IRIS PSEUDACORUS, *ABOVE, LIKE THE SIBERIAN IRIS,*
is easy. Flowers are short-lived, but foliage is interesting year-round.
I. douglasiana, TOP RIGHT, *is an iris for the West Coast.*

SOME BOG PLANTS ARE carnivorous. Sarracenia *is the pitcher plant. The flowers of* S. flava, ABOVE, *are globular and about the height of its hooded leaves.* Ligularia dentata *'Desdemona,'* BELOW, *has reddish foliage in spring that deepens to bronze by summer.*

the flag iris's. It doesn't take a linguist to recognize that *Iris pseudacorus* is named for this plant: "iris-false-acorus." The curious inflorescence is insignificant, and to me so is the foliage of the species. You might as well grow the iris. However, *A. c.* 'Variegatus' is sensational. In early spring it is suffused with rose, then quickly grows two to four feet tall (there are dwarf species and varieties, such as *A. gramineus* and its variegated form, which top out at twelve inches). Acorus has a flat, fleshy rhizome, quite a bit like the iris's. One of the most striking variegated plants for the water garden, it will grow in a bog as well as in a pot set in water—with the rim above the surface or as deep as six inches.

Among the weird but lovable spire plants are the horsetails, which grow throughout the United States. *Equisetum* spp. make ferns look modern. They are simply hollow tubes with nodes like the joints of the bamboo culms or canes. *E. hyemale* is the one most available and grows in zones 3–9, where it is semi-evergreen. Its segmented stems with ragged brown rings at each joint were used as pot scrubbers in colonial times, and it is still sometimes called scouring rush.

Rushes and sedges lend the vertical or fountain shape to plantings. Many need sun, but most of the *Carex* species can do with less light. *Carex stricta* 'Bowles Golden' is a showy, moisture-loving plant called golden variegated sedge, and is about two to three feet tall.

THE BEAUTIFUL FLOATING LEAVES ABOVE ARE NOT THOSE OF A CLOVER.

Amazingly, it is the fern Marsilea mutica, *whose leaves are about two inches across. There are some sixty-five species distributed throughout the world.*

C. grayi, Gray's sedge, is for moist shade, too, as is *C. pendula,* the dropping sedge grass, which is evergreen.

When I was in Northern California recently, the landscape architect Ron Lutsko asked me if I knew the "fiber optic plant." This new name for a plant I know as spike rush (*Eleocharis montevidensis*) is certainly apt. To me, it looks like long blades of grass topped by brown cotton-swab tips. It is a marvelous plant for moist places or in pots directly in the water. I don't know how hardy it is. It survived a bad winter to come back, not just in its original site, but in several wet spots where seeds sprouted with

SARRACENIA PURPUREA, ABOVE, *is another native pitcher plant. This one has low-foliage from which foot-tall, downward-facing flowers bloom in summer.*

a vengeance. It grows and flowers in shade but it flops a bit, there, and I think it looks better standing tall, so I recommend at least three hours of direct sun. And this is one plant that can take midday sun if that's all you have—a lack of leaves helps it retain moisture.

Beautiful water clover (*Marsilea* spp.) floats on the surface of the shaded pool, and must either be planted in soil in the natural pool edge or, better, in a submerged pot. Giant cloverlike leaves with colorful zones and brown markings float on the water, or rise just above it. This is not really a clover, or *Oxalis,* but, amazingly, a fern. *M. mutica* is said to be hardy in zones 6–10. I'll find out if the *koi* leave it alone. The European *M. quadrifolia* is hardy in New England, where it has naturalized in some ponds. Shellflower or floating lettuce (*Pistia stratiotes*) is a fascinating annual to float in the shady pond. Lush rosettes of pale-green leaves can be ordered and replaced yearly.

You have probably never seen *Lathyrus vernus,* a sweet-pea relative allegedly known as spring vetchling or bitter spring vetch. There is a white form and one with salmon pink blossoms, but the species has an abundance of three-quarter-inch purple pealike blooms that turn sapphire with age and then fall—self-cleaning. It is an excellent ground cover for a moist area. I photographed a substantial colony shaded in very soggy leaf mold (I was up to my ankles in water). But Helen Stoddard used this dainty plant in a retaining-wall crevice at her Massachusetts garden, and Oliver's Nursery in Connecticut displayed a neat mound in a woodland bed. I've read that it is recommended for "full sun" in one source and that "sun is death" in another. British author Margery Fish vouches for its use "for the front of the shady border," and as to its low maintenance, she adds, "I have never done more than admire it." Is this another jack-of-all-plants? Soon you'll find it offered in one catalog, or come across it at a specialty nursery. In a few years it will be as ubiquitous as a newly learned word.

Gentians are magical. I think

ASCLEPIAS INCARNATA,

swamp milkweed, ABOVE, *is shade-tolerant for its clan. It likes some direct sunlight: midday sun will work because the roots are in moist soil.* Cornus florida, *dogwood,* BELOW, *is a small tree for an island or a waterside.*

their mystery stems from the remarkable color of the flowers—mirácle blue, the color of an old bottle, deep and cobalt. *Gentiana andrewsii* is called closed gentian because the flowers never seem to open, but they are large, about two inches long. This species is the best choice for streamside or moist woodland. Willow gentian (*G. asclepiadea*) is another to try. It has flowers that open into stars at the end of tubes that grow along the stem, as do the flowers of *G. septemfida,* the crested gentian. These plants lay their arching stems down to the ground to cover and spread over time. They don't need dividing.

Moisture-loving ground covers include one of the lysimachias and ajugas. *Lysimachia nummularia* is unlike the others in that it creeps along the banks of the water, often dipping right into it. This simple moneywort is pretty enough, but in late spring to early summer, it sports happy yellow flowers; and, of special interest to me, there is a gold-colored, albeit less tenacious, variety, *L. n.* 'Aurea'.

Lobelia cardinalis (cardinal flower) and its blue-flowered cousin, *Lobelia siphilitica,* the great blue lobelia, are both for bog gardens in varying degrees of shade. Look for the cardinal flower with deep red foliage, too, but remember that this species is a short-lived perennial.

Good flowering plants for the waterside include some familiar pinch hitters such as hosta, astilbe, *Aruncus* spp. (goatsbeard), *Filipendula* spp. (meadowsweet), primroses, purple

LYSIMACHIA

nummularia, *creeping Jennie,*
ABOVE, *loves to spill over the*
edge of the pool and into the water.
For much of the season, its stems are
covered with small yellow flowers.
Lobelia siphilitica, BELOW, *is the*
great blue lobelia well-known as a
plant for the waterside.

Asclepias incarnata (swamp milkweed), and *Eupatorium purpureum* (Joe-Pye weed), which needs some sun. *Cardamine pratensis* (cuckooflower) has ferny foliage and clusters of rose-lilac-colored flowers in spring. *C. p.* 'Flore-Pleno' is a showy double form. *Mimulus* spp. and varieties might be tried. The native *M. guttatus* will succeed. This plant, called monkey flower here and musk in Great Britain, has layered rings of yellow flowers, blotched red. It is a short-lived perennial. *M. luteus* (golden monkey flower) performs similarly and also as a ground cover.

There are, of course, many ferns for the waterside. Here's a list of some candidates: *Adiantum* spp., *Asplenium* spp., *Athyrium* spp., *Dryopteris* spp., *Matteuccia* spp., *Onoclea* spp., *Osmunda* spp., *Polypodium* spp., and *Polystichum* spp.

The carnivorous plants grow in bogs in many parts of our country. The sundews and Venus flytrap like sun. In the wet pine barrens, Virginia and south, *Sarracenia flava* trumpets grow. I know they are hardy far north of their homeland. *S. purpurea,* the pitcher plant, is familiar in sphagnum bogs from Canada south to Minnesota, across to Maryland, and down to the coast of Florida. Incredible "leaves," deeply veined and flared, form vases half filled with water, six to eight inches tall. Separate stems shoot up one to two feet, topped by extraordinary nodding spherical flowers colored wine red. I think these are among nature's most wonderful works of art.

THE BEST OF ALL BLUES COMES FROM THE GENTIANS. GENTIANA ANDREWSII HAS
large flowers in late summer that never seem to open all the way. Called closed gentian for that reason, it is a long-lived,
two-foot-tall perennial to grow by a stream or water's edge.

TREES CREATE THE WOODLAND, SUCH AS THESE MAPLES WEARING THEIR
autumnal colors. We can make gardens down below, in the forest understory, RIGHT. *It's a wonderful place for a cool
walk on a summer's day, but most of all, it affords an opportunity to grow extraordinary species.*

THE WOODLAND GARDEN

S o many of the plants we use in the natural
shade garden come from the wooded areas of
the world. What differentiates the woodland garden
from the other plantings of the natural shade garden?
The woodland garden is the planting that more than
any other resembles the wild. It's the place for as
many native plants as possible, but all "wildflowers,"
even plants wild in other parts of the world, are welcome. Think of these plants as *species*—unhybridized
plants. So native jewelweed (*Impatiens capensis*) might
be the counterpart of a 'Dazzler', 'Elfin', or 'Blitz' hybrid impatiens, and frilly parrot tulips would give way
to species stand-ins such as the multiflowered *Tulipa*

clusiana, the candy-stripe tulip.

If you have an area thick with trees, then you have the makings of a woodland garden, and your task might be to create and develop a path. Most wildflowers will be situated along this path. You will want to remove some trees and uninteresting shrubs to let in more light and to make room for the plants you want to introduce. Brush can be cleared away from large rocks to reveal their texture and provide year-round interest through this garden. Bury new rocks so that parts of them stick up above the soil line, so that they look natural. The aesthetic arrangement of plants is important, of course. Unlike bed and border plantings, however, the wildflowers of the woodland look just fine with plenty of mulch around them. This mulch cover—shredded leaves or pine needles, perhaps—acts as if it were a mat for a watercolor.

The woodland plants need a highly moisture-retentive medium that is also very well draining—sounds like a contradiction. If you have poor drainage due to clay soil, then you might consider raised beds held by logs. Turn under and over as much clayey soil as you can and add

A FOUNTAIN OF

Dicentra spectabilis *'Alba',* ABOVE,
blooms above Phlox divaricata.
BELOW: Uvularia grandiflora.
OPPOSITE: *The woodland garden*
in spring. OVERLEAF: Dicentra
flowers and Cimicifuga *buds.*

sand and humus such as leaf mold. Make sure that the medium that goes above ground, perhaps six inches or more, is the best that it can be for a particular plant's needs. Since the bed is raised, it may have a tendency to dry out more quickly. Humus will hold moisture, even in this elevated bed, but this is the time to consider an irrigation system of some kind, probably a soaker hose snaking throughout the planting area above the improved original soil and through the added material that fills the raised bed.

When you prepare the new growing medium, enrich it also with nutrients that are organic and release slowly so as not to burn roots; this is hardly the place for commercial fertilizers. Compost or leaf mold will release a continuous dose of nutrition to the plants over the years. Add a dusting of bone meal so that it turns the surface white, and then enough cottonseed meal to turn it yellow, and fold these nutrient sources into the mix. Cottonseed meal is acidic; bone meal slowly delivers phosphorus, which the woodland plants love (and so do dogs). If you use a fresh wood source, such as new shredded bark or fresh white sawdust, you'll have to add a bit of nitrogen, because, as noted, the microorganisms that break down these materials take nitrogen from the soil, and away from plants. Manure tea—fresh cow manure steeped in water and strained—well-rotted cow or horse manure, or liquid seaweed are organic sources of nitrogen.

It is very important not to walk on garden soil. Compacted soil, even from occasional foot traffic, is the menace of many plants, especially the wildflowers, which need a loose, open medium. You planned for stepping-stones as a utility path among the perennial and shrub plantings of the shady border. For access to the woodland garden, you can lay flat boards over the mulch to stand on.

WOODLAND WILDFLOWERS, FROM LEFT TO RIGHT, TOP ROW TO BOTTOM ROW:

Stylophorum diphyllum, *celandine poppy;* Pulmonaria saccharata; Sanguinaria canadensis *'Multiplex', double bloodroot;* Anemone ranunculoides; Dicentra spectabilis, *bleeding heart;* Anemone quinquefolia; Cardamine pentaphyllos; Anemone nemorosa; Dicentra eximia, *native bleeding heart;* Chrysogonum virginianum, *green and gold;* Epimedium grandiflorum; Anemonella thalictroides *'Shoaf's Double'.* OPPOSITE: Dodecatheon meadia *'Album'.*

PRIMROSES

Primulas are perhaps the most magical and beautiful of all the flowers of the open woodland. The most familiar ones are native to the British Isles, but primroses come from many parts of the world. There are American hybrids and cultivars, many developed by H. Lincoln Foster. They are naturals for us because they naturalize freely—that is, they increase over the years from offsets, little plants that grow beside the parent, and from self-sown seeds.

The cowslips (*P. veris*) and oxlips (*P. elatior*) are the British spring bloomers that started the

PRIMULAS *(SUCH AS*

P. polyantha, ABOVE) *are*

intensely romantic flowers. And yet,

some people curse them for their

finicky requirements; others find

them easy to grow. At the Berkshire

Botanical Garden, OPPOSITE,

they bloom freely beneath ancient

apple trees.

whole thing, and to some extent, these plants are taken for granted by the Brits. A single stem rises above the crinkly basal foliage and produces a floppy cluster of drooping, tousled bells. The oxlip is similar but the flowers are not as shy; they turn up to the light and come in a color range from pale yellow to deep orange, and occasionally, wine red. These plants, crossed with *P. vulgaris* (the wild primrose), gave us the Polyanthus group (*P.* x *polyantha*). They come in inconceivable colors and bicolors. You've probably seen them at the florist shop in late winter. Incredible navy blue flowers edged in sulphur yellow are irre-

sistible. *P. vulgaris* has pale yellow flowers, each one rising above the foliage, one to a stem.

Another wilding, *P. vulgaris* var. *rubra,* has pretty pink flowers and comes from Turkey. Hybridized with the English species, it gave rise to the ones usually called *Primula acaulis,* whose flowers can be pink or red, white, yellow, lavender, wine, bronze, peach-pink, orange, indigo, violet, or palest blue. But these of the "vernal" group are not the first or last to bloom. *Primula rosea* 'Grandiflora' may bloom with a covering of snow.

P. denticulata is an easy one. Mine are lavender violet, but

PRIMULA VERIS, *CALLED cowslip,* ABOVE, *is a member of the "vernal" group.* OPPOSITE: Primula vulgaris *subsp.* Sibthorpii, ABOVE, *and* P. auricula (Auricula spp.), BELOW, *a species for a well-drained site, perhaps the rock garden.*

there are white, lilac, pink, rose, red, and others. The round flower heads are unmistakable. It comes from the Himalayas and is tolerant even of a moist location, but the crown must not be wet, especially in winter—excellent drainage is imperative. These plants self-sow and may be divided just after flowering. They have wide-ranging wiry roots, and must have time to become established. Winter heaving means death to the primulas.

Primula juliae, Julianas, as they are called, are also supposed to be easy to grow. They come in a wide range of colors and originated in the Caucasus. The fo-

liage of the species is small, and the roots very close to the surface. They should have a carefully chosen site, perhaps right along the path edge. Julianas introduce the vernal group.

The primulas with which I have had the most success are the candelabra types, *P. japonica,* which extend the primula season into summer. These are typified by layers of flowers in rings around the stem. The colors range from white to Crayola red. I've seen them in bog gardens, so I know they can take it wet, but it baffles me a bit to see that so many of these plants, which hate poor drainage, do so well in a

nearly swampy condition. The japonicas will sow their heads off in such a site and produce thousands of variably colored offspring. Perhaps these are places that are fed by spring streams and dry a bit by summer's end, staying dry until the thaw, by which time the new season's growth has begun.

As with most primulas they are best started from fresh seed, and if you can beg some, collect them from the fading flowers and scatter them where you want them to grow. Cover the seeds with a bit of fine soil. Small plants will emerge and probably bloom in their second year.

PLANTING PRIMULAS

To see primroses is to fall in love with them. As with many of the wildflowers, some are hard to grow, best left clinging to rocky Russian steppes, but others are quite easy. If you can simply supply: a relatively open site that is shaded in summer—especially from the noon sun—with deep, rich soil loaded with organic matter, ample moisture throughout the season, excellent drainage, wonderful breezes in summer, shelter from winter winds, and a cool "root run," you can grow many primulas. I can't. I can't devote the space to them. And I can't seem to do much about the hot, humid New York summer.

There are ways to get around the heat, besides moving north. I've seen them growing in among rocks buried in the soil to keep them cool. They must not be smothered by other plants, and even their needs for mulching are picky. In cool places, pine needles are great, but primroses do very well with crushed rock or gravel: more cool stones to shelter their roots. No mulch should cover the crowns of the plants. A shelter from winter winds is important, and pine-tree branches are the perfect winter mulch.

They must have excellent drainage. To a mix of one part clay, one part sand, and one part humus, you might add another part of crushed rock—coarse gravel. I have found that plants requiring very good drainage and oxygen at the roots respond very well to an addition of unscented, untreated, *unused* kitty litter: crushed fired clay. It is coarse and holds both moisture and air. Try one part clayey garden soil (or loam), one part humus, and one part terracotta-colored cat litter.

The noted primula expert Doretta Klaber explained that she was unable to grow the distinctive *Auricula* group until she added a splash of wood ashes and bone meal to the soil mix. I think these are valuable additions for most primulas.

Dig a generous hole for planting, and drop in some well-rotted cow manure, followed by your enriched soil medium. Place the plant in the hole so that the crown is at soil level, or just above. Carefully pry the root ball apart a bit, and fill in all the space with soil mix, making absolutely sure that there are no air pockets. Fill with medium, gently but with determination.

Try the primulas. Do the best you can, and be willing to try again in a more or less open site, until you have success. Remember the words of one gardener who had them all about: "Once they find the spot they like, they're yours forever."

NATURALIZED PRIMULA JAPONICA

at Winterthur, LEFT, *and* Primula denticulata, RIGHT.

TRILLIUMS

Besides the remarkable native orchids, the most exquisite flowers of the woodland must be the trilliums, called wake-robins because their first flowers appear with the arrival of that early bird. Their habitats are endangered, but the plants can be propagated, and should be—otherwise, they'll stop being rare and become extinct. They are distributed throughout the United States. California has a few, *T. ovatum, T. chloropetalum,* for example, and there is even a prairie trillium, *T. recurvatum,* from Iowa to Ohio.

I think that the trillium should have been chosen as the national flower. Unfortunately, when Congress decided to pick a botanical to represent the nation, the choice was narrowed down to two plants: the marigold (from Central and South America), and the rose (admittedly, from all over the Northern Hemisphere). I wrote to Senator Ted Kennedy, one of the advocates of the bill, suggesting that a native plant might be a better choice. He wrote back, "Rose is the name of a beautiful flower, and a beautiful mother." I'm afraid the trillium lobby isn't as big as those for the seed industry (marigold) or nursery plant growers (hybrid tea rose). The rose probably won because a lot of Americans think marigolds smell bad.

There are thirty or so trillium species native to North America. They all have one thing in common—the arrangement of three

FROM TOP, TRILLIUM relative Paris polyphylla, T. chloropetalum, *and* T. viride luteum. OPPOSITE: T. cuneatum *with yellow* Stylophorum diphyllum, *blue* Mertensia virginica *and* Disporum maculatum.

leaves. The plants have a single stem and a single flower at the top. The flowers too are constructed in clusters of three: three petals, three green sepals. The roots are tuberous, and for that reason, they are sometimes offered in bulb catalogs. The plants are usually started from divisions including one tuber eye, or from seed. The seeds can take more

than a year to germinate, and seedlings will take three or more years to flower.

If you grow them from tubers, plant them two to four inches deep in rich, loose, moisture-retentive soil—like the woodlands they love. Most want an acid soil; some species, such as the painted trillium, *T. undulatum,* need exceedingly acidic soil, about pH 4.5. A relative, *Medeola virginiana,* Indian cucumber root, also needs this acidity, and is distinguished for two sets of nodding tripetal flowers from its three-leaved top. (*Paris polyphylla,* from Europe, is a cousin for the woodland or border, and there are a few related Asian species.) Most of the trilliums want more light than deep shade provides. They are often seen under deciduous trees, especially ones that leaf out late, because they appreciate even oblique rays of sun in the early shade garden. Trilliums should be mulched at all times.

Probably the easiest of all to grow is *T. grandiflorum,* called large-flowered wake-robin, or snow or white trillium. They bloom in midspring and the flowers may last a full month—often shading to delicate pink or even red as they nod and fade. They like soil that is slightly acidic, but will tolerate neutral soil, and in fact, ordinary garden conditions will do as long as there is sufficient protection from summer sun. The spreading rhizome will increase your stand if the site suits. And although they are gems alone in any setting, they are extraordinary en masse.

The purple or red trillium, *T. erectum,* has large flowers as well. These plants usually form a substantial clump almost like a short shrub, somewhat the way the hellebores grow. They are also easy and tolerate more shade than *T. grandiflorum.* The common painted trillium has a slender stalk about a foot tall. The flowers are white with pink streaks. Take care to label your plants. They may disappear into dormancy by summer.

I have my favorites, though, and some are not to the norm. Two have incredibly mottled foliage and flowers with narrow petals that point to the sky. *T. viride luteum,* yellow trillium, has one set of colorful leaves, and twisted lemon yellow flowers that are fragrant—they even smell a little lemony. It is very hardy, and like most, wants fall planting if from a dormant tuber. When in bloom, it needs filtered light—some sun. At other times, shade is fine. My passion is *T. cuneatum,* the whippoorwill flower. The flecked leaves are silver and green and the flower is the color of chocolate.

The jewel in the crown of the trillium clan is a cultivar, not a species. It's the double *T. grandiflorum* 'Flore Pleno'. This is the plant that announces your arrival as a world-class native-plant aficionado, and garners more attention in the spring woodland garden than any other plant. Suppliers will be pleased to soak you for this treasure. I've seen it sold for thirty dollars. My *T. sessile* cost $12, but you can buy *T. grandiflorum* for as little as $5.

THERE ARE ABOUT THIRTY SPECIES OF TRILLIUM; however, individual plants may present floral variations, such as these pointed petals, ABOVE. T. erectum, BELOW.
OPPOSITE: T. grandiflorum *'Flore Pleno' is a cultivar that must be nursery propagated.*

A GALLERY OF

SHADE GARDENS

A NATURALIST'S GARDEN

Neil Jorgensen is a landscape designer who has been creating naturalistic schemes for over a decade. He works with an enormous range of native plants, imported species, and hybrids, placing them perfectly in designs that complement the local environment. You won't find a lot of paving in a Jorgensen design.

He tests his theories right in his own backyard. The property has a generous area of sheltered lawn (shown in fall on the next pages) made up of grass varieties that can tolerate shade. This space is surrounded by wildflowers and spring-flowering shrubs. He has developed a nursery to supply plants to his own garden and to clients who share his vision. Often these are propagated species of plants that grow in the wild spaces nearby.

Outcasts are particularly welcome. Jorgensen cultivates plants such as *Peltiphyllum peltatum* (*Darmera peltatum, opposite,* foreground), and the Himalayan mayapple, *Podophyllum hexandrum,* having elevated them from

the so-called waste places. Moosewood, *Acer pensylvanicum*, a small maple with striped bark and canary-yellow autumn leaves, has a position of honor here. And a massive chestnut tree trunk has been allowed to disintegrate over the past thirty years—a sculptural reminder of the ebb and flow of life in the natural landscape.

It takes a certain sophistication and devotion to appreciate this subtle concept—to recognize the beauty of the land that "grows" all around a property. Neil Jorgensen practices a landscape ideal in which nature and man share a common goal.

(A plan for this garden appears on page 275.)

AN AMERICAN
MASTERPIECE

H. Lincoln Foster died a few
weeks before I visited Millstream for the last time. One of
the great American plantsmen,
he not only grew thousands of
plants, but introduced new varieties from every corner of the
globe, and even "invented"
some of the hybrids we grow
today.

Millstream Garden, created
about forty years ago with his
wife, Laura Louise ("Timmy")
Foster, tells the story of a great
love. The Fosters' partnership—
of artist and master gardener—
has become a legend in the realm
of rock gardening. Foster's great
work, *Rock Gardening: A Guide
to Growing Alpines and Other
Wildflowers in the American Garden,* published in 1968, was illustrated with drawings Timmy
Foster sketched in the open land
that stretches out behind their
gray 1730s farmhouse (*above*).

Other parts of the property present ideas for our gardens in the shade. We should look to places beneath the ancient oaks and pines, where primroses, epimediums (*right*), spring vetch (*above*), phloxes, iris, and daffodils (*opposite*), rhododendrons, azaleas, kerrias, and andromeda grow; or among the giant rocks where Virginia blue bells and palmate-leaved mayapple naturalize in spring (*previous pages*). And there's the stream itself, whose rushing song echoes throughout the landscape.

A HILLSIDE IN THE NORTHWEST

Jim Hammond is a serious collector who counts among his treasures nearly 2,000 botanicals. To help create a suitable showcase for the plants, he called upon Seattle garden maker Todd Paul.

Todd scoffs at the term "designer"; he sees himself as a "gardener" in the old sense of the word. Charged with taming a 25′ × 65′ hillside behind the house (*above*), he embarked on clearing the site of briers and brush himself. Every boulder was placed by hand; every bit of soil, gravel, and mulch was carried up in buckets.

Much of the area is shaded not only by the tall trees that surround the property, but also by the small trees and large shrubs they planted early on in the garden—rhododendrons and Japanese maples (*opposite*). Climbing a path (*left*) allows close inspection of the perfectly sited perennials and ferns. Both gardeners' loving care is evident in this beautiful, compact garden every month of the year.

(A plan for this garden appears on page 274.)

A STREAMSIDE GARDEN REVISTED

Jean Pope is an inspiration. She and her husband, Dan, created an Eden from what might have seemed a catastrophe to anyone with less vision. Years ago, they bought an old stone house in north central New Jersey (*left*). Unfortunately, it overlooked a swamp backed by a landslide. The site had even been a dumping ground (at one point, they unearthed an overturned car). To Jean and Dan, it was an irresistible challenge.

Jean designed while Dan provided a lot of the muscle. Together, they accentuated the hillside with rocks and terraced plantings. They diverted the marsh waters into a stream bed lined with rocks (*right*), and then directed the tamed stream into

three branches spanned by bridges (*previous page, below left*). Today the garden is filled with flowering shrubs, intricate plantings of wildflowers gathered through native plant societies, ornamental shade perennials such as hostas and ferns, and hundreds of Japanese primroses that bloom in late spring (*opposite*). An old pump house was saved and enhanced with stones and plantings (*above*).

Jean Pope has become well-known for her work with native plant groups and horticultural

institutions, and as a designer. Among her projects was her discovery and restoration of a formal garden on the grounds of the Cross estate. This great achievement, accomplished at first by her own hand, and then with the aid of volunteers, is now part of The New Jersey Historical Garden Foundation (P.O. Box 8, Madison, NJ 07940) and is open to the public.

(*A plan for this garden appears on page 273.*)

A TINY URBAN REFUGE

Jon Rowen grew up in a suburban garden filled with roses, peonies, and summer phlox. When he moved to New York City he knew he had to have a garden. In a world of concrete and asphalt, garden spaces are few and far between and Jon ended up carving one out of a little space behind his apartment.

Jon knew that every garden begins from the ground up, but in this case, the earth consisted of paving stones. He removed the stones only to find more rocks and red clay. In order to make a garden, he had to first make *soil*.

Topsoil was brought in, to which he added manure and peat moss. The plan was for a "woodsy" scheme in keeping with the the shady location. After preparing the planting medium, Jon used two small trees, a dogwood and a viburnum, to provide the framework, or "bones," of his garden. Next came herbaceous perennials and flowering shrubs for the garden's middle layer. The tiny space took shape. It appears on these pages as it looks through the growing season: spring (*below left*); early summer (*top*); and late summer (*opposite*).

The shadowy garden has changed over the twenty years he has cultivated it. For him, gardening is a continual process of fine-tuning: old plants are divided to make gifts for friends or moved elsewhere to give room to new additions.

The small trees change, too. Flowers bloom in spring, fruits form in summer (*left*, viewed from above), foliage colors appear in autumn, and in winter the tracery of twigs and branches looks wonderful with a dusting of snow. In spring, the garden awakes anew with flowering bulbs and rhododendrons (*above*). Although this isn't the lavish garden he remembers from childhood, it's an endless fascination of postage stamp proportions. Regardless of the setting, it has evolved into an anything-but-urban jewel.

(A plan for this garden appears on page 274.)

THE GARDEN IN THE WOODS

WILL C. Curtis drove a second-hand truck down a meandering road in Framingham, Massachusetts, on a cold, clear day in 1930. Something beckoned the landscape designer to veer off the rural street onto a dirt road that wound its way up a hillside and into the woods. As he drove along, he became more and more excited. What he had stumbled upon was an unusually diverse landscape rich with trees, glacier-made ridges, valleys, natural bogs, a meadow, and even a pond. He bought 30 acres for $1,000.

In 1933, Howard O. Stiles joined Curtis in making a wild-flower and endangered plant preserve that was to become known worldwide as the "Garden in the Woods." As the town grew up around them, their work became endangered by the encroachment of creeping developments. Fortunately, The New England Wild Flower Society acquired the property and raised an endowment. It is now a forty-five acre botanical garden and sanctuary with nearly 1,500 wildflowers (like golden seal, *center*), trees, shrubs, and grasses, 200 of which are rare or endangered. They raise wild-flowers in several solar greenhouses (the first, shown *above left*), and hope to introduce new, unusual plants, such as the variegated daylily (*below left*). With good fortune and the support of visitors and members, this national treasure will be open to the public forever.

THE AUTHOR'S TOWNHOUSE GARDEN

I moved from my sunny rooftop garden in Manhattan to a brownstone backyard in Brooklyn in 1987. When these row houses were built in the 1870s, the backyards were designed for drying clothes; the 20′ × 50′ lot was contained by a bluestone path surrounding the lawn. My backyard faces east. A building about a hundred feet away casts early-morning shade, and then the yard receives sun until my building's shadow begins to creep across the garden after noon. It would have a clear southern exposure, except for a tree in my neighbor's yard. They say the fabled tree that grew in Brooklyn was an *Ailanthus,* but Norway maples grow behind nearly all the houses on my block, making a miniature hardwood forest. Norway maples cast deep shade from their thick, overlapping leaves, and they also reproduce like crazy; their seedlings are my only weed problem. (To add insult to injury, they have shallow moisture-stealing roots.)

I bought the house in autumn, so I had the luxury of observing this space over a winter before I could start. I began by planning my wish list. I wanted a paved patio for entertaining (*below right*), a raised area with comfortable chairs (*above right*), a "woodland" path lined with wildflowers (*above left* and *opposite*), a rock garden, and a

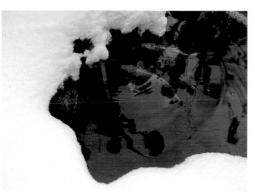

stream, waterfall, and pond for
koi (*below left*).

I wanted a trellis for flowering
vines, a spot to summer my
houseplants, and of course,
flowers from spring to fall. The
garden is shown through the
seasons on these pages: early
spring (*opposite*); summer and
fall, (*above left and right*); and
winter (*left*). I'm an incurable
collector, so I must try every
single plant that will possibly fit
my climate and conditions. The
results may seem somewhat
shaggy and overgrown, in much
the way that nature gardens. But
I wouldn't have it any other
way.

(A plan for this garden appears on page 272.)

SOURCES

Acquiring Wildflowers

There are few truly wild places left in America. What you might imagine as wild and untouched woods was probably pasture not too long ago; in colonial days, much of the land was cleared. Over time the forest has reclaimed these areas with native plants and a host of "naturalized citizens" that found the open ground irresistible. Plants often considered wild, such as daylilies, came from Asia via colonial gardens and are usually referred to as being from garden origin, while plants like Queen Anne's lace, which crept down from Canada, are called aliens. A lot of wildings are deemed noxious weeds, such as French broom, purple loosestrife, and *Ailanthus* (tree of heaven). That tree grows all over, especially in urban areas (you can see them growing beneath the sidewalk subway grates in New York City). But most wildflowers are precious—and precious few. The last thing we want to do is contribute to their extinction.

For years, conservationists cried "Don't touch!"—don't take plants from the wild. Today an enlightened, more active approach advocates "conservation through propagation," the idea being that the more plants that are cultivated in home gardens, the more opportunities there will be for survival. I've written a lot about collecting plants; I use the term in the sense of acquiring specimens to form a collection, not as a polite word for stealing plants. There is only one excuse for taking wild plants and that is when their habitat is threatened. In such cases, I would call the act one of rescue. If a local habitat is to be developed for a highway or building site, by all means go and get the wildflowers out. Secure permission first; the rescue attempt should not resemble a midnight raid. I think it is a good idea to bring along some friends for support. Local wild-

flower societies can also be very helpful for such ventures.

If you have the luxury of time, then you will be virtually guaranteed of success. Most plants fare best if moved when they are dormant. Go to the site when the plants are in bloom and carefully mark the wildings with stakes and name tags, and return after they have died down to the ground in the fall, or, in the case of deciduous woody plants, dropped their leaves. The best times of year are after the first frost in fall and very early spring, providing the ground is not frozen solid.

If the rescue mission is an emergency, as it all too often is, then be prepared to do some serious harvesting. The best conditions are a cloudy day following a rainy one. The rain makes the soil moist and workable and the cloudy, humid weather reduces the chances of wilting and dehydration. If possible, remove about two-thirds of a plant's growth above ground to compensate for root loss below. I know this seems drastic, but you will have a much better success rate, and the plants will take this pruning as a signal to put on vigorous new roots and shoots come spring. Herbaceous and woody perennials should be dug up with a spade. Cut a generous area around the plant, and, trying to take as much of the soil as you can, dig down at least eight inches and lift the section. Then wrap the roots and soil in a wet cloth or a sheet of plastic or aluminum foil. (If you use plastic, don't let the sunlight hit it or you'll create a minigreenhouse and heat the soil.) Keep the root mass moist, and, if you can help it, don't keep the plants in the trunk of your car; cardboard boxes on the floor of the backseat would be better. Take the plant to its new home as soon as you can and plant it.

There's no point in moving annual wildflowers. Instead, mark the plants and return when the seed-bearing fruits, capsules, and the like are ripe so you can collect seed. Fruits of plants usually change color or soften when they are ripe. Keep track of the process, as seed pods

sometimes burst to disseminate seeds and it's best if you can gather them promptly.

Many mail-order companies sell seeds of cultivated varieties or hybrids that have been bred to have very high germination rates. This is not true of the wildings. Nature guarantees the continuance of the species partly by producing enormous quantities of seed. Because the seeds might be eaten, or fall on top of leaves or debris that will keep them from coming in contact with soil, and because emerging seedlings may be covered with similar detritus, high numbers are necessary. Theoretically this means you'll have a bigger crop, because you can provide a growing environment cleaner and safer than nature's. On the other hand, many seeds from the wild will need to have their native conditions mimicked for success, and this usually means that they will have to go through a period of chilling, warming, and chilling again, called stratification. (The packaged seeds we buy for flowering annuals are usually those of tropical plants—ones that are best germinated fresh and come up quickly.) If you've never grown plants from seeds, wildflowers are not ideal for your first effort.

First and foremost, keep good notes. Jot down the dates of sowing, the period of chilling if needed, the date of germination, and anything else that seems relevant. If you can, provide a sowing medium that is similar to the environment of the original plant. That might mean making a soil test. An often suitable alternative is milled sphagnum moss —about the best sowing medium. It is slightly acid and moisture-retentive, and has a natural ability to counter the enemies of all seedlings: fungal diseases collectively known as damping-off, which cause sprouts' stems to collapse. You can store flats of hardy plant seeds in a protected place outdoors, or place them in their damp medium in the refrigerator for four to six months. Most seeds should be planted to a depth that equals their thickness. Some seeds need light for germination, while others require darkness. Some take two years to germinate. Check a detailed reference source for specific information.

At sowing time many plants benefit from bottom heat, supplied by a soil-heating cable. All need a lot of light once they germinate. A south-facing window will work, but fluorescent lights are better, because they can be controlled, and seedlings won't have to be turned daily to keep from leaning toward the light. The flats of seeds should be placed about four inches below two four-foot-long (forty-watt) fluorescent tubes that are balanced to simulate sunlight's color. Leave the lights on for sixteen to eighteen hours; a timer will help. And keep the atmosphere humid. You may want to enclose the lights and all in a plastic tent.

The medium must be kept moist—but not waterlogged—during the entire process. If just-sprouted seedlings are allowed to dry out, it's over. Water from below by setting flats or containers in a saucer or tray of water until the top of the medium

darkens. You probably won't have to water again until the seeds have germinated, and in order not to dislodge the seeds or seedlings, again, water from below.

Taking stem cuttings of woody plants may seem easier than starting from seeds, but it won't be like making a soft, succulent cutting of a prized begonia, a tropical plant eager to grow new roots. You will take either hard- or soft-wood cuttings: last year's growth or this year's new green growth, depending on the subject. The cuttings can be rooted in sphagnum moss, but pure coarse builder's sand is my choice. A combination of both can also be used.

Professional nurseries have intricate misting systems that keep the humidity very high for the rooting of cuttings. They also use rooting hormones of various strengths to form calluses on the cut ends and to prevent rotting. Some people set a container of sand into a closed plastic bag. I've found that this minigreenhouse can be as encouraging to fungal diseases as it is to new growth. A

plastic bag left open is fine, but I prefer to simply set the container in a humid part of the garden, away from direct sunlight. You can buy rooting hormones at the garden center. Read the packages for specific recommendations. Again, keep good records, including the dates that the cuttings were "struck."

You might be able to tell if a cutting has rooted if it produces new top growth, or if it resists a gentle tug. Woody plants may take a year to form new roots, and they will have to be kept cool over winter—protected in a cold frame or even buried.

Starting new plants is one of the greatest joys of gardening. But don't be put off by a failed attempt. This is not a simple process and you'll have to do some research. You might visit a local grower and see if you can talk to the person who does the propagating. It's important to succeed, not only for the exhilaration of experiencing the "birth" of a new plant, but also to perpetuate the wild species.

USDA Plant Hardiness Zone Map

RANGE OF AVERAGE ANNUAL MINIMUM TEMPERATURES FOR EACH ZONE (IN FAHRENHEIT)

zone 1	below −50°
zone 2	−50° to −40°
zone 3	−40° to −30°
zone 4	−30° to −20°
zone 5	−20° to −10°
zone 6	−10° to 0°
zone 7	0° to 10°
zone 8	10° to 20°
zone 9	20° to 30°
zone 10	30° to 40°
zone 11	above 40°

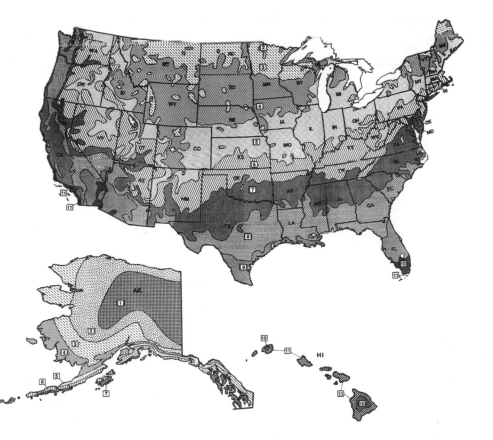

HERBACEOUS PERENNIALS

The following herbaceous perennials, many culled from edges of the woodland, thrive in various degrees of shade. Some need more light than others; many will need to be staked or allowed to flop against a neighboring shrub. They are arranged by flower color, with their Latin name first. Since few of us know every plant's botanical name, plants are listed in the index by their common names as well. When many species and cultivated varieties of one genus are recommended, the plant is listed by genus followed by spp., the abbreviation for plural species. Each listing contains basic information about the plant: its light requirements (partial shade, light shade, filtered light, bright light, shade or dense shade); height; season of bloom; color range; and hardiness zone (indicated by USDA zones). Actual blooming time varies across the country, as do temperatures within a zone and shade tolerance.

KEY

L = light recommendations
Ht = height
S = season of bloom
C = shades and range of colors
Z = temperature range (see USDA map, page 251)

BLUE

ACONITUM spp., monkshood. L: partial shade. Ht: 3'–4'. S: summer to early fall by variety. C: mostly blue shades. Z: 2–9.

AMSONIA TABERNAEMONTANA, bluestar flower. L: partial shade. Ht: 2'. S: early summer. C: pale blue. Z: 3–9.

AQUILEGIA spp., columbine. L: partial shade. Ht: 1'–3' by variety. S: late spring to early summer. C: all. Z: 3–10.

BRUNNERA MACROPHYLLA, Siberian bugloss. L: partial shade to shade. S: spring. Ht: 1.5'. C: blue. Z: 3–10.

CAMPANULA spp., bellflower. L: partial shade. Ht: various by species. S: variable. C: white to blue. Z: variable.

CODONOPSIS spp., bonnet bellflower. L: partial shade. Ht: 1'–2'. S: summer. C: blue. Z: 5–9.

DEINANTHE CAERULEA, deinanthe. L: shade. Ht: 1.5'. S: summer. C: blue. Z: 6–9.

ECHINOPS RITRO, globe thistle. L: partial shade. Ht: 2'–3'. S: mid- to late summer. C: steel blue. Z: 3–10.

EUPATORIUM COELESTINUM, hardy ageratum, mistflower. L: partial shade to filtered light. Ht: 3'. S: late summer to early fall. C: violet blue. Z: 6–10.

GENTIANA spp., gentian. L: partial shade to shade. Ht: various. S: summer to fall. C: blue. Z: 5–9.

MERTENSIA VIRGINICA, Virginia bluebells. L: partial shade to shade. Ht: 1.5'. S: late spring to early summer. C: blue with pink. Z: 3–10.

OMPHALODES spp., blue-eyed Mary. L: partial shade to shade. Ht: 6"–9". S: spring. C: blue. Z: 5–9.

POLEMONIUM CAERULEUM, Jacob's ladder. L: partial shade to shade. Ht: 1'–3'. S: late spring to midsummer. C: pale to medium blue, white. Z: 3–9.

P. REPTANS, Jacob's ladder, creeping polemonium. L: partial shade to shade. Ht: 1'. S: spring to early summer. C: pale blue. Z: 3–9.

PULMONARIA spp., lungwort. L: partial shade to shade. Ht: 1'. S: spring. C: blue, white, pink. Z: 3–10.

TRACHYSTEMON ORIENTALIS, trachystemon. L: partial shade to shade. Ht: 2'. S: spring. C: blue. Z: 7–9.

VERONICA spp., veronica, speedwell. L: partial shade. Ht: various. S: various. C: blue common, various. Z: 3–10 (varies by species and hybrid).

GREEN TO BROWN

ALCHEMILLA MOLLIS, lady's-mantle. L: partial to light shade. Ht: 1.5'. S: late spring to summer. C: chartreuse. Z: 3–9.

ARISAEMA spp., jack-in-the-pulpit. L: light to dense shade. Ht: 1'. S: spring to early summer. C: green-brown. Z: 4–9.

ASARUM spp., wild ginger (evergreen species and varieties). L: filtered light to dense shade. Ht: 6". C: brown. Z: 5–9.

A. CANADENSE, Canada wild ginger. L: filtered light to dense shade. Ht: 6". C: brown. Z: 2–9.

CHASMANTHIUM LATIFOLIUM, Northern sea oats. L: partial shade. Ht: 3'. C: brown. S: late summer to winter. Z: 5–9.

EUPHORBIA (selected) spp., euphorbia, spurge. L: partial shade to bright light. Ht: various. C: yellow-green, white, orange. Z: varies by species.

HELLEBORUS ARGUTIFOLIUS, Corsican hellebore. L: partial shade. Ht: 1'–3'. S: spring to early summer. C: pale green. Z: 6–10.

H. FOETIDUS, stinking hellebore. L: partial to dense shade. Ht: 1.5'. S: early spring. C: green fading to purple along the edges. Z: 3–10.

PARIS POLYPHYLLA, Paris. L: partial shade to dense shade. Ht: 2'. S: summer. C: green. Z: 4–8.

VERATRUM spp., false hellebore. L: partial to light shade. Ht: 4'+. S: summer. C: green to white to brown. Z: 3–9.

PINK

ANEMONE spp., windflower (woodland species). L: partial shade to shade. Ht: 6″–12″. S: spring. C: pink, white. Z: 6–10.

ANEMONE hybrids, fall-blooming anemone (tall garden flowers). L: partial shade. Ht: 2′–4′. S: midsummer to fall. C: pink, white. Z: 6–10.

AQUILEGIA spp., columbine. L: partial shade. Ht: 1′–3′. S: spring to early summer. C: all. Z: 3–10 by species and variety.

ASTILBE spp., false spiraea. L: partial shade to filtered light. Ht: 1′–4′, varies by species and variety. S: summer. C: pink, lavender, white, red. Z: 4–8.

BEGONIA GRANDIS (B. EVANSIANA), hardy begonia. L: partial shade to bright light. Ht: 1.5′. S: late summer to fall. C: pink, white. Z: 7–10.

BERGENIA CORDIFOLIA, bergenia. L: partial shade to shade. Ht: 1.5′. S: spring and sporadically. C: pink, white, rose. Z: 3–10.

CHELONE LYONII, turtlehead. L: partial shade. Ht: 3′–4′. S: late summer to fall. C: pink. Z: 4–10.

DICENTRA spp., bleeding heart. L: partial shade to shade. Ht: various. S: early spring to summer by species. C: pink, red, white. Z: 3–9.

DIGITALIS spp., foxglove. L: partial shade. Ht: 2′–6′ by species. S: late spring to summer. C: pink, white, yellow. Z: 4–10.

EPIMEDIUM spp., barrenwort. L: partial shade to shade. Ht: 1′. S: spring. C: all but blue. Z: 4–9.

FILIPENDULA spp., meadowsweet. L: partial to light shade. S: summer. C: pink to white. Z: 6–9 (some Z 3).

GERANIUM spp., geranium, cranesbill. L: partial shade. Ht: 1′–2′. S: spring to fall by species. C: pink to blue. Z: 4–9 various.

HEMEROCALLIS spp., daylily. L: partial shade. Ht: 1′–4′, varies. S: summer. C: pink, melon shades, red, yellow, grape. Z: 3–9.

HEUCHERA spp., coralbells, alumroot. L: partial to light shade. Ht: 2′ (flower spike). S: summer. C: pink, coral, white. Z: 3–10.

x HEUCHERELLA, heucherella. L: partial to light shade. Ht: 1.5′. S: late spring to early summer. Z: 3–10.

LATHYRUS VERNUS, spring vetchling. L: partial to light shade. Ht: 1′. S: spring to early summer. C: deep pink fading to sapphire blue. Z: 4–9.

LYCHNIS spp., campion. L: partial shade. Ht: various. S: summer. C: magenta, white, red. Z: 3–10.

LYTHRUM SALICARIA (hybrids), purple loosestrife. L: partial shade. Ht: various to 4′. S: summer. C: deep pink. Z: 3–10.

MACLEAYA CORDATA, plume poppy. L: partial to light shade. Ht: 8′. S: summer. C: buff-pink. Z: 4–9.

MONARDA PUNCTATA, horsemint. L: partial shade. Ht: 2′. S: summer. C: pink and yellow. Z: 5–10.

PAEONIA spp., peony. Experiment with species, especially in north coastal areas.

PETASITES spp., butterbur. L: partial shade to shade. Ht: various to 3′. S: early spring. C: pink. Z: 4–9.

PHLOX ADSURGENS, periwinkle phlox. L: partial shade to shade. Ht: 1′. S: spring. C: pink. Z: 7–9.

P. STOLONIFERA, creeping phlox. L: partial shade to shade. Ht: 6″. S: late spring. C: pink, white, blue. Z: 3–9.

PHYSOSTEGIA VIRGINIANA, false dragonhead, obedient plant. L: partial to light shade. Ht: 3′. S: summer to fall. C: pink. Z: 3–10.

PRIMULA JAPONICA, Japanese primrose. L: partial shade. Ht: 2′. S: late spring to early summer. C: pink, red, white. Z: 5–9.

PULMONARIA spp., lungwort. L: partial shade to shade. Ht: 1′. S: spring. C: blue, white, pink. Z: 3–10.

RODGERSIA spp., rodgersia. L: partial to light shade. Ht: 3′ + . S: early summer. C: pink, buff. Z: 4–9.

SEDUM (selected) spp., stonecrop. L: partial to light shade. Ht: varies by species. S: summer to fall. C: pink, yellow, red (by variety). Z: 4–10.

VERONICA spp., veronica, speedwell. L: partial shade. Ht: varies by variety. S: summer. C: pink, blue, white. Z: 3–10 by variety.

RED

AQUILEGIA spp., columbine. L: partial shade. Ht: 1′–3′, varies by species and hybrid. S: spring to early summer. C: all. Z: 2–10.

ASTILBE spp., false spiraea. L: partial shade to filtered light. Ht: 1′–4′, varies by species and variety. S: summer. C: red, pink, white, lavender. Z: 4–8.

DICENTRA spp., bleeding heart. L: partial shade to shade. Ht: various. S: early spring through summer by variety. C: red, pink, white. Z: 3–10.

HELLEBORUS spp., hellebore. L: partial to dense shade. Ht: 1′–2′. S: late winter to spring. C: red, green, purple, white. Z: 3–10 (various by species).

HEMEROCALLIS spp., daylily. L: partial shade. Ht: 1′–4′, varies. S: late spring to summer. C: red, pink, melon shades, yellow, grape. Z: 3–9.

LOBELIA CARDINALIS, cardinal flower. L: partial shade to shade. Ht: 2′–3′. S: summer. C: red. Z: 2–9.

LYCHNIS spp., campion. L: partial shade. Ht: various. S: summer. C: red, white, or magenta. Z: 3–10.

PAEONIA TENUIFOLIA, fernleaf peony. L: partial shade. Ht: 1.5′. S: spring. C: red. Z: 4–10.

PRIMULA JAPONICA, Japanese primrose. L: partial shade. Ht: 2′. S: late spring to early summer. C: red, pink, white. Z: 5–9.

SEDUM (selected) spp., stonecrop. L: partial to light shade. Ht: various (from 2″–24″). S: summer to fall by species. C: red, various. Z: 4–10.

TOVARA VIRGINIANA 'Variegata', tovara. L: partial shade to shade. Ht: 3′ (flower spike). S: fall. C: cerise buds along stalk. Z: 6–9.

VIOLET

ADENOPHORA CONFUSA, ladybells. L: partial to light shade. Ht: 2′. S: summer. C: violet blue. Z: 3–9.

ANEMONOPSIS MACROPHYLLA, false anemone. L: partial shade. Ht: 3′. S: summer to late summer. C: violet. Z: 6–9.

ASTER spp., aster. L: partial shade. Ht: 3′–6′. S: late summer to fall. C: violet, white. Z: 2–8.

CARDAMINE spp., bitter cress. L: partial shade. Ht: 1′ +. S: mid- to late spring. C: purple. Z: 3–9.

GERANIUM spp., geranium, cranesbill. L: partial shade. Ht: 1′. S: varies. C: purple, violet, blue, pink. Z: 4–9 (varies).

HEMEROCALLIS spp., daylily. L: partial shade. Ht: 1′–4′, varies. S: late spring to summer. C: grape, lavender, red, pink, melon shades, yellow. Z: 3–9.

HESPRIS MATRONALIS, dame's rocket. L: partial to light shade. Ht: 3′. S: late spring to early summer. C: violet to white. Z: 4–8.

HOSTA spp., hosta, plantain lily. L: partial to dense shade. Ht: varies by species and variety. S: varies from early summer to fall. C: lilac to white. Z: 3–9.

LIRIOPE spp., lilyturf. L: partial shade to shade. Ht: 1′. S: summer to fall. C: violet to white. Z: 5–10.

LUNARIA REDEVIVA, perennial honesty. L: partial shade to shade. Ht: 2′–3′. S: late spring to early summer. C: deep lilac to white. Z: 6–9.

MENTHA spp., mint. L: partial shade. Ht: 1.5′. S: summer. C: lavender. Z: 5–10.

OPHIOPOGON spp., mondo grass. L: partial shade to shade. Ht: 6″. S: summer. C: lavender to white by species. Z: 7–10.

PHLOX DIVARICATA, wild sweet William. L: partial shade to shade. Ht: 1′. S: spring. C: lavender-blue, white. Z: 4–9.

THALICTRUM AQUILEGIFOLIUM, meadow rue. L: partial shade to bright light. Ht: 3′–4′. S: late spring. C: lavender. Z: 5–10.

TRADESCANTIA X ANDERSONIANA, spiderworts. L: partial shade. Ht: 2′. S: late spring, intermittently to fall. C: lavender-blue, white. Z: 5–10.

TRICYRTIS spp., toad lily. L: partial shade to dense shade. Ht: varies, around 2.5′. S: summer to fall by species. C: violet, yellow, white. Z: 5–9.

WHITE

ACANTHUS MOLLIS, bear's-breech. L: partial shade. Ht: 4′ +. S: late spring to summer. C: white with purple and brown. Z: 8–10.

A. SPINOSISSIMUS, bear's-breech. L: partial shade. Ht: 3′ + (flower spike). S: spring to summer. C: white with purple and brown. Z: 7–10.

ACTAEA PACHYPODA, baneberry. L: filtered light to dense shade. Ht: 2′. S: spring. C: white. Z: 2–9.

ANAPHALIS CINNAMOMEA, pearly everlasting. L: partial shade. Ht: 2′. S: late summer to fall. C: white. Z: 3–9.

A. TRIPLINERVIS, pearly everlasting. L: partial shade. Ht: 2′. S: summer to early fall. C: white. Z: 3–9.

ANEMONE hybrids, windflower. L: partial shade. Ht: 2′–4′. S: early spring to early fall. C: white to pink. Z: 6–10.

ANGELICA ARCHANGELICA, wild parsnip. L: partial shade. Ht: 5′–7′. S: summer. C: white. Z: 4–9.

AQUILEGIA spp., columbine. L: partial. Ht: 1′–3′ by species and variety. S: spring to early summer. C: all. Z: 3–10.

ARUM ITALICUM, Italian arum. L: partial shade to filtered light. Ht: 1.5′. S: late spring. C: greenish white. Z: 6–10.

ARUNCUS DIOICUS, goatsbeard. L: partial shade. Ht: 5′. S: summer. C: white. Z: 3–9.

ASTER spp., aster. L: partial shade. Ht: 3′–6′. S: late summer to fall. C: white, violet. Z: 2–8.

ASTILBE hybrids, false spiraea. L: partial shade to filtered light. Ht: 1′–4′, varies by species and variety. S: summer. C: white, pink, lavender, red. Z: 4–8.

ASTRANTIA MAJOR, masterwort. L: partial shade. Ht: 3′. S: summer. C: white. Z: 4–9.

BEGONIA GRANDIS 'Alba', (B. EVANSIANA), hardy begonia. L: partial shade to bright light. Ht: 1.5′. S: late summer to fall. C: white. Z: 7–10.

BERGENIA CORDIFOLIA, bergenia. L: partial shade to shade. Ht: 1.5′. S: spring and sporadically. C: white, pink, rose. Z: 3–10.

CAMPANULA spp., bellflower. L: partial shade. Ht: various. S: various. C: white, blues. Z: various.

CHRYSANTHEMUM PARTHENIUM 'Aureum', golden feverfew. L: partial shade. Ht: 1.5′. S: summer. C: white. Z: 4–10.

CIMICIFUGA spp., bugbane. L: partial shade to bright light. Ht: 5′. S: late spring to fall by species. C: white. Z: 3–9.

DICENTRA spp., bleeding heart. L: partial shade to shade. Ht: various. S: various by species. C: white, pink, red. Z: 3–10.

DIGITALIS PURPUREA, foxglove. L: partial shade. Ht: 5′. S: late spring. C: white, purple. Z: 4–10.

DIPHYLLEIA CYMOSA, umbrella leaf. L: partial shade. Ht: 3′. S: late spring. C: white. Z: 6–8.

EOMECON CHIONANTHA, snow poppy. L: partial shade to shade. Ht: 1'–1.5'. S: spring. C: white. Z: 6–10.

EPIMEDIUM spp., barrenwort. L: partial shade to shade. Ht: 1'. S: spring. C: white (all but blue). Z: 4–9.

EUPATORIUM RUGOSUM, white snakeroot. L: partial shade to shade. Ht: 3'. S: late summer to fall. C: white. Z: 3–9.

FILIPENDULA spp., meadowsweet. L: partial to light shade. Ht: to 5' by species. S: summer. C: white, pink to rose. Z: 6–9 (some species tolerant to Z 3).

GALAX URCEOLATA, galax. L: light to dense shade. Ht: 1.5'. S: late spring to early summer. C: white. Z: 3–8.

HERACLEUM MANTEGAZZI-·ANUM, cow parsnip, giant hogweed. L: partial shade. Ht: 8'. S: summer. C: white. Z: 3–9.

HESPRIS MATRONALIS, dame's rocket. L: partial to light shade. Ht: 3'. S: late spring to early summer. C: white to blue violet. Z: 4–8.

HEUCHERA spp., coralbells, alum-root. L: partial shade to filtered light. Ht: 1'–1.5'. S: spring to summer. C: white, pink, coral. Z: 3–10.

HOSTA spp., hosta, plantain lily. L: partial to dense shade. Ht: various. S: early summer to fall. C: white, violet. Z: 3–9.

HOUTTUYNIA CORDATA, hout-tuynia, chameleon plant. L: partial shade to shade. Ht: 1'. S: summer. C: white. Z: 6–10.

LIRIOPE spp., lilyturf. L: partial to dense shade. Ht: 1'. S: summer to fall. C: white, violet. Z: 5–10.

LYSIMACHIA CLETHROIDES, gooseneck loosestrife. L: partial shade. Ht: 2.5'. S: summer to fall. C: white. Z: 4–9.

MYRRHIS ODORATA, myrrh, cow parsley. L: partial shade. Ht: 4'. S: early summer. C: white. Z: 4–9.

OPHIOPOGON spp., mondo grass. L: partial shade to shade. Ht: 6"–24", varies by species. S: summer. C: white. Z: 7 (some, 6)–10.

PAEONIA spp., peony. Experiment in north coastal areas. .

PELTIPHYLLUM PELTATUM (DARMERA PELTATUM), um-brella plant. L: partial shade. Ht: 3'. S: spring. C: white. Z: 5–9.

PHLOX CAROLINA, Carolina phlox, wedding phlox. L: partial shade. Ht: 2.5'. S: early summer. C: white, pink. Z: 4–9.

PODOPHYLLUM PELTATUM, mayapple. L: partial shade. Ht: 1.5'. S: spring. C: white. Z: 3–9.

POLYGONATUM spp., Solomon's seal. L: partial shade to shade. Ht: varies by species and variety, to 3'. S: mid- to late spring. C: white. Z: 4–9.

PRIMULA JAPONICA, Japanese primrose. L: partial shade. Ht: 2'. S: late spring to early summer. C: white, pink, red. Z: 5–9.

SAXIFRAGA STOLONIFERA, strawberry begonia. L: partial shade to shade. Ht: 1.5' (flower spikes). S: late spring to early summer. C: white. Z: 7–10.

S. X URBIUM, London pride. L: partial shade to shade. Ht: 1.5'. S: early summer. C: white. Z: 6–9.

SMILACINA RACEMOSA, false Solomon's seal. L: partial shade to shade. Ht: 2'. S: spring. C: cream. Z: 3–9.

TELLIMA GRANDIFLORA, false alumroot. L: partial shade to shade. Ht: 1.5'. S: late spring to early summer. C: white. Z: 4–9.

TIARELLA CORDIFOLIA, foam-flower. L: partial to light shade. Ht: 1.5'. S: late spring to early summer. C: white. Z: 3–9.

TRADESCANTIA X ANDER-SONIANA, spiderworts. L: partial shade. Ht: 2'. S: late spring to fall. C: white, violet. Z: 5–10.

VERONICA spp., veronica, speed-well. L: partial shade. Ht: varies by species and variety. S: various. C: white, blue, pink. Z: 3–10 (varies).

YUCCA FILAMENTOSA 'Varie-gata', Adam's needle. L: partial shade. Ht: 4'. S: summer. C: white. Z: 4–10.

YELLOW

ADONIS spp., adonis. L: partial shade. Ht: 1'. S: early spring. C: yel-low. Z: 4–8.

AQUILEGIA spp., columbine. L: partial shade. Ht: 1'–3' by species and hybrid. S: spring to early summer. C: all. Z: 3–10.

CORYDALIS LUTEA, yellow fu-matory, yellow corydalis. L: partial shade to shade. Ht: 1'. S: spring to late summer. C: yellow. Z: 5–10.

DIGITALIS GRANDIFLORA, yel-low foxglove. L: partial shade. Ht: 2.5'. S: summer. C: yellow. Z: 3–8.

D. LUTEA, straw foxglove. L: par-tial shade. Ht: 2.5'. S: summer. C: creamy yellow. Z: 3–8.

DORONICUM CORDATUM, leop-ard's-bane. L: partial shade. Ht: 1'–2'. S: spring. C: yellow. Z: 4–9.

EPIMEDIUM PERRALDERANUM, barrenwort. L: partial shade to shade. Ht: 1'. S: spring. C: yellow. Z: 5–9.

HEMEROCALLIS spp., daylily. L: partial shade. Ht: 1'–4', varies. S: late spring to summer. C: yellow, red, pink, melon shades, grape. Z: 3–9.

HYLOMECON JAPONICUM, hy-lomecon. L: partial shade to shade. Ht: 1'. S: spring. C: yellow. Z: 5–9.

KIRENGESHOMA PALMATA, kir-engeshoma. L: partial shade to shade. Ht: 3'–4'. S: late summer to fall. C: creamy yellow. Z: 5–9.

LAMIASTRUM GALEOBDOLON 'Herman's Pride', yellow archangel. L: partial shade to shade. Ht: 1'. S: late spring. C: yellow. Z: 3–9.

LIGULARIA spp., ligularia. L: par-tial shade to filtered light. Ht: 3'. S: early to late summer (varies by species and variety). C: yellow. Z: 4–10.

LYSIMACHIA spp., loosestrife. L: partial shade. Ht: varies by species (around 2.5'). S: summer. C: yellow. Z: 4–9.

MECONOPSIS CAMBRICA, Welsh poppy. L: partial shade to filtered light. Ht: 1.5'. S: late spring to summer. C: yellow, orange. Z: 6–9.

MIMULUS spp., monkey flower. L: partial shade. Ht: varies by species. S: various. C: yellow, others. Z: 6–9.

RUTA GRAVEOLENS, rue. L: partial shade. Ht: 2'. S: summer. C: sulphur yellow. Z: 4–9.

STYLOPHORUM DIPHYLLUM, celandine poppy. L: partial shade to dense shade. Ht: 1.5'. S: early spring to summer. C: yellow. Z: 4–8.

TRICYRTIS spp., toad lily. L: partial shade to shade. Ht: 2'. S: early summer to fall by species and variety. C: yellow, violet shades. Z: 5–9.

TROLLIUS spp., globeflower. L: partial shade. Ht: 2', varies. S: spring, varies. C: yellow, orange. Z: 3–10.

UVULARIA GRANDIFLORA, merrybells. L: partial shade to shade. Ht: 2.5'. S: spring. C: yellow. Z: 3–9.

ORNAMENTAL SHRUBS

This list includes deciduous and evergreen shrubs for varying degrees of shade. While some like the oakleaf hydrangea (*Hydrangea quercifolia*) will bloom in shade to deep shade, many will not. But there will be surprises, especially among the broadleaved evergreens. You will have to experiment a bit.

Many shrubs resent being dragged from the sunny nursery fields to the deep and dark. To help them adjust, move new plants gradually, if possible, into the shade while they are still in their containers. Keep the container or balled-and-burlapped roots well watered at all times.

The plants, alphabetized by Latin name, are arranged by height at ten

years of age. Some shrubs may grow up a bit after this point and nearly all will spread out, but these heights will give you a good idea for placement in the landscape. Plan for the effect at ten years; you might choose a dwarf variety for a place in front of a window or in a mixed planting of herbaceous perennials.

KEY

S = season of interest from flowers or fruit

C = color and form of blossoms or fruit

Z = USDA zone range (see page 251)

DECIDUOUS SHRUBS AND SMALL TREES

LOW:
TO 2.5 FEET

COTONEASTER HORIZONTALIS, cotoneaster. S: fall. C: red berries. Z: 5–9.

DAPHNE X BURKWOODII 'Carol Mackie', Burkwood's daphne. S: spring. C: pink stars. Z: 6–8.

ZENOBIA PULVERULENTA, dusty zenobia. S: spring. C: white bells. Z: 4–9.

MEDIUM:
2.5 FEET TO 6 FEET

ABELIOPHYLLUM DISTICHUM, white forsythia. S: early spring. C: pink fading to white. Z: 6–8.

ACER PALMATUM 'Dissectum', cut-leaf maple. S: spring. C: small flowers, fall foliage colors. Z: 3–10.

AZALEA, see RHODODENDRON

BERBERIS spp., barberry. S: spring. C: small yellow flowers. Z: 5–9, varies by species.

B. THUNBERGII 'Atropurpurea', red-leaved Japanese barberry. S: spring. C: small yellow flowers, foliage color. Z: 5–9.

B. VULGARIS, common barberry. S: spring. C: small yellow flowers. Z: 5–9.

CALYCANTHUS FLORIDUS, sweet shrub. S: summer. C: brown, fragrant flowers. Z: 5–9.

CEPHALANTHUS OCCIDENTALIS, buttonbush. S: summer. C: white balls. Z: 5–9.

CLETHRA ALNIFOLIA, sweet pepperbush. S: summer. C: white spires (pink varieties). Z: 4–9.

COMPTONIA ASPLENIFOLIA, sweet fern. S: spring. C: brown catkins. Z: 5–9.

CORYLUS AVELLANA 'Contorta', Harry Lauder's walking stick. S: early spring. C: brown catkins. Z: 2–9.

COTONEASTER spp., deciduous spp. S: late summer to fall. C: red berries. Z: 5–9.

DEUTZIA GRACILIS, deutzia. S: spring. C: white. Z: 5–8.

EUONYMUS ALATA, winged euonymus. S: fall. C: red berries and fall foliage color. Z: 4–7.

FOTHERGILLA MAJOR, large fothergilla. S: spring. C: fuzzy white. Z: 6–8.

HYDRANGEA ARBORESCENS 'Annabelle', tree hydrangea. S: summer. C: huge white umbels. Z: 4–9.

H. ASPERA, rough-leaved hydrangea. S: summer. C: lavender, flat umbels. Z: 6–9.

H. MACROPHYLLA, large-leaved hydrangea. S: summer. C: huge pink-to-blue flower heads. Z: 6–9.

H. QUERCIFOLIA, oakleaf hydrangea. S: summer. C: white panicles turn pink to rust. Z: 5–9.

KERRIA JAPONICA, kerria. S: early spring and sporadically. C: bright yellow. Z: 5–9.

K. j. 'Variegata', variegated kerria. S: early spring and sporadically. C: bright yellow. Z: 5–9.

MAGNOLIA STELLATA, star magnolia. S: early spring. C: white stars (pink varieties). Z: 4–8.

M. X LOEBNERI, star magnolia. S: early spring. C: white stars (pink varieties). Z: 4–8.

MYRICA PENSYLVANICA, bayberry. S: fall. C: gray berries. Z: 5–9.

PAEONIA SUFFRUTICOSA, Japanese tree peony. S: spring. C: various, large single and double flowers. Z: 5–8.

RHODODENDRON spp., azaleas. S: spring (varies by species and variety). Z: variable.

ROSA RUBRIFOLIA (R. GALBRA), red-leaved rose. S: early summer. C: pink. Z: 2–8.

RUBUS ODORATUS, flowering bramble. S: summer. C: rose-colored flowers, berries. Z: 2–8.

R. PHOENICOLASIUS, wineberry. S: summer. C: pinkish white flowers, edible berries. Z: 3–8.

R. TRIDEL, flowering bramble. S: early summer. C: white. Z: 3–8.

SPIRAEA X BUMALDA (varieties, including 'Anthony Waterer'), spirea. S: summer. C: white-to-magenta umbels. Z: 5–10.

S. TOMENTOSA, steeplebush. S: summer. C: rose-purple. Z: 2–8.

S. X VANHOUTTEI, spirea, bridal wreath. S: spring. C: white, along stems. Z: 5–10.

SYMPHORICARPOS ALBUS, snowberry. S: fall. C: fleshy white berries. Z: 3–9.

S. ORBICULATUS, Indian currant, coralberry. S: fall. C: red berries. Z: 3–9.

VACCINIUM CORYMBOSUM, highbush blueberry. S: summer. C: edible blue-black berries. Z: 2–8.

VITEX AGNUS-CASTUS, chaste tree. S: late summer. C: blue-violet spires. Z: 7–10.

TALL:
6 FEET OR MORE

ACANTHOPANAX SIEBOLDIANUS, five-leaved aralia. S: summer. C: white-green. Z: 5–9.

AESCULUS PARVIFLORA, bottlebrush buckeye, buckeye. S: summer. C: white-buff. Z: 5–8.

AMELANCHIER spp., shadbush. S: spring. C: white. Z: 3–9.

ARALIA SPINOSA, devil's-walking-stick, angelica tree. S: late summer. C: white. Z: 4–9.

ARONIA ARBUTIFOLIA, chokeberry. S: spring. C: white-red. Z: 5–9.

BENZOIN AESTIVALIS (LINDERA BENZOIN), spicebush. S: early spring. C: yellow. Z: 2–8.

CALLICARPA BODINIERI (C. GIRALDIANA), beauty-berry. S: late summer to late fall. C: purple, or violet or white fruits by variety. Z: 5–9.

CHAENOMELES JAPONICA, Japanese flowering quince. S: early spring. C: pink, yellow, orange by variety. Z: 5–9.

CLERODENDRUM TRICHOTOMUM, same. S: summer. C: white with red. Z: 6–10.

CORNUS ALBA (C. SIBIRICA), red-twig dogwood, Tartarian dogwood. S: late spring. C: white. Z: 3–9.

CORYLOPSIS spp., winter hazel. S: late winter. C: yellow teardrops. Z: 4–8.

C. PAUCIFLORA, winter hazel. S: late winter. C: yellow teardrops. Z: 4–8.

C. SINENSIS, Chinese winter hazel. S: late winter. C: yellow teardrops. Z: 4–8.

C. SPICATA, winter hazel. S: late winter. C: yellow teardrops. Z: 4–8.

CORYLUS AVELLANA, filbert. S: fall. C: nuts. Z: 2–8.

C. MAXIMA 'Purpurea', purple-leaved filbert. S: fall. C: colorful fruits in clusters. Z: 3–8.

DIERVILLA SESSILIFOLIA, southern bush honeysuckle. S: late spring. C: yellow. Z: 3–8.

ENKIANTHUS CAMPANULATUS, enkianthus. S: spring. C: pink. Z: 5–9.

E. CERNUUS RUBENS, enkianthus. S: spring. C: red. Z: 5–9.

FORSYTHIA spp., forsythia. S: late winter. C: yellow. Z: 5–9.

HAMAMELIS X INTERMEDIA, hybrid witch hazel. S: winter. C: yellow to red. Z: 6–8.

H. MOLLIS, Chinese witch hazel. S: winter. C: yellow. Z: 6–8.

H. VIRGINIANA, American witch hazel. S: late fall. C: yellow. Z: 5–9.

HIBISCUS SYRIACUS, rose of Sharon. S: mid- to late summer. C: pink, red, white, violet-blue. Z: 5–9.

HYDRANGEA PANICULATA, tree hydrangea. S: late summer. C: large white panicles. Z: 4–9.

ILEX VERTICILLATA, winterberry. S: winter. C: red berries. Z: 4–8.

ITEA VIRGINICA, Virginia sweet-spire. S: summer. C: white. Z: 3–8.

KERRIA JAPONICA 'Pleniflora', double-flowered kerria. S: early spring and sporadically. C: bright yellow double pompons, green bark in winter. Z: 5–9.

KOLKWITZIA AMABILIS, beauty bush. S: late spring. C: pink. Z: 5–8.

LIGUSTRUM OBTUSIFOLIUM, privet. S: summer. C: white flowers, black berries in fall. Z: 4–10.

LONICERA TATARICA, Tartarian honeysuckle. S: late spring. C: pink to white. Z: 4–9.

LYONIA LIGUSTRINA, he-huckleberry. S: spring. C: white. Z: 2–8.

MAGNOLIA VIRGINIANA, sweet bay magnolia. S: spring. C: green-white. Z: 3–9.

PHILADELPHUS CORONARIUS, mock orange. S: early summer. C: white. Z: 5–8.

PHYSOCARPUS OPULIFOLIUS 'Aureus', eastern ninebark. S: late spring. C: white. Z: 3–8.

RHUS spp., sumac. S: late spring, fall. C: rust-colored flowers and brilliant fall foliage. Z: various.

SALIX spp., shrub willows (osier, pussy willows). S: early spring. C: catkins. Z: 5–9.

SAMBUCUS CANADENSIS, American elder. S: late spring, summer. C: small flowers, purple-black fruits. Z: 2–8.

S. C. 'Aurea', golden elder. S: late spring, summer. C: small flowers, purple-black fruits. Z: 2–8.

STEWARTIA OVATA, mountain camellia. S: summer. C: white like single camellias. Z: 5–9.

S. PSEUDOCAMELLIA, Japanese stewartia. S: summer. C: white like single camellias. Z: 5–9.

SYMPLOCOS PANICULATA, Asiatic sweetleaf. S: late spring. C: white flowers, blue-black berries. Z: 3–8.

VIBURNUM spp., viburnum. S: early spring, fall. C: white, fragrant flowers, red berries by variety. Z: variable.

XANTHORHIZA SIMPLICISSIMA, yellowroot. S: spring. C: purple-brown, seedpods. Z: 3–10.

ZANTHOXYLUM AMERICANUM, prickly ash. S: spring. C: greenish. Z: 3–8.

SMALL TREES

ACER HERSII, snake-bark maple. S: all. C: interesting bark, fall foliage. Z: 4–8.

A. JAPONICUM, Japanese maple. S: spring to fall. C: flowers and foliage. Z: 4–8.

A. NEGUNDO 'Elegans', A. N. 'Flamingo', box maple, ash-leaved maple. S: spring to fall. C: pink foliage in spring, variegated white and green through summer. Z: 6–9.

A. SPICATUM, mountain maple. S: spring. C: green flowers. Z: 2–8.

ALNUS spp., alders. S: all. C: catkins in spring, fall cones persist to following spring. Z: 5–8.

CERCIS CANADENSIS, redbud. S: early spring. C: magenta. Z: 3–8.

C. CHINENSIS, Chinese redbud. S: early spring. C: magenta or white by variety. Z: 7–8.

CORNUS FLORIDA, dogwood. S: early spring, fall. C: green-white or pink flower bracts, red fruits in fall. Z: 4–9.

C. KOUSA, Japanese dogwood. S: flowers late spring to midsummer by variety, fall. C: white, pink, red, large red fruits in fall. Z: 4–9.

C. MAS, cornelian cherry. S: early spring, fall. C: yellow fuzzy flowers, scarlet edible fruits in fall. Z: 3–8.

C. NUTTALLII, Pacific dogwood. S: early spring. C: white flowers. Z: 7–9.

HALESIA CAROLINA, Carolina silver bell. S: spring. C: white bells. Z: 3–9.

MAGNOLIA X SOULANGIANA, saucer magnolia. S: spring. C: usually purple and white. Z: 2–8.

OXYDENDRUM ARBOREUM, sorrel tree. S: spring, summer, fall. C: white flowers in racemes followed by similar-looking fruit and deep red fall color. Z: 3–8.

PTELEA TRIFOLIATA, hop tree. S: spring. C: greenish. Z: 2–9.

RHAMNUS spp., buckthorn. S: summer. C: yellow to black berries. Z: 3–8.

SORBARIA SORBIFOLIA, tree spirea. S: early summer. C: white umbels. Z: 1–8.

STAPHYLEA COLCHICA, bladdernut. S: summer. C: odd green, dangling papery pods. Z: 3–8.

STEWARTIA KOREANA, stewartia. S: summer. C: white flowers (bark year-round). Z: 5–9.

S. PSEUDOCAMELLIA, stewartia. S: summer. C: camellialike white flowers. Z: 5–9.

STYRAX JAPONICA, Japanese snowbell. S: early summer, summer. C: white bells, green teardrop fruits. Z: 3–9.

EVERGREEN SHRUBS

LOW: TO 2.5 FEET

ANDROMEDA GLAUCOPHYLLA, bog rosemary. S: spring. C: pink bells. Z: 2–9.

A. POLIFOLIA, bog rosemary. S: spring. C: pink bells. Z: 2–9.

ARCTOSTAPHYLOS spp., bearberry. S: spring, fall. C: pink flowers in drooping clusters, red berries. Z: 2–6.

COTONEASTER spp., cotoneaster. S: fall. C: red berries on some varieties. Z: 5–10, variable.

DANAE RACEMOSA, Alexandrian laurel. S: spring, fall. C: white flowers, red berries. Z: 7–10.

DAPHNE X BURKWOODII, Burkwood daphne (semievergreen). S: early spring. C: fragrant pink stars fade to white. Z: 5–8.

D. LAUREOLA, spurge laurel. S: early spring. C: whitish green flowers, blue-black fruits. Z: 5 (with protection)–9.

D. ODORA, fragrant daphne, winter daphne. S: early spring. C: scented rosy purple flowers. Z: 7–10.

EPIGAEA REPENS, trailing arbutus. S: spring. C: flowers pink or white in clusters. Z: 3–8.

EUONYMUS RADICANS (E. FORTUNEI), wintercreeper. S: year-round. C: foliage most interesting; some flowers and fruit, most insignificant. Z: 5–9.

GAULTHERIA SHALLON, gaultheria, wintergreen. S: spring, fall, winter. C: pink urn-shaped flowers; black, purple berries. Z: 5–9.

ILEX CRENATA, box-leaved holly, Japanese holly. S: fall. C: insignificant flowers, small black berries. Z: 5–9.

I. GLABRA 'Compacta', inkberry (semievergreen in northern areas). S: fall. C: black berries once used for ink. Z: 3–8.

KALMIA ANGUSTIFOLIA, sheep laurel. S: spring. C: lilac. Z: 2–7.

MAHONIA AQUIFOLIUM, Oregon holly grape. S: spring. C: yellow clusters. Z: 5–9.

RHODODENDRON spp., rhododendron, rosebay, small species and varieties. S: spring to early summer. C: trusses in all colors but true blue. Z: variable.

SARCOCOCCA HOOKERANA, sarcococca, sweet box. S: fall. C: red or black berries. Z: 7–10.

S. H. 'Humilis', sweet box. S: fall. C: red or black berries. Z: 6–9.

SKIMMIA JAPONICA, Japanese skimmia. S: spring, fall. C: yellowish white flowers and red berries in fall. Z: 7–9.

VINCA MAJOR, periwinkle. S: spring. C: blue flowers. Z: 7–10.

MEDIUM: 2.5 FEET TO 6 FEET

ABELIA X GRANDIFLORA, glossy abelia (semievergreen). S: early to late summer. C: white trumpets flare pink. Z: 5–9.

AUCUBA JAPONICA, aucuba. S: fall to spring. C: scarlet berries. Z: 7–10.

BERBERIS DARWINII, Darwin's barberry. S: spring, fall. C: yellow flowers, black berries. Z: 5–8.

B. JULIANAE, wintergreen barberry. S: fall. C: bluish black glaucous berries. Z: 6–8.

BUXUS SEMPERVIRENS, boxwood. S: evergreen. C: known for foliage alone. Z: 5–8.

CAMELLIA SASANQUA, camellia. S: late winter to spring. C: single or double roselike flowers, white, pink, or red. Z: 7(with protection)–10.

CHOISYA TERNATA, Mexican orange. S: early spring. C: fragrant white flowers. Z: 8–10.

COTONEASTER spp., cotoneaster. S: fall. C: berries. Z: various.

ELAEAGNUS X EBBINGEI, elaeagnus. S: spring. C: tiny, fragrant yellow flowers. Z: 7–9.

X FATSHEDERA LIZEI, tree ivy. S: spring to fall. C: greenish flowers followed by berries. Z: 7–10.

KALMIA LATIFOLIA, mountain laurel. S: late spring. C: pink, white, or red. Z: 3–8.

LEUCOTHOE FONTANESIANA, drooping leucothoe. S: early summer, fall. C: white flowers, fall color. Z: 4–8.

NANDINA DOMESTICA, heavenly bamboo. S: all. C: pinkish white flowers, red berries, red fall foliage. Z: 7–10.

PHILLYREA spp., jasmine box. S: early summer, fall. C: fragrant flowers, purple-black fruits. Z: 7–9.

PIERIS spp., andromeda. S: spring. C: white or pink flowers, red new growth. Z: 5–9.

RHODODENDRON spp., rhododendron, rosebay. S: early spring to early summer by variety. C: all colors but true blue. Z: various by species and variety.

TALL: 6 FEET OR MORE

CAMELLIA JAPONICA, camellia. S: late winter to spring. C: single or double roselike flowers, white, pink, or red. Z: 7(with protection)–10.

EUONYMUS JAPONICUS, Japanese euonymus, Japanese spindle tree. S: early summer, fall. C: yellow-green flowers, pink berries (rarely form). Z: 5–9.

FATSIA JAPONICA, castor-oil plant, Japanese fatsia. S: spring, summer. C: large clusters of white flowers followed by ivylike black berries. Z: 7–10.

ILEX spp., holly. S: fall-winter. C: yellow-to-red berries by variety. Z: various.

I. GLABRA, American holly, inkberry. S: fall. C: black berries. Z: 4–10.

LAURUS NOBILIS, sweet bay. S: early summer. C: yellow tufts. Z: 8–10.

LIGUSTRUM spp., privet. S: summer. C: fragrant white flowers. Z: various by species and variety.

LONICERA FRAGRANTISSIMA, winter honeysuckle (semievergreen). S: winter. C: fragrant creamy green flowers. Z: 4–8.

MAHONIA JAPONICA, mahonia. S: all. C: yellow flowers in early spring, blue-black berries through winter. Z: 5–8.

M. 'Undulata' (M. AQUIFOLIUM 'Undulata'), mahonia. S: late winter on. C: showy pale yellow flowers, berries from fall on. Z: 6–9.

MYRICA CERIFERA, wax myrtle. S: fall. C: gray berries. Z: 4–8.

OSMANTHUS spp., tea olive, osmanthus. S: fall to winter. C: intensely fragrant tiny flowers. Z: various (7, 8 south).

PITTOSPORUM spp., pittosporum. S: summer. C: orange-blossom fragrant flowers. Z: 8–10.

PYRACANTHA spp., fire thorn, pyracantha. S: fall. C: orange berries. Z: various (6,7 south).

RHODODENDRON spp., rhododendron, rosebay. S: early spring to early summer. C: trusses in all colors but true blue. Z: various.

VIBURNUM spp., viburnum (evergreen species and varieties). S: spring to summer. C: white flowers, varies. Z: various by species and variety.

SMALL TREES

PRUNUS LAUROCERASUS (LAUROCERASUS OFFICINALIS), cherry laurel. S: early spring, summer. C: white flowers, purple fruits. Z: 6–8.

RHAMNUS spp., buckthorn (evergreen species). S: fall. C: berries. Z: various (8 south).

MAIL-ORDER NURSERIES

There are many places to buy plants. Local nurseries stock those that do well in your area; garden clubs and botanical gardens often have plant sales as fundraisers. One of the best ways to find unusual plants, however, is through mail-order suppliers. They have a wider range than your nursery could hope to carry. The growers are arranged according to their specialty: native plants, bulbs, herbaceous perennials, shrubs, water and bog plants, and a miscellaneous guide for seeds, vines, and ground covers. Prices for catalogs are noted (a *d* means the price is deductible from your first order). Whenever possible phone numbers are included; many of these nurseries are open to the public, so you might call ahead.

NATIVE PLANTS

Nearly every state has a native-plant group. Consult your local county extension agent, usually affiliated with the state university, for names and addresses of societies. Often these organizations have sales of plants propagated by members. I checked to the best of my ability that the native plants and wildflower growers listed are propagating wildflowers and not lifting them from their natural sites. Try to support these passionate growers and let them know you share their concern for the future of the wildings and their habitats.

APPALACHIAN GARDENS
P.O. Box 82
Waynesboro, PA 17268
(717) 762-4312
Rare plants, hardy ornamentals.
Catalog: free

APPALACHIAN WILDFLOWER NURSERY
Route 1, Box 275-A
Honey Creek Road
Reedsville, PA 17084
(717) 667-6998
Plants native to the New Jersey Pine Barrens, Soviet Union, Caucasus. Catalog: $1.25d

BAY VIEW GARDENS
1201 Bay Street
Santa Cruz, CA 95060
(408) 423-3656
Pacific Coast native iris.
Catalog: $1.50

BEAVER CREEK NURSERY
7526 Pelleaux Road
Knoxville, TN 37938
(615) 922-3961
Rare and unusual plants.
Catalog: 45¢

BEERSHEBA WILDFLOWER GARDEN
P.O. Box 551
Stone Door Road
Beersheba Springs, TN 37305
(615) 692-3575
Hardy native perennial wildflowers and ferns. Catalog: free

BERNARDO BEACH NATIVE PLANT FARM
Star Route 7, Box 145
Veguita, NM 87062
Various plants of the Southwest. Catalog: $1

BOEHLKE'S WOODLAND GARDENS
W. 140 North 10829
Country Aire Road
Germantown, WI 53022
Native marsh and woodland perennials. Catalog: $1

COASTAL GARDENS & NURSERY
4611 Socastee Boulevard
Myrtle Beach, SC 29575
(803) 293-2000
Ornamental grasses, ferns, perennials: participates in worldwide seed exchange.
Catalog: $2

COLORADO ALPINES, INC.
P.O. Box 2708
Avon, CO 81620
(303) 949-6464 or 6672
Alpines and miniature plants.
Catalog: $2

COLVOS CREEK NURSERY & LANDSCAPING
1931 Second Avenue, #215
Seattle, WA 98101
(206) 441-1509
Unusual Pacific Coast natives.
Catalog: $2

COMPANION PLANTS
7247 North Coolville Ridge Road
Athens, OH 45701
(614) 592-4643
Mostly herbs, some native plants. Catalog: $2

COUNTRY WETLANDS NURSERY
P.O. Box 126
Muskego, WI 53150
(414) 679-1268
Wetland plants, woodland plants and seeds. Catalog: $1

CROWNSVILLE NURSERY
P.O. Box 797
Crownsville, MD 21032
(301) 923-2212
Ornamental perennials, natives, propagated cyclamen: excellent quality. Catalog: $2d

DONAROMA'S NURSERY
P.O. Box 2189
Upper Main Street
Edgartown, MA 02539
(508) 627-8366 or 3036
Wildflowers and ornamental perennials. Catalog: $3

FANCY FRONDS
1911 Fourth Avenue West
Seattle, WA 98119
Ferns from everywhere, excellent source. Catalog: $1d

FIELDSTONE GARDENS, INC.
620 Quaker Lane
Vassalboro, ME 04989-9713
(207) 923-3836
Perennials: familiar and rare.
Catalog: $1.50

FOLIAGE GARDENS
2003 128th Avenue SE
Bellevue, WA 98005
(206) 747-2998
Ferns: all spore-grown.
Catalog: $1

FORESTFARM
990 Tetherow Road
Williams, OR 97544
(503) 846-6963
Excellent source of woody natives and unusual plants. Informative catalog: one of the best sources. Catalog: $3

FROSTY HOLLOW NURSERY
P.O. Box 53
Langley, WA 98260
(206) 221-2332
Specializes in ecological restoration, rescues and propagates plants of Pacific Northwest. List: SASE

GARDEN PLACE
P.O. Box 338
6780 Heisley Road
Mentor, OH 44061
Perennials including wildings.
Catalog: $1

INDIGO KNOLL PERENNIALS
16236 Compromise Court
Mount Airy, MD 21771
(301) 489-5131
Border and rock-garden plants, native herbs. Catalog: free

MARY'S PLANT FARM
2410 Lanes Mill Road
Hamilton, OH 45013
(513) 892-2055 or 894-0022
Native perennials, ferns, flowering shrubs and trees: shade-tolerant plants. Catalog: $1d

MARYLAND AQUATIC NURSERIES
3427 North Furnace Road
Jarrettsville, MD 21084
Native bog and water plants and others. Catalog: free

NATIVE GARDENS
Route 1, Box 494
Greenback, TN 37742
(615) 856-3350
Native herbaceous perennials, a few woody plants. Catalog: $1

NATURAL GARDENS
113 Jasper Lane
Oak Ridge, TN 37830
(615) 856-3350
Native woodland and marsh plants from the Southeast. Catalog: $1d

OAKRIDGE NURSERIES
P.O. Box 182
East Kingston, NH 03827
(603) 642-8227
Rescued plants and propagated natives. Catalog: free

SCOTT O'CONNER
North Temperate Wildflowers
R.F.D. 1, Box 317-A
Newcastle, ME 04553
Large list of native plants. Catalog: free

OLD FARM NURSERY
5550 Indiana Street
Golden, CO 80403
(303) 278-0754 or 0755
Native plants. Catalog: free

ORCHID GARDENS
6700 Splithand Road
Grand Rapids, MN 55744
(612) 755-0205
Native plants of north central states, including orchids. Catalog: $1

OWL RIDGE ALPINES
5421 Whipple Lake Road
Clarkston, MI 48016
Alpine and woodland species. Catalog: free

PRIMROSE PATH, THE
R.D. 2, Box 110
Scottdale, PA 15683
(412) 887-6756
Woodland plants and other perennials. Catalog: $2d

RICE-CREEK GARDENS, INC.
11506 Highway 65
Blaine, MN 55432
(612) 754-8090
Wildflowers. Catalog: $2

SILVER SPRINGS NURSERY
H.C.R. 62, Box 86
Moyie Springs, ID 83845
(208) 267-5753
Native ground covers. Catalog: free

SISKIYOU RARE PLANT NURSERY
2825 Cummings Road
Medford, OR 97501
(503) 772-6846
Incredible selection of wild plants: specializing in, but not limited to, alpines and rock-garden plants. Catalog: $2d

SUNLIGHT GARDENS
Route 1, Box 600-A
Andersonville, TN 37705
(615) 494-8237
Plants native to the eastern United States. Catalog: $2

WE-DU NURSERIES
Route 5, Box 724
Marion, NC 28752
(704) 738-8300
Woodland plants. Catalog: $1d

WILDWOOD FLOWER, THE
Route 3, Box 165
Pittsboro, NC 27312
(919) 542-4344
Wildflowers, some woody shrubs and ferns. List: SASE

WOODLANDERS, INC.
1128 Colleton Avenue
Aiken, SC 29801
(803) 648-7522
Native trees and shrubs and some herbaceous perennials. Catalog: free.

WYRTTUN WARD
18 Beach Street
Middleboro, MA 02346
Woodland wildflowers. Catalog: $1

BULBS

AMBERGATE GARDENS
8015 Krey Avenue
Waconia, MN 55387
(612) 443-2248
Unusual plants, martagon lily. Catalog: $1

ANTONELLI BROTHERS, INC.
2545 Capitola Road
Santa Cruz, CA 95062
(408) 475-5222
Tuberous begonias and shade bulbs. Catalog: free

B & D LILIES
330 P Street
Port Townsend, WA 98368
(206) 385-1738
Some native lilies and many hybrids, nice catalog. Catalog: $2d

BIO-QUEST INTERNATIONAL
P.O. Box 5752
Santa Barbara, CA 93150-5752
(805) 969-4072
Some native bulbs, specializes in South African bulbs. Catalog: $2

BUNDLES OF BULBS
112 Green Springs Valley Road
Owings Mills, MD 21117
(301) 581-2188
Rare and unusual bulbs. Catalog: $1d

FAIRYLAND BEGONIA & LILY GARDEN
1100 Griffith Road
McKinleyville, CA 95521
(707) 839-3034
Mostly lilies. Catalog: 50¢

GRANT MITSCH NOVELTY DAFFODILS
P.O. Box 218
Hubbard, OR 97032
(503) 651-2742
Large list, many old varieties. Catalog: $3

HONEYWOOD LILIES
R.R. 1
723 Robson Road
Waterdown, Ont., Canada
L0R 2H0
(416) 689-6984
Lilies. Catalog: $1

MARY WALKER BULB COMPANY
P.O. Box 256
Omega, GA 31775
(912) 386-1919
Callas, caladiums, summer-blooming bulbs. Catalog: free

McCLURE & ZIMMERMAN
P.O. Box 368
108 West Winnebago
Friesland, WI 53935
(414) 326-4220
Netherlands importers, good quality. Catalog: free

MESSELAAR BULB CO.
P.O. Box 269
County Road, Route 1-A
Ipswich, MA 01938
(508) 356-3737
Netherlands importers, summer-blooming bulbs. Catalog: free

NANCY R. WILSON
6525 Briceland-Thorn Road
Garberville, CA 95440
(707) 986-7336
Species and miniature narcissus. Catalog: free

RUSSELL GRAHAM
4030 Eagle Crest Road NW
Salem, OR 97304
(503) 362-1135
Wonderful collection of ferns, shade plants, and bulbs. Catalog: $2d

SISTERS' BULB FARM, THE
Route 2, Box 170
Gibsland, LA 71028
(318) 843-6379
Species daffodils and varieties from 1920s and 30s. Catalog: free

VELDHEER TULIP GARDENS
12755 Quincy Street
Holland, MI 49424
(616) 399-1900
Importer of various bulbs. Catalog: free

WAUSHARA GARDENS, THE
Route 2, Box 570
Plainfield, WI 54966
(715) 335-4462
Lilies, callas, summer-blooming bulbs. Catalog: $1

WILLIAM R. P. WELCH
43 East Gorgas Road
Carmel Valley, CA 93924-9450
(408) 659-3830
Narcissus species, N. tazetta. Catalog: free

WORLD CALADIUM
P.O. Box 629
Sebring, FL 33871-0629
(813) 385-0663 or 655-3530
Caladiums. Catalog: free

FLOWERING HERBACEOUS PERENNIALS

AITKIN'S SALMON CREEK GARDEN
608 NW 119th Street
Vancouver, WA 98685
(206) 573-4472
Iris and orchids. Catalog: $1d

AMERICAN DAYLILY & PERENNIALS
P.O. Box 210
Grain Valley, MO 64029
(816) 224-2852
Daylilies and others. Catalog: $3d

ANDRE VIETTE FARM & NURSERY
Route 1, Box 16
State Route 608
Fishersville, VA 22939
(703) 943-2315
Huge list including many perennials classified for shade. Catalog: $2

ART FORM NURSERIES
156 Chillicothe Road
Chagrin Falls, OH 44022
(216) 338-8100
Perennials. Catalog: free

BLUESTONE PERENNIALS
7211 Middle Ridge Road
Madison, OH 44057
(800) 952-5243
Inexpensive seedlings in flats (three, six, twelve, etc.) four hundred varieties. Catalog: free

BUSSE GARDENS
Route 2, Box 238
Cokato, MN 55321
(612) 286-2654
Hard-to-find perennials. Catalog: $2d

CAMELOT NORTH
R.R. 2, Box 398
Piquot Lakes, MN 56472
(218) 568-8922
Perennials. Catalog: $1d

CANYON CREEK NURSERY
3527 Dry Creek Road
Oroville, CA 95965
(916) 533-2166
Uncommon perennials, large collection of fragrant violets and hardy geraniums. Catalog: $1

CAPRICE FARM
15425 SW Pleasant Hill Road
Sherwood, OR 97140
(503) 625-7241
Old-fashioned and hard-to-find perennials. Catalog: $1

CARMEN'S NURSERY
16201 Mozart
Los Gatos, CA 95030
Hostas and Siberian iris. Catalog: free

CARROLL GARDENS
P.O. Box 310
444 East Main Street
Westminster, MD 21157
(800) 638-6334
Extensive, well-written catalog. Catalog: $2d

CLIFFORD'S PERENNIAL & VINE
Route 2, Box 320
East Troy, WI 53120
(414) 968-4040 April–September, 642-7156 October–March
General nursery material. Catalog: $1d

COASTAL GARDENS
4611 Socastee Boulevard
Myrtle Beach, SC 29575
(803) 293-2000
Perennials. Catalog: $1.50d

COOPER'S GARDENS
212 West Country Road
Roseville, MN 55113
(612) 484-7878
Shade perennials. List: SASE

CRICKLEWOOD NURSERY
11907 Nevers Road
Snohomish, WA 98290
(206) 568-2829
Herbaceous border perennials. Catalog: $2d

CROWNSVILLE NURSERY
P.O. Box 797
Crownsville, MD 21032
(301) 923-2212
Outstanding list with good descriptions; hosta and familiar and unusual perennials. Catalog: $2d

CRUICKSHANK'S, INC.
1015 Mount Pleasant Road
Toronto, Ont., Canada
M4P 2M1
(416) 488-8292
Perennials and bulbs. Catalog: free

ECO-GARDENS
P.O. Box 1227
Decatur, GA 30031
(404) 294-6468
Shade perennials. Catalog: $1

FAIRWAY ENTERPRISES
114 The Fairway
Albert Lea, MN 56007
(507) 373-5290
Hosta. List: SASE

FANCY FRONDS
1911 Fourth Avenue West
Seattle, WA 98119
Ferns. Catalog: $1d

FLORIDA WILDFLOWERS, INC.
1224 South Military Terrace, #2324
Deerfield Beach, FL 33434
Southern-grown perennials.

GARDEN PERENNIALS
Route 1
Wayne, NE 68787
(402) 375-3615
Daylilies, familiar perennials. Catalog: $1d

GARDEN PLACE
P.O. Box 388
6780 Heisley Road
Mentor, OH 44061-0388
(216) 255-3705
General perennials. Catalog: $1

GARDENIMPORT, INC.
P.O. Box 760
Thornhill, Ont., Canada
L3T 4A5

(406) 731-1950
Largest selection of hostas in Canada. Catalog: $3

GILSON GARDENS
P.O. Box 277
U.S. Route 20
Perry, OH 44081
(216) 259-4845
Perennials and ground covers. Catalog: free

HAUSER'S SUPERIOR VIEW FARM
Route 1, Box 199
County Highway J
Bayfield, WI 54814
(715) 779-5404
All field-grown perennials. Catalog: free

HOLBROOK FARM AND NURSERY
Route 2, Box 223
Fletcher, NC 28732
(704) 891-7790
Perennials for shade. Catalog: $2d

HORTICO, INC.
R.R. 1
723 Robson Road
Waterdown, Ont., Canada
L0R 2H0
(416) 689-6984
Perennials, ground covers, shrubs, and vines. Catalog: $2

JERNIGAN GARDENS
Route 6, Box 593
Dunn, NC 28334
(919) 567-2135
Ferns, daylilies, irises. List: SASE

KELLY'S PLANT WORLD
10266 East Princeton
Sanger, CA 93657
(209) 294-7676 or 292-3505
Ligularia, tricyrtis, summer-blooming bulbs. Catalog: free

KURT BLUEMEL, INC.
2740 Greene Lane
Baldwin, MD 21013-9523
(301) 557-7229
The ornamental grass supplier: look for sedges and rushes for shade and marsh areas. Catalog: $2

LAMB NURSERIES
East 101 Sharp Avenue
Spokane, WA 99202
(509) 328-7956
Perennials for shade. Catalog:
free

LEE BRISTOL NURSERY
Bloomingfields Farm
Route 55
Gaylordsville, CT 06755-
0005
(203) 354-6951
Daylilies. Catalog: free

LOGEE'S GREENHOUSES
141 North Street
Danielson, CT 06239
(203) 774-8038
*Mostly greenhouse plants
(tropical and subtropical);
camellias, herbs, and some
hardy perennials including
Chrysanthemum parthenium
'Aurea'.* Catalog: $3d

LOUISIANA NURSERY
Route 7, Box 43
Highway 182
Opelousas, LA 70570
(318) 948-3696, 942-6404
Native iris and others.
Catalog: $3

MARY'S PLANT FARM
2410 Lanes Mill Road
Hamilton, OH 45013
(513) 892-2055 or 894-0022
Wide variety of perennials.
Catalog: $1d

MEADOWLAKE GARDENS
Route 4, Box 709
Walterboro, SC 29488
(803) 844-2359 or 2545
Hostas. Catalog: $2

MOUNT TAHOMA NURSERY
28111 112th Avenue East
Graham, WA 98338
(206) 847-9827
Alpines. Catalog: $1

NOVELTY NURSERIES
P.O. Box 382
Novelty, OH 44072
(216) 338-4425
Ferns and hostas. Catalog: free

PIEDMONT GARDENS
533–577 Piedmont Street
Waterbury, CT 06706

(203) 754-8534 or 3535
Hostas. Catalog: 50¢

POWELL'S GARDENS
Route 3, Box 21
Highway 70
Princeton, NC 27569
(919) 936-4421
Perennials, hostas. Catalog:
$2.50

PRIMROSE PATH, THE
R.D. 2, Box 110
Scottdale, PA 15683
(412) 887-6756
Primulas and natives. Catalog:
$2d

RICE-CREEK GARDENS, INC.
11506 Highway 65
Blaine, MN 55432
(612) 754-8090
*Eight hundred varieties of rare
and familiar perennials.*
Catalog: $2

ROCKKNOLL NURSERY
9210 U.S. 50 East
Hillsboro, OH 45133-8546
(513) 393-1278
*Perennials and rock-garden
plants.* List: 50¢ or two first-
class stamps

RUSSELL GRAHAM
4030 Eagle Crest Road NW
Salem, OR 97304
(503) 362-1135
*Wonderful collection of ferns,
shade plants, and bulbs.*
Catalog: $2d

SAVORY'S GARDENS, INC.
5300 Whiting Avenue
Edina, MN 55439-9612
(612) 941-8755
Hostas. Catalog: $2

SHADY OAKS NURSERY
700 Nineteenth Avenue NE
Waseca, MN 56093
(507) 835-5033
Shade plants. Catalog: $1d

SISKIYOU RARE PLANT
NURSERY
2825 Cummings Road
Medford, OR 97501
(503) 772-6846

*Unusual perennials, mostly
alpines, incredible selection.*
Catalog: $2d

SPRINGVALE FARM NURSERY,
INC.
Mozier Hollow Road
Hamburg, IL 62045
(618) 232-1108
Dwarf and alpine perennials.
Catalog: $2

STOECKLEIN'S NURSERY
135 Critchlow Road
Renfrew, PA 16053
(412) 586-7882
Wildflowers, shade plants.
Catalog: $1

SUNLIGHT GARDENS
Route 1, Box 600-A
Andersonville, TN 37705
(615) 494-8237
Shade perennials, too.
Catalog: $2d

SURRY GARDENS
P.O. Box 145
Surry, ME 04684
(207) 667-4493
General nursery plants.
Catalog: $2

TRANS PACIFIC NURSERY
16065 Oldsville Road
McMinnville, OR 97128
(503) 472-6215
*General nursery stock,
perennials, vines.* Catalog:
$1d

TRIPPLE BROOK FARM
37 Middle Road
Southampton, MA 01073
(413) 527-4626
Hardy nursery stock. Catalog
free

WALDEN-WEST
5744 Crooked Finger Road
NE
Scotts Mills, OR 97375
(503) 873-6875
Hostas. Catalog: free

WAYSIDE GARDENS
P.O. Box 1
Hodges, SC 29695
(800) 845-1124
*Vast selection of usual and
unusual woody plants and
perennials, full-color catalog.*
Catalog: $1d

WEISS BROTHERS NURSERY
11690 Colfax Highway
Grass Valley, CA 95945
(916) 272-7657
Perennials. Catalog: $1

WHITE FLOWER FARM
Route 63
Litchfield, CT 06759
(203) 567-0801
*Wonderful catalog, great
information.* Catalog: $5d

WINTER GREENHOUSE
Route 2, Box 24
Winter, WI 54896
(715) 226-4963
Primroses, columbines.
Catalog: $1

WOODLANDERS, INC.
1128 Collection Avenue
Aiken, SC 29801
(803) 648-7522
Perennials for shade. List:
SASE

SHRUBS

BAMBOO SHOOT, A
1462 Darby Road
Sebastopol, CA 95472
(707) 823-0131
Catalog: $1

BAMBOO SOURCERY
666 Wagnon Road
Sebastopol, CA 95472
(707) 823-5866
Catalog: $1

BERNARDO BEACH NATIVE
PLANT FARM
Star Route 7, Box 145
Veguita, NM 87062
*Various plants of the
Southwest.* Catalog: $1d

BRIARWOOD GARDENS
R.F.D. 1
14 Gully Lane
East Sandwich, MA 02537
(508) 888-2146
Rhododendrons. Catalog: $1

BROKEN ARROW NURSERY
13 Broken Arrow Road
Hamden, CT 06518
(203) 288-1026
*Mountain laurel, uncommon
trees and shrubs.* List: SASE

BROWN'S KALMIA & AZALEA NURSERY
8527 Semiahmoo Drive
Blaine, WA 98230
(206) 371-2489
Hybrid mountain laurel and rhododendrons. List: SASE

BULL VALLEY RHODODENDRON NURSERY
214 Bull Valley Road
Aspers, PA 17304
(717) 677-6313
Sells only rhododendrons (soon will add magnolias). Catalog: $2d

BURPEE, W. ATLEE, CO.
300 Park Avenue
Warminster, PA 18974
(215) 674-4900
Primarily seeds, but offers some ground covers and shrubs. Catalog: free

CAMELLIA FOREST NURSERY
P.O. Box 291
125 Carolina Forest
Chapel Hill, NC 27516
(919) 967-5529
Camellias, conifers. Catalog: $1

CARDINAL NURSERY
Route 1, Box 316
State Road, NC 28676
(919) 874-2027
Rhododendrons. Catalog: free

CARLSON'S GARDENS
P.O. Box 305 NSG
South Salem, NY 10590
(914) 763-5958
Native azaleas: northern grown and acclimated. Catalog: $2d

CHAMBERS NURSERY
26874 Ferguson Road
Junction City, OR 97448
(503) 998-2467
Rhododendrons and azaleas. Catalog: free

COLD STREAM FARM
2030 Free Soil Road
Free Soil, MI 49411-9752
(616) 464-5809
Evergreen and deciduous trees and shrubs. Catalog: free

CROWNSVILLE NURSERY
P.O. Box 797
Crownsville, MD 21032
(301) 923-2212
Some shrubs and hybrid azaleas. Catalog: $2d

CUMMINS GARDEN, THE
22 Robertsville Road
Marlboro, NJ 07746
(201) 536-2591
Dwarf and unusual rhododendrons and azaleas, mountain laurels. Catalog: $2d

DAYSTAR
Route 2, Box 250
Litchfield-Hallowell Road
(West Gardiner)
Litchfield, ME 04350
(207) 724-3369
Dwarf conifers, unusual shrubs. Catalog: $1

FLORA LAN NURSERY
Route 1, Box 357
Forest Grove, OR 97116
(503) 357-3500
Rhododendrons, camellias. Catalog: free

FORESTFARM
990 Tetherow Road
Williams, OR 97544
(503) 846-6963
Excellent source for native and unusual woody plants; consider second-day air for cross-country orders. Catalog: $3

GIRARD NURSERIES
P.O. Box 428
6839 North Ridge East, Route 20
Geneva, OH 44041
(216) 466-2881 or 969-1636
Rare and unusual trees and shrubs. Catalog: free

GOSSLER FARMS NURSERY
1200 Weaver Road
Springfield, OR 97478-9663
(503) 746-3922 or 747-0749
Magnolias and stewartia; 200–300 varieties of plants. Catalog: $1

GREER GARDENS
1280 Goodpasture Island Road
Eugene, OR 97401-1794
(503) 686-8266
Excellent source of rhododendrons, extensive list. Japanese maples and rare shrubs. Catalog: $3

HALL RHODODENDRONS
P.O. Box 62
6924 Highway 38
Drain, OR 97435
(503) 836-2290
Sixteen hundred varieties of rhododendron. Catalog: $1

HORTICO, INC.
R.R. 1
723 Robson Road
Waterdown, Ont., Canada
L0R 2H0
(416) 689-6984
Shrubs, ground covers, vines. Catalog: $2

KELLY NURSERIES
Catalog Division
Department BK123L
Louisiana, MO 63353
(314) 754-4525
Assorted woody plants. Catalog: free

KRISTICK, MICHAEL & JANET
155 Mockingbird Road
Wellsville, PA 17365
(717) 292-2962
Dwarf conifers and Japanese maples. Catalog: free

LAMTREE FARM
Route 1, Box 162
Warrensville, NC 28693
(919) 385-6144
Franklinia, stewartia, native azaleas. Catalog: $2

LOUISIANA NURSERY
Route 7, Box 43
Highway 182
Opelousas, LA 70570
(318) ... *Magnolias and many unusual shrubs.* Catalog: $5

MARY'S PLANT FARM
2410 Lanes Mill Road
Hamilton, OH 45013
(513) 892-2055 or 894-0022
Native perennials, ferns, flowering shrubs, and trees: shade-tolerant plants. Catalog: $1d

MELLINGER'S INC.
2310 West South Range Road
North Lima, OH 44452
(216) 549-9861 or (800) 321-7444
Eccentric variety of plants and products. Catalog: free

MORDEN NURSERIES, LTD.
P.O. Box 1270
Morden, N.B., Canada
R0G 1J0
(204) 822-3311
Shade trees. Catalog: free

MOUNT LEO NURSERY
P.O. Box 135
603 Beersheba Street
McMinnville, TN 37110
(615) 473-7833
Flowering shrubs and ground covers. Catalog: free

MOUNT TAHOMA NURSERY
28111 112th Avenue East
Graham, WA 98338
(206) 847-9827
Dwarf conifers. Catalog: $1

MOWBRAY GARDENS
3318 Mowbray Lane
Cincinnati, OH 45226
(503) 321-0694
Rhododendrons, dwarf conifers. Catalog: free

MUSSER FORESTS INC.
P.O. Box 340
Route 119 North
Indiana, PA 15701
(412) 465-5686
Tree seedlings, some shrubs, conifers. Catalog: free

NUCCIO'S NURSERIES
P.O. Box 6160
3555 Chaney Trail
Altadena, CA 91003
(818) 794-3383
Camellias, azaleas. Catalog: free

OAK HILL FARM
204 Pressly Street
Clover, SC 29710
(803) 222-4245
*Hardy evergreens, species
rhododendrons.* Catalog: free

OWENS FARMS
Route 3, Box 158-A
Curve-Nankipoo Road
Ripley, TN 38063
(901) 635-1588
Native deciduous hollies.
Catalog: $2d

RED'S RHODIES
15920 SW Oberst Lane
Sherwood, OR 97140
(503) 625-6331
Rhododendrons. List: SASE

ROSLYN NURSERY
211 Burrs Lane
Dix Hills, NY 11746
(516) 643-9347
*Extensive catalog of rare and
familiar woody plants,
rhododendrons, pieris, kalmias,
azaleas.* Catalog: $2

**SHERWOOD AKIN'S
GREENHOUSES**
P.O. Box 6
Sibley, LA 71073
(318) 377-3653
Unusual fruiting plants. List:
SASE

SMITH NURSERY CO.
P.O. Box 515
Charles City, IA 50616
(515) 228-3239
Native trees. Catalog: free

**SPRINGVALE FARM NURSERY,
INC.**
Mozier Hollow Road
Hamburg, IL 62045
(618) 232-1108
Dwarf conifers, alpines.
Catalog: $2

**STEVE RAY'S BAMBOO
GARDENS**
909 Seventy-ninth Place
South
Birmingham, AL 35206
(205) 833-3052
*Excellent source for many hardy
bamboos.* Catalog: $2

STUBBS SHRUBS
23225 SW Bosky Dell Lane
West Linn, OR 97068
(503) 638-5048
Evergreen azaleas. Catalog:
$2d

SURRY GARDENS
P.O. Box 145
Surry, ME 04684
(207) 667-4493
General nursery stock.
Catalog: $2

THOMASVILLE NURSERIES
P.O. Box 7
1842 Smith Avenue
Thomasville, GA 31799-
0007
(912) 226-5568
Azaleas. Catalog: free

TRANSPLANT NURSERY
Parkertown Road
Lavonia, GA 30553
(404) 356-8947
*Native rhododendrons; azaleas,
too.* Catalog: $1

TRILLIUM LANE NURSERY
18855 Trillium Lane
Fort Bragg, CA 95437
(707) 964-3282
Rhododendrons. Catalog: free

TRIPPLE BROOK FARM
37 Middle Road
Southampton, MA 01073
(413) 527-4626
Hardy nursery stock. Catalog:
free

VALLEY NURSERY
P.O. Box 4845
2801 North Montana
Avenue
Helena, MT 59601
(406) 442-8460
Hardy trees and shrubs. List:
Long SASE

**VERNON BARNES & SON
NURSERY**
P.O. Box 250
McMinnville, TN 37110
(615) 668-8576 or 2165
Shade trees, flowering shrubs.
Catalog: $1

**WASHINGTON EVERGREEN
NURSERY**
P.O. Box 388
Brooks Branch Road
Leicester, NC 28748
*Dwarf kalmias, rhododendrons
and conifers.* Catalog: $2d

WAVECREST NURSERY
2509 Lakeshore Drive
Fennville, MI 49408
(616) 543-4175
*Japanese maples, unusual trees
and shrubs.* Catalog: free

WAYSIDE GARDENS
P.O. Box 1
Hodges, SC 29695
(800) 845-1124
*Vast selection of usual and
unusual woody plants and
perennials, full-color catalog.*
Catalog: free

WESTGATE GARDEN NURSERY
751 Westgate Drive
Eureka, CA 95501
(707) 442-1239
Rhododendrons. Catalog: $4d

WHITMAN FARMS
1420 Beaumont Street
Salem, OR 97304
(503) 363-5020
*Unusual shrubs and trees, some
natives.* List: SASE

WHITNEY GARDENS
P.O. Box F
31600 Highway 101
Brinnon, WA 98320
Rhododendrons. Catalog: $3

WATER AND
BOG PLANTS

BLACK COPPER KITS
111 Ringwood Avenue
Pompton Lakes, NJ 07442
(201) 831-6484
Carnivorous plants. Catalog:
25¢

BLUEMEL, KURT, INC.
2740 Greene Lane
Baldwin, MD 21013-9523
(301) 557-7229
*Sedges and grasslike water
plants.* Catalog: $2

LILYPONS WATER GARDENS
P.O. Box 10
6800 Lilypons Road
Buckeystown, MD 21717-
0010
*Everything for the water
garden, including animals.*
Catalog: $5

**MARYLAND AQUATIC
NURSERIES**
3427 North Furnace Road
Jarrettsville, MD 21084
(301) 557-7615
*Water and bog plants, including
natives.* Catalog: $2

**MOORE WATER GARDENS,
LTD.**
P.O. Box 340
Highway 4
Port Stanley, Ont., Canada,
N0L 2A0
(519) 782-4052
Aquatic plants and supplies

PRAIRIE NURSERY
Route 1, Box 365
Westfield, WI 53964
(608) 296-3679
Waterside plants. Catalog: $2

PARADISE WATER GARDENS
62 May Street
Whitman, MA 02382
(617) 447-4711
General water-garden supplier.
Catalog: $3

PERRY'S WATER GARDENS
191 Leatherman Gap Road
Franklin, NC 28734
(704) 524-3264 or 369-5648
*Many plants, complete
supplies.* Catalog: $2

**SANTA BARBARA WATER
GARDENS**
P.O. Box 4353
160 East Mountain Drive
Santa Barbara, CA 93140
(805) 969-5129
Bog plants and others, books.
Catalog: $1.50

SCHERER, S., & SONS
104 Waterside Road
Northport, NY 11768
(516) 261-7432
*Complete supplies, colocasias
and giant taros, third
generation.* Catalog: free

SLOCUM WATER GARDENS
1101 Cypress Gardens
Boulevard
Winter Haven, FL 33884-
1932
(813) 293-7151
*Water plants, marsh plants, and
supplies.* Catalog: $3

TILLEY'S NURSERY/THE
WATER WORKS
111 East Fairmount Street
Coopersburg, PA 18036
(215) 282-4784
*Bog plants, fish, scavengers,
and supplies.* Catalog: free

WILLIAM TRICKER, INC.
7125 Tanglewood Drive
Independence, OH 44121
(216) 524-3491
*General supplies, plants and
fish, color catalog.* Catalog:
free

VAN NESS WATER GARDENS
2460 North Euclid Avenue
Upland, CA 91786-1199
(714) 982-2425
The works. Catalog: free

WATER WAYS NURSERY
Route 2, Box 247
Lovettsville, VA 22080
(703) 822-9050
Aquatic plants. List: SASE

WATERFORD GARDENS
74 East Allendale Road
Saddle River, NJ 07458
(201) 327-0721
*Good color catalog, helpful
people.* Catalog: $4

WICKLEIN'S AQUATIC FARM
& GARDEN NURSERY, INC.
1820 Cromwell Bridge Road
Baltimore, MD 21234
(301) 823-1335
Aquatic and bog plants.
Catalog: $1

MISCELLANEOUS

ALLEN, STERLING & LOTHROP
191 U.S. Route 1
Falmouth, ME 04105
(207) 781-4142
Lawn and garden seed.
Catalog: $2d

ARCHIAS' SEED STORE
106 East Main Street
Dedalia, MO 65301
(816) 826-1330
*Seeds of perennials and other
garden plants.* Catalog: free

ARTHUR H. STEFFEN, INC.
P.O. Box 184
1259 Fairport Road
Fairport, NY 14450
(716) 377-1665
Vines, especially clematis.
Catalog: $2

BOTANIC GARDEN COMPANY
9 Wyckoff Street
Brooklyn, NY 11201
(718) 624-8839
Wide range of wildflower seeds.
Catalog: free

CALLAHAN SEEDS
6045 Foley Lane
Central Point, OR 97502
(503) 855-1164
Native tree and shrub seeds.
Catalog: free

EARLY'S FARM & GARDEN
CENTRE, INC.
P.O. Box 3024
2615 Lorne Avenue South
Saskatoon, Sask., Canada
S7K 3S9
(306) 931-1982
Wildflower seeds. Catalog: $2d

IVIES OF THE WORLD
P.O. Box 408
Highway 42
Weirsdale, FL 32195
(904) 821-2201 or 2322
*Over two hundred varieties of
ivies—hardy and tender.*
Catalog: $1.50

LIFE-FORM REPLICATORS
P.O. Box 857
Fowlerville, MI 48836
(517) 223-8750
*Bob Stewart has an amazing
list of wild and rare plant seeds,
and he will propagate to order
—useful for large sites.*
Catalog: $2d

MAPLEWOOD SEED COMPANY
311 Maplewood Lane
Lake Oswego, OR 97470-
9236
(503) 672-1023
Seeds for rare maples. List:
Long SASE

MOON MOUNTAIN
WILDFLOWERS
P.O. Box 34
864 Napa Avenue
Morro Bay, CA 93442-0032
(805) 772-2473
*Seeds, supplies, and books on
wildflowers.* Catalog: $1

NATIVE SEED FOUNDATION
Star Route
Moyie Springs, ID 83845
(208) 267-7938
*Pacific Northwest woody plant
seeds.* Catalog: free

NORTHPLAN/MOUNTAIN
SEED
P.O. Box 9107
Moscow, ID 83843-1607
(208) 882-8040
Wildflower seed. Catalog: $1

PEEKSKILL NURSERIES
Shrub Oak, NY 10588
(914) 245-5595
Ground covers. Catalog: free

PRENTISS COURT GROUND
COVERS
P.O. Box 8662
Greenville, SC 29604
(803) 277-4037
Ground covers. Catalog: 50¢

SCHUMACHER, F. W., CO.
36 Spring Hill Road
Sandwich, MA 02563-1023
(508) 888-0659
*Seeds of rhododendrons, azaleas,
shrubs, trees.* Catalog: $1

SORUM'S NURSERY
Route 4, Box 308-J
Sherwood, OR 97140
(503) 628-2354
Rhododendrons and pieris. List:
SASE

TER-EL NURSERY
P.O. Box 112
Orefield, PA 18069
(215) 435-5411
Ground covers. Catalog: $1d

ORGANIC PRODUCTS AND SUPPLIES

AGE-OLD GARDEN SUPPLY
P.O. Box 1556
Boulder, CO 80306
(303) 499-0201
Time-tested natural products.
Catalog: free

AMERICAN ARBORIST
SUPPLIES
882 South Matlack Street
West Chester, PA 19382
(800) 441-8381, (800) 352-
3458 (in Pennsylvania)
Tools and books. Catalog: free

AQUACIDE COMPANY
P.O. Box 10748
1627 Ninth Street
White Bear Lake, MN 55110
Algae-control products.
Catalog: free

ARBORIST SUPPLY HOUSE,
INC.
P.O. Box 23607
215 SW Thirty-second Street
Fort Lauderdale, FL 33307
(305) 561-9527
Tools. Catalog: free

BENEFICIAL INSECTARY
14751 Oak Run Road
Oak Run, CA 96069
(916) 472-3715
Biological insect control.
Catalog: free

BETTER YIELD INSECT &
GARDEN HOUSES
P.O. Box 3451
Tecumseh Station
Windsor, Ont., Canada
N8N 3C4
(519) 727-6108
Biological insect control.
Catalog: free

BIO-CONTROL COMPANY
P.O. Box 337
57-A Zink Road
Berry Creek, CA 95916
(916) 589-5227
Biological insect control.
Catalog: free

BIO-GARD AGRONOMICS
P.O. Box 4477
Falls Church, VA 22044
(703) 536-4076
Organic products.
Catalog: free

BIO-RESOURCES
P.O. Box 902
1210 Birch Street
Santa Paula, CA 93060
(805) 525-0526
Biological insect control.
Catalog: free

BIOLOGIC
P.O. Box 177
Springtown Road
Willow Hill, PA 17271
(717) 349-2789
Biological insect control.
List: SASE

BRICKER'S ORGANIC FARM
842 Sandbar Ferry Road
Augusta, GA 30901
(404) 722-0661
Organic products. Catalog: $1

BRONWOOD WORM GARDENS
P.O. Box 28
Bronwood, GA 31726
(912) 995-5994
Worms. Catalog: free

CAPE COD WORM FARM
30 Center Avenue
Buzzards Bay, MA 02532
(506) 759-5664
Worms. Catalog: free

CARTER FISHWORM FARM
Plains, GA 31780
Presidential worms.
Catalog: free

JOHN DEERE CATALOG
1400 Third Avenue
Moline, IL 61265
(800) 544-2122
Tools, gifts. Catalog: free

DIRT CHEAP ORGANICS
5645 Paradise Drive
Corte Madera, CA 94925
(415) 924-0369
Organic products.
Catalog: free

EARLEE, INC.
2002 Highway 62
Jeffersonville, IN 47130
(812) 282-9134
Organic products.
Catalog: free

EARTHLY GOOD FARM &
GARDEN SUPPLY
Route 3, Box 761
Mounds, OK 74047
(918) 827-3238
Organic products.
Catalog: free

FOOTHILL AGRICULTURAL
RESEARCH, INC.
510½ West Chase Drive
Corona, CA 91720
(714) 371-0120
Biological insect control.
Catalog: free

FREEDOM SOIL LAB
P.O. Box 1144
42 Hangar Way
Freedom, CA 95019
(408) 724-4427
Soil testing. Catalog: free

FULL CIRCLE FARM PRODUCTS
P.O. Box 6
77 Avenue of the Giants (in
Phillipsville)
Redway, CA 95560
(800) 426-5511
Supplies. Catalog: free

FULL MOON FARM PRODUCTS
P.O. Box 4865
217 SW Second Street
Corvallis, OR 97339
(503) 757-2532,
(800) 888-5765
Supplies. Catalog: free

GARDENER'S EDEN
Box 7307
San Francisco, CA 94120
(415) 428-9292
Tools. Catalog: free

GARDENER'S SUPPLY
COMPANY
128 Intervale Road
Burlington, VT 05401
(802) 863-1700
Supplies. Catalog: free

GREAT LAKES IPM
10220 Church Road NE
Vestaburg, MI 48891
(517) 268-5693
Pest control. Catalog: free

GREEN EARTH ORGANICS
9422 144th Street East
Puyallup, WA 98373
(206) 845-2321
Organic products.
Catalog: free

GREENER THUMB, THE
P.O. Box 704
Littlefield, TX 79339
Organic products, tools.
Catalog: free

GROWING NATURALLY
P.O. Box 54
Pineville, PA 18946
(215) 598-7025
Organic supplies.
Catalog: free

HARMONY FARM SUPPLY
P.O. Box 451
3320 Gravenstein Highway
North (in Sebastopol)
Graton, CA 95444
(707) 823-9125
Organic supplies. Catalog: $2

I.F.M.
333 Ohme Garden Road
Wenatchee, WA 98801
(509) 662-3179,
(800) 332-3179
*Organic products, biological
insect control.* Catalog: free

INNOVATIVE GEOTEXTILES
CORP.
P.O. Box 34221
Charlotte, NC 28234
(704) 553-1125
Weed-retardant landscape fabric.
Catalog: free

DAVID KAY GARDEN & GIFT
CATALOGUE, INC.
4509 Taylor Lane
Cleveland, OH 44128
(216) 464-5125,
(800) 872-5588
Supplies, gifts. Catalog: free

LARAMIE SOILS SERVICE
P.O. Box 255
Laramie, WY 82070
(307) 742-4185
Soil testing. Catalog: (only
instructions)

MAESTRO-GRO
P.O. Box 310
121 Lincoln Drive
Lowell, AR 72745
(501) 770-6154
Organic products.
Catalog: free

MISTI MAID, INC.
5500 Boscell Common
Fremont, CA 94538
(415) 656-5777,
(800) 634-2104
Irrigation. Catalog: free

MOSS PRODUCTS, INC.
P.O. Box 72
Palmetto, FL 34220
(813) 729-5433
Irrigation supplies.
Catalog: free

MOTHER NATURE'S WORM
CASTINGS
P.O. Box 1055
Avon, CT 06001
(203) 673-3029
Organic products.
Catalog: free

THE NATURAL GARDENING
COMPANY
217 San Anselmo Avenue
San Anselmo, CA 94960
*Supplies, small plants, books,
and gifts.* Catalog: free

NATURAL GARDENING
RESEARCH CENTER
P.O. Box 149
Sunman, IN 47041
(812) 623-3800
*IPM (integrated pest
management) supplies.*
Catalog: free

NATURE'S CONTROL
P.O. Box 35
Medford, OR 97501
(503) 899-8318
Biological insect control.
Catalog: free

NECESSARY TRADING CO.
P.O. Box 305
422 Salem Avenue
New Castle, VA 24127
(703) 864-5103
Biological insect control.
Catalog: $3

NEMATEC—Biological
Control Agents
P.O. Box 93
Lafayette, CA 94549
(415) 866-2800
Biological insect control.
Catalog: free

NETAFIM IRRIGATION
10 East Merrick Road
Valley Stream, NY 11580
(516) 561-6650
Irrigation supplies.
Catalog: free

WALTER NICKE COMPANY
P.O. Box 433
36 McLeod Lane
Topsfield, MA 01983
(508) 887-3388
*Garden tools, many unusual
finds, great catalog.*
Catalog: free

NITRON INDUSTRIES, INC.
P.O. Box 1447
4605 Johnson Road
Fayetteville, AR 72702
(510) 750-1777,
(800) 835-0123
Organic products.
Catalog: free

OHIO EARTH FOOD, INC.
13737 Duquette Avenue NE
Hartville, OH 44632
(216) 877-9356
Organic products.
Catalog: free

ORGANIC CONTROL, INC.
P.O. Box 781147
Los Angeles, CA 90016
(213) 937-7444
Biological insect control.
Catalog: free

ORGANIC PEST MANAGEMENT
P.O. Box 55267
Seattle, WA 98155
(206) 367-0707
Organic products.
Catalog: free

BARGYLA RATEAVER
9049 Covina Street
San Diego, CA 92126
(619) 566-9884
Organic products.
List: long SASE

RINGER CORPORATION
9959 Valley View Road
Eden Prairie, MN 55344
(612) 941-4180
Organic products.
Catalog: free

SMITH & HAWKEN
25 Corte Madera
Mill Valley, CA 94941
(415) 383-8070
Tools, books, gifts, and clothes.
Catalog: free

SUBMATIC IRRIGATION
SYSTEMS
P.O. Box 246
Lubbock, TX 79408
(806) 747-9000,
(800) 858-4016
Irrigation supplies.
Catalog: free

TFS SYSTEMS
P.O. Box 710038
8733 Magnolia, Suite 100
Santee, CA 92071
(619) 449-6408
Irrigation supplies.
Catalog: $2.50

TEC LABORATORIES, INC.
P.O. Box 1958
Albany, OR 97321
(503) 926-4577,
(800) ITCHING
Poison-ivy cleanser.
Catalog: free

THURSTON DISTRIBUTING,
INC.
914 Lee Street
Boise, ID 83702
(208) 342-1212
Organic pest control.
Catalog: free

UPCP IRRIGATION
P.O. Box 206
Bouse, AZ 85325
(602) 851-2506
Irrigation supplies.
Catalog: free

UNIQUE INSECT CONTROL
5504 Sperry Drive
Citrus Heights, CA 95621
(916) 961-7945
Biological insect control.
Catalog: free

THE URBAN FARMER STORE
2833 Vicente Street
San Francisco, CA 94116
(415) 661-2204
Irrigation supplies.
Catalog: $1

WEST COAST LADYBUG SALES
P.O. Box 903
Gridley, CA 95948
(916) 534-0840
Biological insect control.
Catalog: free

WICKATUNK MARINE, INC.
P.O. Box 156
Wickatunk, NJ 07765
(201) 946-8326
Pond liners. Catalog: $1

WINTERTHUR MUSEUM &
GARDENS CATALOGUE
DIVISION
102 Enterprise Place
Dover, DE 19735
(302) 678-9200,
(800) 767-0500
Garden ornaments, some plants.
Catalog: free

ZOOK & RANCK, INC.
R.D. 1, Box 243
Gap, PA 17527
(717) 442-4171
Fertilizers. Catalog: free

BOOKSELLERS

THE AMERICAN BOTANIST
1103 West Truitt Avenue
Chillicothe, IL 61523
(309) 274-5254
Books. Catalog: $1

BARK SERVICE COMPANY
P.O. Box 637
Troutman, NC 28166
(800) 999-2275
Books. Catalog: free

BELL'S BOOK STORE
536 Emerson Street
Palo Alto, CA 94301
(415) 323-7822
Books. Send want list

THE BOOK TREE
12 Pine Hill Road
Englishtown, NJ 07726
(201) 446-3853
Books. Catalog: free

BROOKS BOOKS
P.O. Box 21473
Concord, CA 94521
(414) 672-4566
Books. Catalog: $1

BUILDERS BOOKSOURCE
1817 Fourth Street
Berkeley, CA 94710
(415) 845-6874,
(800) 843-2028
Books. Catalog: free

CALENDULA
Box 930
Picton, Ont., Canada
K0K 2T0
*Rare and out-of-print gardening
books.* Catalog: free

CAPABILITY'S BOOKS
P.O. Box 144
Highway 46
Deer Park, WI 54007
(800) 247-8154,
(715) 269-5346
Books. Catalog: free

CEDAR HILL BOOKS
Route 8, Box 883
Tulsa, OK 74127
(918) 425-2590
Books. Catalog: free

FLORA & FAUNA BOOKS
121 First Avenue South
Seattle, WA 98104
(206) 623-4727
Books. Catalog: free

THE GARDEN BOOK CLUB
333 East 38th Street
New York, NY 10016
(212) 455-5000
Books. Write for
membership information.

GARDEN VARIETY, LIMITED
P.O. Box 40721
5230 Sherier Place
Northwest
Washington, DC 20016
(202) 686-1229
Books. Catalog: free

GRAY BOOKS
255 Fifty-fifth Street
Boulder, CO 80301
(800) 343-2757
*Classic books on gardens,
architecture, and design.*
Catalog: free

LAURELBROOK BOOK
SERVICES
5468 Dundas Street West,
Suite 600
Toronto, Ont., Canada
M9B 6E3
(416) 234-6811
Books. Catalog: free

THE NATURAL GARDENING
COMPANY
217 San Anselmo Avenue
San Anselmo, CA 94960
*Supplies, small plants, books,
and gifts.* Catalog: free

NATURAL GARDENS
113 Jasper Lane
Oak Ridge, TN 37830
(615) 856-3350
Books. Catalog: $1d

NELSON-MILLER
318 Drummond Street
Nevada City, CA 95959
Books. Catalog: free

SMITH & HAWKEN
25 Corte Madera
Mill Valley, CA 94941
(415) 383-8070
Tools, books, gifts, and clothes.
Catalog: free

ELISABETH WOODBURN
P.O. Box 398
Booknoll Farm
Hopewell, NJ 08525
(609) 466-0522
Books. Catalogs: Various
categories of books, $2 each

SUGGESTED READING

Considering the fact that every gardener has to deal with shade to some extent or another, I was surprised to discover relatively few books on this subject. Now you have *The Natural Shade Garden,* and here are some other titles that might be useful. Most of them are in print or have been reissued.

Aden, Paul. *The Hosta Book.* Edited and compiled by Paul Aden. Portland, Ore.: Timber Press, 1988.

Armitage, Allan M. *Herbaceous Perennial Plants, A Treatise on Their Identification, Culture, and Garden Attributes.* Athens, Ga.: Varsity Press, 1989.

Bailey, Liberty Hyde. *Hortus Third: A Concise Dictionary of Plants Cultivated in the United States and Canada.* Revised and expanded by the staff of the Liberty Hyde Bailey Hortorium, Cornell University. New York: Macmillan, 1976.

Birdseye, Clarence and Eleanor G. *Growing Woodland Plants.* New York: Dover Publications, 1972.

Brickell, Christopher, editor in chief. *Royal Horticultural Society Gardeners' Encyclopedia of Plants and Flowers.* London: Dorling Kindersley, 1989.

Chatto, Beth. *The Green Tapestry.* New York: Simon and Schuster, 1982.

Clausen, Ruth Rogers, and Ekstrom, Nicholas H. *Perennials for American Gardens.* New York: Random House, 1989.

Coombes, Allen J. *Dictionary of Plant Names.* Portland, Ore.: Timber Press, 1985.

Davis, Brian. *The Gardener's Illustrated Encyclopedia of Trees and Shrubs.* Emmaus, Pa.: Rodale Press, 1987.

Druse, Ken. *The Natural Garden.* New York: Clarkson N. Potter, 1989.

Fish, Margery. *Gardening in the Shade.* Boston: Faber and Faber, 1984.

Foster, F. Gordon. *Ferns to Know and Grow.* Portland, Ore.: Timber Press, 1982.

Foster, H. Lincoln. *Rock Gardening: A Guide to Growing Alpines and Other Wildflowers in the American Garden.* Portland, Ore.: Timber Press, 1982.

Fretwell, Barry. *Clematis.* Deer Park, Wis.: Capability's Books, 1989.

Klaber, Doretta. *Primroses and Spring.* New York: M. Barrows and Company, 1966.

Morse, Harriet K. *Gardening in the Shade.* Beaverton, Ore.: Timber Press, 1982.

Ottesen, Carole. *Ornamental Grasses: The Amber Wave.* New York: McGraw-Hill, 1989.

Parcher, Emily Seaber. *Shady Gardens.* New York: Prentice-Hall, 1955.

Patterson, Allen. *Plants for Shade.* London, Melbourne, Toronto: J. M. Dent and Sons, 1981.

Peterson, Roger Tory, and McKenny, Margaret. *A Field Guide to Wildflowers.* Boston: Houghton Mifflin, 1968.

Phillips, Roger, and Rix, Martyn. *The Random House Book of Bulbs.* New York: Random House, 1989.

Phillips, Roger, and Rix, Martyn. *The Random House Book of Shrubs.* New York: Random House, 1989.

Schenk, George. *The Complete Shade Gardener.* Boston: Houghton Mifflin, 1984.

Sperka, Marie. *Growing Wildflowers: A Gardener's Guide.* New York: Harper and Row, 1973.

Steffek, Edwin F. *The New Wild Flowers and How to Grow Them.* Portland, Ore.: Timber Press, 1983.

Taylor, Norman. *Taylor's Guide to Ground Covers, Vines and Grasses* (based on *Taylor's Encyclopedia of Gardening,* 4th ed., 1961). Boston: Houghton Mifflin, 1987.

PLACES TO VISIT

My favorite kind of garden re-creates to some extent the natural or native environment. Increasingly, public gardens are featuring wildlife, naturalistic plantings that simulate the native plant community. Some of these places blend natives with related plants from similar climates around the world. The following places to visit feature either wildflower and woodland collections or shade plantings of merit. Call ahead for seasons and hours.

ALABAMA

BIRMINGHAM BOTANICAL GARDENS
2612 Lane Park Road
Birmingham, AL 35223
(205) 879-1227

UNIVERSITY OF ALABAMA ARBORETUM
P.O. Box 1927
Tuscaloosa, AL 35487
(205) 553-3278

CALIFORNIA

QUAIL BOTANICAL GARDENS
230 Quail Gardens Drive
Encinitas, CA 92024
(619) 753-4432

RANCHO SANTA ANA BOTANIC GARDEN
1500 North College Avenue
Claremont, CA 91711
(714) 625-8767

REGIONAL PARKS BOTANIC GARDEN
Tilden Regional Park
Berkeley, CA 94708
(415) 841-8732

STRYBING ARBORETUM AND BOTANICAL GARDENS
Ninth Avenue and Lincoln Way
San Francisco, CA 94122
(415) 558-3622

UNIVERSITY OF CALIFORNIA, BERKELEY, BOTANICAL GARDEN
Centennials Drive
Berkeley, CA 94720
(415) 642-3343

WILLIAM JOSEPH MCINNES BOTANIC GARDEN AND THE CAMPUS ARBORETUM OF MILLS COLLEGE
Box 9949
Oakland, CA 94613
(415) 430-2158

CONNECTICUT

AUDUBON FAIRCHILD GARDEN OF THE NATIONAL AUDUBON SOCIETY
North Porchuck Road
Greenwich, CT 06830
(203) 869-5272

CONNECTICUT ARBORETUM AT CONNECTICUT COLLEGE
New London, CT 06320
(203) 447-7700

DELAWARE

MOUNT CUBA CENTER FOR THE STUDY OF PIEDMONT FLORA
P.O. Box 3570
Greenville, DE 19807
(302) 239-4244

WINTERTHUR MUSEUM AND GARDENS
Winterthur, DE 19735
(302) 656-8591

DISTRICT OF COLUMBIA

KENILWORTH AQUATIC GARDENS
Anacostia Avenue and Douglass Street NE
Washington, D.C. 20020
(202) 426-6905

UNITED STATES NATIONAL ARBORETUM
3501 New York Avenue NE
Washington, D.C. 20002
(202) 475-4815

FLORIDA

BOK TOWER GARDENS
P.O. Box 3810
Lake Wales, FL 33859
(813) 676-1408

THE MARIE SELBY BOTANICAL GARDENS
811 South Palm Avenue
Sarasota, FL 33577
(813) 366-5730

GEORGIA

IDA CASON CALLAWAY FOUNDATION
Highway 27
Pine Mountain, GA 31822
(404) 663-2281

UNIVERSITY OF GEORGIA BOTANICAL GARDEN
2450 South Milledge Avenue
Athens, GA 30605
(404) 542-1244

HAWAII

HAWAII TROPICAL BOTANICAL GARDEN
248 Kahan Road
Hilo, HI 96720
(808) 935-4703

HONOLULU BOTANIC GARDENS
50 North Vineyard Boulevard
Honolulu, HI 96817
(808) 533-3406

WAIMEA ARBORETUM AND BOTANICAL GARDEN
59-864 Kamehameha Highway
Haleiwa, Oahu, HI 96712
(808) 638-8655

ILLINOIS

CENTER FOR NATURAL LANDSCAPING
2100 Ridge Avenue
Evanston, IL 60204
(312) 328-2100

CHICAGO BOTANIC GARDEN
P.O. Box 400
Glencoe, IL 60022
(312) 835-5440

THE MORTON ARBORETUM
Route 53
Lisle, IL 60532
(312) 968-0074

INDIANA

HAYES REGIONAL ARBORETUM
801 Elks Road
Richmond, IN 47374
(317) 962-3745

UPPER WABASH BASIN NATURAL RESEARCH CENTER
2303 College Avenue
Huntington, IN 46750
(219) 356-6000

IOWA

BICKELHAUPT ARBORETUM
340 South Fourteenth Street
Clinton, IA 52732
(319) 242-4771

UNIVERSITY OF NORTHERN IOWA
UNI Biological Preserves
Cedar Falls, IA 50614
(319) 273-2456

KANSAS

DYKE ARBORETUM OF THE PLAINS
Hesston College
P.O. Box 3000
Hesston, KS 67062
(316) 327-8127

LOUISIANA

HODGES GARDENS
Box 921
Many, LA 71449
(318) 586-3523

SHADOWS-ON-THE-TECHE
Box 254
New Iberia, LA 70560
(318) 369-6446

MAINE

WILD GARDENS OF ACADIA
Sieur de Monts Spring
Acadia National Park
Bar Harbor, ME 04609
(207) 228-3338

FAY HYLAND BOTANICAL PLANTATION
Department of Botany
University of Maine
Orono, ME 04469
(207) 581-7461

MARYLAND

LONDON TOWN PUBLIK
HOUSE AND GARDENS
839 London Town Road
Edgewater, MD 21037
(301) 956-4900

PERKINS GARDEN
6101 Wilson Lane
Bethesda, MD 20034
(301) 320-3200

MASSACHUSETTS

THE ARNOLD ARBORETUM OF
HARVARD UNIVERSITY
Arborway
Jamaica Plain, MA 02130
(617) 524-1718 or 2919

BERKSHIRE GARDEN CENTER,
INC.
Stockbridge, MA 01262
(413) 298-3926

GARDEN IN THE WOODS
Hemenway Road
Framingham, MA 01701
(617) 877-7630

HERITAGE PLANTATION OF
SANDWICH
Box 566 Grove Street
Sandwich, MA 02563
(617) 888-3300

WALTER HUNNEWELL
PINETUM
845 Washington Street
Wellesley, MA 02181
(617) 235-0422

MOUNT AUBURN CEMETERY
580 Mount Auburn Street
Cambridge, MA 02138
(617) 547-7105

MINNESOTA

ELOISE BUTLER WILDFLOWER
GARDEN
Theodore Wirth Parkway
Minneapolis, MN 55415
(612) 348-4448

MINNESOTA LANDSCAPE
ARBORETUM
3075 Arboretum Drive
Chanhassen, MN 55317
(612) 443-2460

MISSISSIPPI

THE CROSBY ARBORETUM
1801 Goodyear Boulevard
Picayune, MS 39466
(601) 798-6961

MISSOURI

MISSOURI BOTANICAL
GARDEN
P.O. Box 299
Saint Louis, MO 63166
(314) 577-5100

SHAW ARBORETUM OF
MISSOURI BOTANICAL
GARDEN
P.O. Box 38
Gray Summit, MO 63039
(314) 577-5238

NEW JERSEY

CORA HARTSHORN
ARBORETUM AND BIRD
SANCTUARY
324 Forest Drive South
Short Hills, NJ 07078
(201) 376-3587

LEAMING'S RUN BOTANICAL
GARDEN
Box 286, R.D. 1
Cape May Courthouse, NJ
08210
(609) 465-5871

LEONARD J. BUCK GARDENS
P.O. Box 565
Far Hills, NJ 07931
(201) 234-2677

SKYLANDS GARDENS
Box 1304
Ringwood, NJ 07456
(201) 962-7031

NEW YORK

BROOKLYN BOTANIC GARDEN
1000 Washington Avenue
Brooklyn, NY 11225
(718) 622-4433

CLARK GARDEN
193 I.U. Willets Road
Albertson, NY 11507
(516) 621-7568

CORNELL PLANTATIONS
One Plantations Road
Ithaca, NY 14850
(607) 255-3020

INSTITUTE OF ECOSYSTEM
STUDIES, THE MARY FLAGLER
CARY ARBORETUM
Box AB
Millbrook, NY 12545
(914) 677-5343

THE NEW YORK BOTANICAL
GARDEN
Southern Boulevard
Bronx, NY 10458
(212) 220-8700

OLD WESTBURY GARDENS
Box 430
Old Westbury, NY 11568
(516) 333-0048

PLANTING FIELDS ARBORETUM
P.O. Box 58
Oyster Bay, NY 11771
(516) 922-9206

WAVE HILL
675 West 252nd Street
Bronx, NY 10471
(212) 549-2055

NORTH CAROLINA

NORTH CAROLINA
BOTANICAL GARDEN
3375 Totten Center
University of North
Carolina-Chapel Hill
Chapel Hill, NC 27514
(919) 967-2246

UNIVERSITY BOTANICAL
GARDENS AT ASHEVILLE, INC.
6 Northwood Road
Asheville, NC 28804
(704) 274-1551

OHIO

THE DAWES ARBORETUM
7770 Jacksontown Road SE
Newark, OH 43055
(614) 323-2355

THE HOLDEN ARBORETUM
9500 Sperry Road
Mentor, OH 44060
(216) 946-4400

OREGON

BERRY BOTANIC GARDEN
11505 SW Summerville
Avenue
Portland, OR 97219
(503) 636-4112

CRYSTAL SPRINGS
RHODODENDRON GARDEN
Route 3, Box 233-B
Sherwood, OR 97140

HOYT ARBORETUM
4000 SW Fairview
Boulevard
Portland, OR 97221
(503) 228-8732

PENNSYLVANIA

BRANDYWINE CONSERVANCY
GARDENS
Box 141
Chadds Ford, PA 19317
(215) 388-7601

BOWMAN'S HILL
WILDFLOWER PRESERVE
P.O. Box 103
Washington Crossing, PA
18977
(215) 862-2924

HENRY FOUNDATION FOR
BOTANICAL RESEARCH
Box 7, 801 Stoney Lane
Gladwyne, PA 19035
(215) 525-2037

JENKINS ARBORETUM
631 Berwyn Baptist Road
Devon, PA 19333
(215) 647-8870

LONGWOOD GARDENS
P.O. Box 501
Kennett Square, PA 19348
(215) 388-6741

MORRIS ARBORETUM OF THE
UNIVERSITY OF
PENNSYLVANIA
9414 Meadowbrook Avenue
Philadelphia, PA 19118
(215) 247-5777

THE TYLER ARBORETUM
P.O. Box 216
Lima, PA 19037
(215) 566-5431

RHODE ISLAND

BLITHEWOLD GARDENS AND
ARBORETUM
Ferry Road
Bristol, RI 02809
(401) 253-2707

WILCOX PARK
71½ High Street
Westerly, RI 02891
(401) 348-8362

SOUTH CAROLINA
BROOKGREEN GARDENS
U.S. 17 South
Murrells Inlet, SC 29576
(803) 237-4218

MAGNOLIA PLANTATIONS AND
GARDENS
Route 4
Charleston, SC 29407
(803) 571-1266

TENNESSEE
MEMPHIS BOTANIC GARDEN
750 Cherry Road
Memphis, TN 38117
(901) 685-1566

TEXAS
MERCER ARBORETUM AND
BOTANIC GARDENS
22306 Aldine-Westfield
Road
Humble, TX 77338
(713) 443-8731

VIRGINIA
ORLAND E. WHITE
ARBORETUM
P.O. Box 175
Boyce, VA 22620
(703) 837-1758

WASHINGTON
BLOEDEL RESERVE
7571 NE Dolphin Drive
Bainbridge Island, WA
98110
(206) 842-7631

JOHN A. FINCH ARBORETUM
West 4-21st Avenue
Spokane, WA 99203
(509) 456-4331

RHODODENDRON SPECIES
FOUNDATION
P.O. Box 3798
Federal Way, WA 98063
(206) 838-4646

WISCONSIN
UNIVERSITY OF WISCONSIN
ARBORETUM
1207 Seminole Highway
Madison, WI 53711
(608) 262-2746

CANADA
NIKKA YUKO CENTENNIAL
GARDEN
Box 751
Lethbridge, Alta. T1J 3Z6
(401) 328-3511

UNIVERSITY OF BRITISH
COLUMBIA BOTANICAL
GARDEN
6501 NW Marine Drive
Vancouver, B.C. V6T 1W5
(604) 228-3928 or 4186

MEMORIAL UNIVERSITY
BOTANICAL GARDEN
MEMORIAL UNIVERSITY OF
NEWFOUNDLAND
St. John's, Newfoundland
A1C 5S7
(709) 737-8590

THE ARBORETUM
UNIVERSITY OF GUELPH
Guelph, Ont. N1G 2W1
(519) 824-4120, extension
2113

HUMBER ARBORETUM
205 Humber College
Boulevard
Rexdale, Ont. M9W 5L7
(416) 675-3111, extension
445

ROYAL BOTANICAL GARDENS
P.O. Box 399
Hamilton, Ont. L8N 3H8
(416) 527-1158

JARDIN BOTANIQUE DE
MONTRÉAL
4101 rue Sherbrooke est
Montréal, Que. H1X 2B2
(514) 872-1400

THE AUTHOR'S TOWNHOUSE GARDEN

A plan of the author's 20' × 50' garden shows the planting areas, developed spaces, and selected plants from the collection.

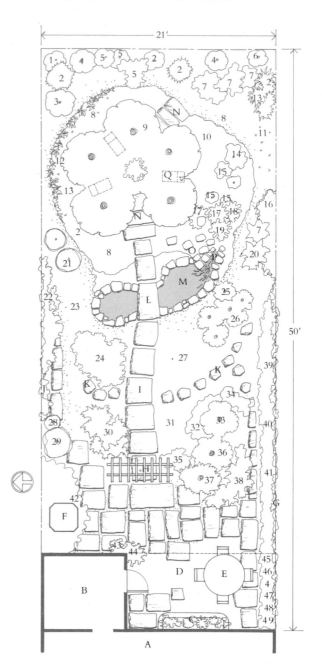

A. House
B. Mud room for
   wintering plants
C. Houseplant stand
D. Patio
E. Table and chairs
F. Compost pile
G. Slatted fence
H. Trellis

I. Path
J. Mirror
K. Utility path
L. Bridge
M. Pond
N. Steps
O. Rock garden
P. Waterfall
Q. Adirondack chairs

1. *Rodgersia pinnata*
2. Bamboo varieties
3. *Salix sachalinensis* 'Sekka'
4. *Salix matsudana* 'Tortuosa'
5. Fastigiate trees
6. *Elaeagnus umbellata*
7. Fern species
8. *Pachysandra terminalis*
9. *Gleditsia triacanthos* var. *inermis* 'Halka'
10. Ground covers
11. *Hemerocallis* spp.
12. *Macleaya cordata*
13. *Lilium* varieties
14. *Viburnum carlesii*
15. Dwarf rhododendrons
16. Rambler rose
17. *Acer palmatum*
18. *Viburnum opulus*
19. *Viburnum plicatum* 'Mariesii'
20. *Hosta* 'Albo-Marginata'
21. *Magnolia* 'Elizabeth'
22. *Weigela florida*
23. Wildflowers
24. Perennials and bulbs
25. *Hibiscus syriacus*
26. *Hydrangea macrophylla*
27. Marsh plants
28. *Abelia grandiflora*
29. *Hydrangea aspera*
30. *Rhus typhina* 'Laciniata'
31. Shade wildflowers
32. *Astilbe taquetii* 'Superba'
33. *Kerria japonica* 'Pleniflora'
34. *Thalictrum* spp.
35. *Hydrangea macrophylla*
36. *Hydrangea quercifolia*
37. *A. p.* 'Aconitifolium'
38. Hostas, ferns, ginger
39. *Schisandra chinensis*
40. *Clematis maximowicziana*
41. *Ampelopsis brevipedunculata* 'Elegans'
42. *Forsythia* x *intermedia*
43. *Lonicera* x *heckrottii*
44. *Hosta lancifolia* in urn
45. *Lonicera periclymenum* 'Serotina Florida'
46. *Hedera helix*
47. *Salix matsudana* 'Tortuosa'
48. *Parthenocissus quinquefolia*

A STREAMSIDE GARDEN REVISITED

The landscape design for Jean and Dan Pope's 80' × 210' property cleverly accommodates all utility and service areas along with places for exquisite plantings. Groups of wildflowers and ornamental perennials grow in the garden beneath the trees.

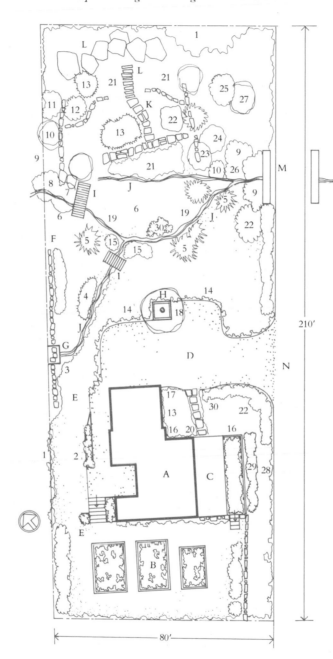

A. House
B. Raised beds for vegetables
C. Entry patio and herb garden
D. Drive
E. Shaded planters
F. Stone walls
G. Spring house
H. Tree well
I. Footbridges
J. Stream
K. Stone steps
L. Quarry area
M. Culvert to lake
N. Main road

1. *Lonicera tatarica*
2. *Hedera helix*
3. Spring house garden: *Cimicifuga* spp., *Mertensia virginica*, *Chelone glabra*, *Filipendula rubra*, *Thalictrum aquilegifolium*, ferns and wildflowers
4. *Liriope muscari*
5. *Hemerocallis* spp.
6. *Pachysandra terminalis*
7. *Salix discolor*
8. *Salix babylonica*
9. *Sambucus canadensis*
10. *Cornus kousa*
11. *Styrax obassia*
12. *Rhododendron schlippenbachii*
13. *Ilex aquifolium*
14. *Ajuga reptens*
15. *Caltha palustris*
16. *Euonymus alatus* 'Compacta'
17. *Viburnum sargentii*
18. *Acer rubrum*
19. *Primula japonica*
20. *Potentila fruticosa*
21. Rock area: *Aconitum fisheri, Acorus calamus, Asarum europaeum, Cimicifuga racemosa, Dicentra* spp., *Digitalis purpurea, Geranium robertianum, Hosta* spp., *Iris cristata, I. pseudacorus, I. sibirica, Macleaya cordata, Primula* spp., ferns and wildflowers
22. *Viburnum plicatum* 'Tomentosum'
23. *Hamamelis mollis*
24. *H. virginiana*
25. *Aesculus parviflora*
26. *Amelanchier laevis*
27. *Cornus mas*
28. *Vinca minor* 'Alba'
29. *Paeonia* spp.
30. *Hosta* spp.

A Hillside in the Northwest

Jim Hammond's garden near Seattle is home to over 2,000 plants. Here are some of the shade plants that love this maritime climate and the long daylight hours.

A. House
B. Paved walkway
C. Fountain
D. Gravel path
E. Foot bridge
F. Open wood canopy

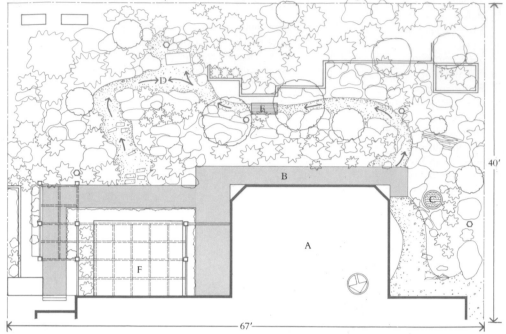

Aconitum napellus
Alchemilla alpina
Alchemilla mollis
Anemone japonica
Chelone glabra
Cimicifuga simplex
Cornus canadensis
Corydalis lutea
Dicentra eximia
Dicentra formosa
Dicentra spectabilis
Dicentra x luxurient
Digitalis purpurea
Dodecatheon amabilis
Doronicum austriacum
Enkianthus campanulatus
Euphorbia characia
Euphorbia polychroma

Galax urceolata
Gaultheria procumbens
Gentiana spp.
Helleborus foetidus
Helleborus lividus
Helleborus niger
Helleborus orientalis
Hepatica spp.
Heuchera sanguineum
Hydrangea anomala petiolaris
Ilex crenata

Iris douglasiana ennomenata
Lamium maculatum
Ligularia 'Desdemona'
Ligularia 'The Rocket'
Lillium hybrids
Lysimachia punctata
Nandina domestica
Oenothera biennis
Omphalodes verna
Oxalis spp.
Phyllostachys nigra

Polygala chameabuxus
Polygonatum biflorum
Polystichum spp.
Primula denticulata
Pulmonaria angustifolia
Pulmonaria saccharata
Rodgersia pinnata
Sanguinaria canadensis
Tradescantia x *andersoniana*
Trillium spp.
Vancouveria chrysantha

A Tiny Urban Refuge

The planting scheme for Jon Rowen's 25' × 30' garden in New York City emphasizes combinations of leaf colors and textures.

A. Apartment
B. Steps
C. Paved patio

1. *Rhododendron* 'Purple Splendor'
2. *R.* 'P.J.M.'
3. *Taxus* x *media* 'Hatfieldii'
4. *Viburnum plicatum* 'Mariesii'
5. *Aucuba japonica*
6, 16. *Ilex aquifolium* 'Argenteo-márginata'

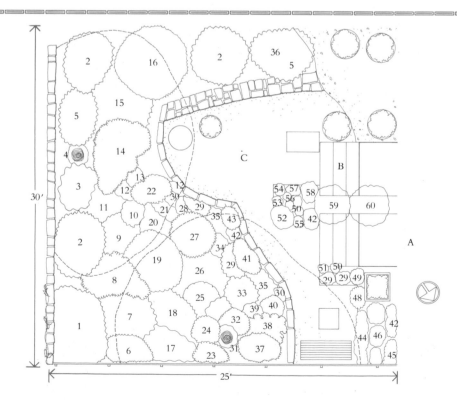

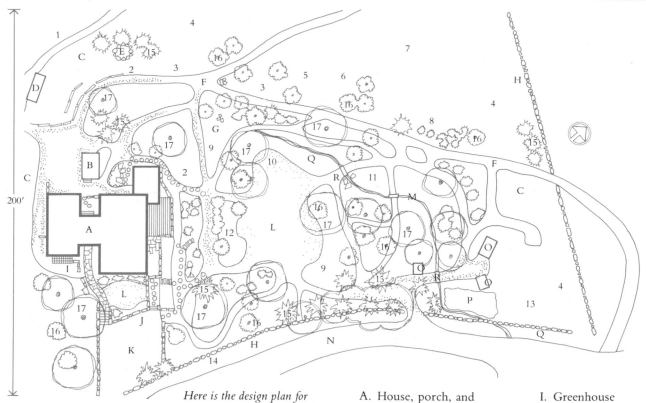

A NATURALIST'S GARDEN

Here is the design plan for Neil Jorgensen's 200' × 300' Massachusetts homesite. The property complements nature and provides a place for recreation and relaxation. It also serves as base for his design business and includes his private nursery.

A. House, porch, and deck
B. Tool shed
C. Nursery growing areas
D. Lathe house
E. Rustic gazebo
F. Woods road
G. Sculpture
H. Stone walls
I. Greenhouse
J. Dry-stone walls
K. Parking area
L. Lawn
M. Marsh garden
N. Main road
O. Storage sheds
P. Vegetable garden
Q. Stream
R. Bridges

7. *Pieris japonica*
8. *R.* 'Rosebud'
9. *Hosta* 'True Blue'
10. *H.* 'Gold Standard'
11. *Polygonatum japonicum* 'Variegatum'
12. *Brunnera macrophylla*
13. *Tricyrtis hirta*
14. *R.* 'Blaauw's Pink'
15. *Mertensia virginica*
17. *Kalmia latifolia*
18. *Hosta* 'Royal Standard'
19. *Hydrangea macrophylla*
20. *Dicentra eximia* 'Alba'
21. *Hosta* 'Blue Moon'
22. *R.* 'Gumpo Pink'
23. *R.* 'Coral Bells'
24. *Skimmia japonica* (male)
25. *Dicentra* x *luxurient*
26. Impatiens and tulips
27. *R.* 'Mother's Day'
28. *Liriope muscari* 'Majestic'

29. *Hosta undulata* 'Albo-marginata'
30. *Hosta sieboldiana* 'Kabitan'
31. *Cornus kousa chinensis*
32. *Skimmia japonica*
33. *Hosta* 'Piedmont Gold'
34. *H.* 'Blue Wedgwood'
35. *Astilbe chinensis* 'Pumila'
36. *Aucuba japonica* 'Picta'
37. *Euonymus fortunei* 'Silver Queen'
38. *Helleborus orientalis*
39. *Tricyrtis formosana stolonifera*
40. *Athyrium nipponicum* 'Metalicum'
41. *Liriope muscari*
42. *Hosta* 'Gold Medallion'
43. *Bergenia cordifolia*
44. *Corydalis lutea*

45. *Ampelopsis brevipedunculata* 'Elegans'
46. *Hosta ventricosa* 'Aureo-marginata'
47. *Lonicera* x *heckrottii*
48. *Hosta* 'Halcyon'
49. *Asarum europaeum*
50. *Tricyrtis sinonome*
51. *Hosta venusta*
52. *Yucca filamentosa* 'Gold Sword'
53. *Geranium* x 'Johnson's Blue'
54. *Hosta* 'Gay Feather'
55. *Heuchera sanguinea*
56. *Ophiopogon planiscapus*
57. *Ajuga pyramidalis*
58. *Hosta* 'Tallboy'
59. *R. macrantha*
60. *Hydrangea arborescens* 'Annabelle'

1. Large rhododendrons
2. Daylilies
3. Small-leaved rhododendrons
4. Woods
5. Rhododendrons
6. Mountain laurels
7. Japanese maple grove
8. Deciduous azaleas
9. Wildflower collections
10. Hosta collection
11. Japanese primroses
12. Spring-blooming wildflowers
13. Northern Lights azaleas
14. Early rhododendrons
15. Evergreens
16. Major understory trees
17. Large trees

Index

Page numbers in **boldface** refer to captions.

The Latin names of plants in this book have been verified in several published sources, including *Hortus Third*, by the Staff of the Liberty Hyde Bailey Hortorium (Macmillan: New York, 1976) and *Dictionary of Plant Names* by Allen J. Combes (Timber Press: Portland, Ore., 1985). I would like to thank members of the staff of the New York Botanical Garden who helped identify certain specimens: Mobee Weinstein, Mike Ruggiero, Greg Piotrowski, John Mickel, and Bob Bartolomei.

Guide to additional plants illustrated, by page number: *iv, Arisaema triphyllum; iv–v, Doronicum caucasicum, Lamium maculatum* 'Beacon Silver'; *v, Fritillaria persica; vi–vii, Epimedium grandiflorum, Sarracenia flava; 1, Anemone virginiana; 33, Hakonechloa macra* 'Alba-Aurea'; *66, Pieris japonica; 67, Anemone japonica (Anemone x hybrida).*